The Queen, RUPERT & me

Desmond Zwar

About The Author

Desmond Zwar began a newspaper cadetship on the *Albury Border Morning Mail,* and then moved to *The Herald,* Melbourne, to be employed by the late Sir Keith Murdoch. (He was to write Sir Keith's Life 30 years later).

He went to Fleet Street, London, and joined the London *Daily Mail,* where he worked as reporter, foreign correspondent, feature writer and latterly acting as Features Editor, remaining with the paper for 11 Years.

He had his own features service in London and concentrated on newspaper and magazine non-fiction series for Sunday newspapers and women's magazines. He was Australian columnist for the *UK Mail* for four years. He worked in Public Relations with a leading Melbourne PR company and latterly had his own weekly newspaper.

Published in Australia by
Temple House Pty Ltd,
T/A Sid Harta Publishers
ACN 092 197 192
Hartwell, Victoria

Telephone: 61 3 9560 9920
Facsimile: 61 3 9545 1742
E-mail: author@sidharta.com.au

First published in Australia 2004
Copyright © Desmond Zwar, 2004
Cover design, typesetting: Chameleon Print Design

Cover photograph of Rupert Murdoch:
NOVEMBER 3, 1999 : News Corp chairman & CEO
Rupert Murdoch during 03/11/99 AGM in Adelaide.
Newspix/Tony Lewis

The right of Desmond Zwar to be identified as the
Author of the Work has been asserted in accordance
with the Copyright, Designs and Patents Act 1988.

National Library of Australia Cataloguing-in-
Publication entry:
Zwar, Desmond
The Queen, Rupert and Me
ISBN: 1-877059-66-8
pp360

Typeset in Book Antiqua

Printed and bound by Everbest Printing, China

For Delphine

Foreword

Can you trust a reporter? Is everything you read in a newspaper, true?

I have been a newsman all my working life; living in fear of getting something wrong. Waking in a sweat at 2 am when the first edition of the paper is being stacked on newsagents' counters or thrown over fences; going over in my mind what was said by a Prime Minister, a call-girl or a criminal and knowing it was on the front page. Did you get it right?

Because if you got it wrong you got the sack; or worse, your newspaper also got sued and if it lost, hundreds of thousands of dollars could be the penalty.

That is why I was one of the first in London's Fleet Street — 50 years ago — to use a tape-recorder for interviews. And it is why the events and the people in the following pages have been faithfully reported.

The first tape-recorder I bought was a cumbersome, reel-to-reel affair, too heavy to be lugged about, but on which I recorded jazz and the odd chat with Dad. It had nothing to do with reporting, but it intrigued me that a voice could be plucked out of the ether and played back forever. The next one I bought was smaller; it used reels, six cms. in diameter which could be conveniently air-mailed from Australia, giving me gossip from my parents in their lounge-room in country Beechworth, Victoria. Their voices filled my small bed-sitter 12,000 miles away in London, where I was a 24-year-old hopeful trying to get a job. But the machine needed mains power and was hardly portable.

Then I bought a smaller, portable recorder called a Fi-Cord, a sophisticated Swiss-made machine not much larger than a small paperback, and I could now sit in the summer sunshine in Hyde Park and hear Dad talk about his garden covered in frost in Australia; or record what Stanley Lowe, King of the English con-men, told me about his profession.

Because my shorthand was bad (I was the dunce of Miss Hopkins' cadet-reporter class at The Herald in Melbourne) I began to use the Fi-Cord in all interviews when I joined the London Daily Mail; however it had an unfortunate battery problem. As the mercury batteries ran down, the resultant interview often sounded like a mad Donald Duck, just transcribable if you listened patiently. The BBC at the time was still using arm-stretching heavy reel-to-reel, far too unwieldy for a reporter on the run, but sturdily reliable for voice broadcast.

One day I started chatting to a Cockney radio serviceman in Soho to whom I regularly went to buy Fi-Cord batteries. What could be done about telephone interviews? I could record my questions, but not the answers I was getting from the other end.

"No problem," said Mick. He went through to his workshop and five minutes later returned with a lead that had a jack at one end — to plug into the tape-recorder — and a suction microphone on the other that wetted with saliva, adhered itself to the telephone hand-piece. The result was a transfer of both my voice and that of the person I was interviewing, onto the little whirring tapes.

This was, he explained, illegal under the UK Post Office telephony regulations. The law, though it had never been tested in court, decreed that: thou shalt not record another person's voice without their permission. This had to be ignored. No reporter worth his expense account was going to warn an interviewee that he was being recorded on tape, innocent electronic note-taking though it might have been. The person being interviewed would have taken fright and hung up.

As tape-recorders became even smaller and more sophisticated I also bought a desk-top answering machine that embraced a recording facility. But it also had a snag: once you pressed the record button, 15 seconds later and every 15 seconds thereafter, there was a loud beep heard by the interviewee, a device installed by the manufacturers by law (and it is still the case) alerting the person talking that they were being 'taped'. This beep always came at the exact moment when a statistic or vital fact was being given, all neatly wiped out by the shrill note.

So I traced Mick again whose little radio repair shop had been forced out of Soho to Essex. "Shit, I can fix that," he grinned. And within a few minutes he removed the pin-head component in the machine's works responsible for the British Post Office's cautionary warning.

By now, the Japanese had produced a palm-sized tape-recorder that I could slip into my top pocket. It used 'mini' cassette tapes and was voice-activated; when I or the interviewee spoke, it jumped into life. Further, should I want to use it on the phone in the reporters' room there was a mini microphone available to stick between my ear and the telephone's ear-piece that led, again, to the recorder jack-socket and perfect reproduction.

I used taped interviews — legal and illegal — to give me interviews for 16 books. On the golf-course in the US once, I was muttering into my recorder to be embarrassingly yelled at by the great Sam Snead. If I didn't desist, he snarled, he might shove the machine in a most uncomfortable place. In the five years that I worked with Colonel Eugene Bird, the Spandau Director, to collaborate on the life of Rudolf Hess in prison, I relied on him sitting hour after hour in Hess's Berlin cell, secretly recording the old Nazi's thoughts on my tape-recorder.

I took two recorders into the lounge-room of Rupert Murdoch's mother, Dame Elisabeth, placing one before her, and one before her billionaire son, so as not to miss a word of their remarkable exchanges about his naughty childhood.

Dr. William McBride, famous for his warnings about the drug Thalidomide, wept into my recorder the night he was struck off. Would-be politicians, who said things to me on tape and then denied them when they were published, were furious that they had been taped, but had to admit their perversity when the tape was played back.

Mr. Richard Adamson, the man who was responsible for the discovery of Tutankhamen's tomb, talked for hours to me on tape, describing in vivid terms what he saw as the wall was broken through and the world's most astounding treasures revealed; eerily filling my room with the scene of the actual moment of opening the world's most astonishing sarcophagus.

Without tape, any reporter could read from his notebook; unable to prove his 'shorthand notes' were jotted down at the time the words were uttered, or even if they were uttered. I never wanted this to happen to me, so I recorded every word I gathered, ready to be played back as irrefutable evidence. Today I still have many of the tapes. This book is the result.

Desmond Zwar
Beechworth, 2004

Chapter 1

Sailing Into The Future

I'm up on the deck in the freezing early morning, peering through the gloom at the little red roofs of England and feeling sick. Not because of any turbulence of the 'Southern Cross', inching its way into Southampton, honking its eerie foghorn across the misty harbour, but the gut-gripping realisation that I'd departed Australia and a safe job, with a single lifeline: a bank account with unfortunately not very much money.

The romantic dream was over. "This is it; sink or swim," I told myself as the icy wind buffeted my face. A seagull cawed at me in sombre agreement. My stomach churned. It had taken six weeks to sail from Melbourne on a new ship. There would be adventure, excitement, sex. What lay on the other side of the world hadn't mattered in the planning.

I had turned 24 the night we made our way into the open sea outside Melbourne. Arriving in the small cabin on 'B' Deck, I had a safe feeling. I was good at journalism; always assuming, cheekily, that Fleet Street, the famed 'Mecca' of the newspaper world, would be waiting patiently, with the red carpet stretched out. I'd danced the tamure with a gorgeous girl in Tahiti, walked the dark, mean streets of The Bowery with the protection of a New York cop; I'd fallen in, and out of, love with a Perth ballet dancer.

In Melbourne, the yellow-bound copies of the London Daily Mirror and Sunday Pictorial I'd bought every week at McGill's bookshop, had for years been my link with British writing. I had avidly consumed every word, every opinion column; every bombastic editorial. The papers might well have been months old arriving by sea, but they were read by more people than any other in the world. Their reporting was the most concise, the most colourful in journalism. Now, as we inched into port, that day's papers had been brought to the ship on the Pilot vessel and I'd shakily bought a selection of five at the ship's shop.

Only an hour away in London stood the great newspaper offices. Which one would give me a job? 'Those who knew', had said back in Melbourne that the answer would be a firm 'none.' The only way into the best journalism in the English-speaking world was via British provincial newspapers and then, after years, perhaps the Manchester offices of the national papers; from there eventually to Fleet Street. "And I mean years," sniffed a stylish Pom sub-editor who'd been hired and shipped over to Australia at great expense by The Herald. "Don't waste your time old boy, just go over and see it all and have a holiday." Wearily, he went on hacking away at a story to make the last edition. (He was surely wrong?)

We got through Customs and I boarded a coach to London with a Melbourne friend. Later, we stood shivering in windswept Earl's Court Road, waiting for our cases to be taken from the bus. A relative had arranged accommodation in a cheerless bed-sitter nearby; a weary room with a gas-ring and heater which devoured shillings at dismaying speed. However it gave John and I a week to look for something permanent and hopefully more luxurious. In the hallway, a notice read: No overnight guests. No noise after 10 pm. Rent Saturday. Cabbage was being boiled in the landlady's kitchen and in the parlour I noticed her husband twiddling with a television set with a screen the size of a paperback novel.

Monday morning dawned. I got out of the stained bath, towelled myself in the freezing cold and put on my suit. As I breakfasted on instant coffee I watched the rain pouring down on the dirty windows. I had a red-and-white London Transport map showing me how to catch a No.6 red bus to what Philip Gibbs had dubbed "The Street of Adventure". I climbed the spiral stairs to the upper deck and tucked under my arm was a grey album with cuttings of articles and news stories I'd written for The Herald. I was proud of them; but deep down reality had set in: I was worried that — just maybe — my reporting might not be good enough for Fleet Street. I'd carefully read eight daily papers the day before. The writing was startlingly brighter and more concise than any paper in Australia. (How could I dare?)

The Daily Express, Daily Mail, Sketch, Mirror, The Times, Daily Telegraph, Guardian and all the Sunday papers had sharply differing styles. Their journalism was spare, slick and 'angled'; six papers might well have covered the same smash-and-grab raid that had killed a security man, but the twist they each gave to it was poles apart. The Telegraph reportage was a grey, matter-of-fact record of the incident. The Sketch, on the other hand, would have discovered the suspect robber's girl-friend and would carry a tearful picture of her pleading with her man to give himself up. The Mirror would have sent out a team of 'Mirror-tecs' to help police track the gunman. I had written from Melbourne to news editors of six daily and four Sunday newspapers and had heard back from only one. I was to meet him at 10 am today. What would happen?

The Daily Express was a massive, black glass pile with

a foyer of awful ostentation, dubbed the Black Gulag. I walked up to Enquiries, and said I had an appointment with the News Editor, Mr. Morley Richards, apologizing for being five minutes early. An aloof, uniformed gentleman with silver pips on his shoulders and a peaked cap, invited me with some disdain to wait while he spoke 'to the desk'. Ten minutes passed and then a pale-faced, middle-aged man without a chin, came down the stairs and was directed to me. "Frightfully sorry, old boy. Nothing at the moment. Mr. Richards says why don't you try again in a month or two?"

I walked back into Fleet Street and drank a coffee and munched at a bun in Mick's cafe, sitting at a counter with workmen in overalls and greasy cloth caps. Most of them were smoking Woodbines, the fug misting the front window so heavily that all I could see of the famous street were the ghostly shapes of passing buses. What next?

Outside into the crisp, winter air to a phone-box where I clunked twopence in at a time, to dial each of the other papers, to ask if I could possibly make an appointment for an interview. Two shillings later I had given up. I had been given no hope by the secretaries. "No point in seeing you, I'm afraid," said one male executive I actually spoke to at the Daily Mail. "Nothing going at the moment. Try again next year."

That week I remained out of work and apart from phone calls I 'did' the crowded, coat-muffled streets of London. Between the Tower, St. Paul's Cathedral, the V&A and Petticoat Lane, the shillings and the large, epistle-sized five-pound notes were starting to flow out of my National Bank account at an alarming rate. I ran into a shipboard mate from Brisbane, outside the stately Coutts Bank in Fleet Street. Could he change his travellers' cheques there, he asked the top-hatted commissionaire. "Not actually," said the ex-colonel. "But one can change them at our branch in the West End."

"No way," said Jack. "I've just sighted St. Paul's Cathedral. I'm not going to lose the bugger now." I looked the other way.

A job of any kind was becoming essential. "Why don't you try a temp agency?" said a Sydney girl who was earning £5 a week as a secretary. "They looked after me."

The idea was ridiculous; temps were girls. Then the bank statement showed I was down to £5 and the rent was due. I found London Temps. A smart lady in a twinset ruffled through a card index and withdrew one: Sir Bruce White and Partners, Engineers; somebody required in the typing pool. "One assumes you can type?" said the aloof woman. Of course! With two fingers search-and-stab; but I could type.

Sir Bruce White's office manager, Mr. Wilkinson, greeted me with aplomb, seemingly ignoring the fact that I was not female, and placed me in front of an electric typewriter in the back row of a room with 20 middle-aged women and young girls. The head of the pool handed me a sheaf of edited engineering instructions. "I want a top and three carbons, dear. All right?"

When she had disappeared I took a stab at the keyboard. Nothing moved. Was the thing plugged in? It was. I poked at letters, figures and keys that carried obscure symbols. Again, nothing. A girl on my left was tittering; I smiled and said this machine was slightly different to the one I had been using and how did it start?

"Hit the KMC key."

I did. And the contraption leapt noisily into life. There was no Key Margin Control on a 30-year-old Herald manual Remington. Plans for great bridges and motorways flowed beneath my fingertips and then it was time for lunch. I was on my way out into The Strand when Mr. Wilkinson bustled out of his office to invite me in.

"There is," he said, looking down at his fingers, "somewhat of a problem. You see," he went on, "the typing-pool expected a … er … typiste. A girl. They will not, I am now told, work with a man." I was at once hurt, indignant and panic-stricken. I had been hired legitimately and now I'd got the typewriter working, nobody had complained about my work. I needed the money. So did the landlord.

Mr. Wilkinson was clearly embarrassed. He wondered if I might work in his own office for the rest of the day. "And I'm afraid," he said sadly, "after that we must sever our relationship."

He paid me at 5 o'clock, the money due to me and after stoppage' of tax, national health contribution for the week and commission to the temp agency, just one and fourpence remained. I walked down The Strand into gloomy Fleet Street, which was dark, wet and miserable. It seemed London had no need for me.

Then at last a breakthrough! A cheery, roly-poly news editor, after weeks of pestering, offered me a casual reporting job at the Sunday Express on Saturdays. £6 for a day's work! A large staff was needed for the next day's paper and reporters, sub-editors and even copy-boys were hired from the dailies to bring the paper out. Every Tuesday I'd gone to see the jovial Mr. Wilson and he shared with me his philosophy and a half-pound block of chocolate, the crumbs dropping over the staff ledger as he looked, always in vain, for 'a spare slot'.

Then at last somebody went on holidays and a position became available. I had a sleepless Friday night and arrived at the black glass edifice ready to change the world. The job lasted three Saturdays and then suddenly it came to a catastrophic end. I had been calling Land's End Radio all day for the actual position of a cadet-crewed yacht that had won some race, and the operator, who said he could actually see the vessel arriving 100 yards off shore, was becoming annoyed. "Look mate, it's down there now. OK? It'll be docking in minutes. Now please, leave me alone!" I sat at my typewriter and reported the yacht's safe arrival as Land's End Radio's cranky operator had assured me, 'to a flag-decked shore'. And it made the Sunday Express first edition front page!

Proudly reading my effort in the paper next morning over breakfast I switched on the BBC News. It announced that my yacht had inexplicably capsized 50 yards from the jetty just when I'd gone off duty. Every paper but the Sunday Express, had the story. Mr. Wilson called me in next day. "It would be wise, Old Boy, if we parted company." This time there was no shared chocolate.

The bitter winter days which became cold and dark at four o'clock in the afternoon, became depressing exercises in hanging on to hope. The nest-egg I'd saved at the National Bank in Melbourne and which I'd transferred to the branch at Australia House in The Strand, was being eaten away again by rent and the outlay of funds for cheap Harris sausages, potatoes and tomato sauce. Salads were out of the question.

In a state of panic I made up my mind to go to Tilbury to join the merchant navy. I'd been told that real desperates could get jobs waiting on ships' waiters at mealtime. The story was correct: but there was a problem, explained the chain-smoking foreman who interviewed me. To get into the navy you had to join the union. And to join the union, you had to first be in the merchant navy.

Shit! Without hope for the future I took the train back to Earl's Court. On the Monday morning I dialled FLE6000, the London Daily Mail, and heard my twopence tumble into the box as I pressed 'Button A'. A charming lady, Ms. Joan Gabbedey, secretary to the News Editor, said how nice it was to speak to an Australian. She had relatives in Australia and why didn't I 'pop in', there might just be a holiday relief job going.

If ever there was instant love, sight unseen, I felt it for Joan Gabbedey. She could have had no idea how 'down'

I was. The chip on the Australian shoulder had grown
progressively heavy as one Englishman after another pat-
ronised me as I opened my mouth. "Oh," said a fat gentleman I shared a table with at the once-a-week 4-shilling
Lyon's evening meal. "It sounds like you are Orstralian.
How are things out in the Colonies?"

Donald Todhunter, News Editor of the Daily Mail,
was a handsome, impeccably-groomed gentleman in a
striped suit and a rose in his buttonhole. The gentle Ms.
Gabbedey, dark-haired and soothing, took me in to meet
him and he asked me about The Herald and Australia. I
proffered my heavy cuttings book. He brushed it aside.
"No, we prefer to look at the man."

"But," I protested, "how can you tell if I can write or
not? These cuttings ..."

He looked hard at me. "Probably re-written by sub-
editors."

"No! What you see there is what I wrote! There's
very little re-writing back in Melbourne. I find it hard to
believe ..."

I knew, and he knew, I'd gone too far. I was actually
with a Fleet Street News Editor who might have given
me a job and I had over-stepped the mark. I'd blown it! I
felt every reporter and sub-editor on the other side of the
glassed-in partition was looking at the surprising confrontation. But suddenly Donald Todhunter grinned.

"You want to run my paper?"

Then, before I made another idiot response he asked,
"When would you like to start?"

My stomach did a flip. "What about this afternoon?"

"OK!" he said. And shook hands. "I'll give you £17 a
week. I'll try you out."

On the first day of my trial I wore a dark blue tie
with white ensigns on it — a purchase from the shop
on the 'Southern Cross'. The reporter sitting next to me
suddenly leaned over and without asking, took it in his

fingers to examine it. "Royal Yacht Club, Old Boy?" "No," I answered. "It's a Shaw Savill line tie."

"Oh," he guffawed. "How very Australian." I tightened my mouth and did not say a word.

Two days later I was on the 5 pm-midnight shift. The Night News Editor called me in. "You live in Earl's Court, don't you, Old Boy?"

"Yes," I admitted.

"You can take the night car home with the driver. So long as you make sure Paul (he named an elderly, veteran reporter) gets home safely. He's hitting the piss a bit lately."

Paul had once been a famous newsman. Now his active days were almost over and he was loitering—mainly in 'Aunties' the nearby pub bar—waiting to retire. I went searching for him around 10.45pm and at last discovered him, fumbling in the urinal. "Paul!" I called to him. No answer. "Paul!" I said again. Still no answer. I took a deep breath, approached the urinal and tapped my senior colleague on the shoulder.

"SHIT!" he exclaimed, almost falling into the urinal. "I was just trying to find my old man, Old Man."

* * *

If you wanted to identify a Daily Mail reporter it was easy: you looked at his fingertips which would be covered in purple. The mass-circulation newspaper, read every morning by millions, was produced on ancient upright typewriters attached to the tops of the reporters' desks. When you wanted to type you reached down and tugged and the hinged mechanism creaked into action replacing the desk-top with a worn Remington on which stories had to be typed on paper called 'Banda'. It was like carbon paper in reverse. Once typed, you took the purple-smudged sheets to a machine which ran off copies from a churning drum which then were distributed by copy boys to sub-editors, the news desk and the Editor.

Laurie Turner, a colleague from The Herald in Melbourne, had joined the paper some months before me and we sat at adjoining desks. Laurie chain-smoked cigarettes which he rolled with one hand while talking on the phone, making him the centre of attention for copy boys scuttling between reporters, sub-editors and the nerve-centre, the news room.

As Laurie and I chatted, reporters and sub-editors would eavesdrop. The Australian accent intrigued them; it was to them uproariously funny.

I sat at my desk, next to Laurie's as I came on shift. "You came over on the Canberra, did you, mate?" I asked him loudly.

"Yeah, mate."

"Buy your camera in Aden?"

"Oh yeah, mate!"

"Get it cheap?"

"Oh God, yeah. Three quid!"

And the Poms would chuckle, nudging each other.

Tall, chain-smoking Laurie was a smart reporter, ruthless tennis player and a man with an eye for the women. His slow West Australian drawl when he was on the phone caused the English reporters to fall about.

The Dalai Lama had just made his historic escape from Tibet, and every reporter—including the intrepid Laurie—was trying to find him.

There were calls put in to possible hiding places in India, Afghanistan, even the Continent of Europe. As each phone on the paper-littered desk jangled, you picked it up in hope, asking Afghans, Indians and even Germans: "Have you seen the Dalai Lama?"

About nine o'clock the phone on Laurie's desk rang. For some reason there was a sudden hush in the vast newsroom as he spoke. He thought he'd found his quarry.

"Hello?" shouted Laurie down the line. "Is that the Dyly Lama? This is the Dyly Mile!"

It was now Friday. All 30-odd reporters could be seen at their uprights, faces concentrating on a task with a determination and seriousness seldom given to the most sensational news story. They were doing their 'exes'.

Expenses (I later learned) formed a large part of their income, and required creativity far surpassing the delicacy of a human-interest story.

It was my first Friday morning and I got out my notebook to recall what I had spent. There was 8d. on telephone calls; I had had to take two Underground rides to the West End on a murder; that came to 1s.6d. I'd taken a taxi on that rush to cover the disturbance in a Soho nightclub. The lot came to 10s 4d.

I placed my expenses form in Joan Gabbedey's In-tray and started work on the day's assignment. About an hour later there was a shout from the glassed-in inner sanctum. 'Toddy' Todhunter, the News Editor, wanted me.

"Zwarrrr!"

He had my expenses sheet in his hand. He looked disturbed, embarrassed even. "What", he wanted to know, "is this total of 10s 4d?"

God! I was being accused of dishonesty in my first week as a reporter in Fleet Street. I hurriedly explained the public phone calls I had made, the taxi to Soho.

"NO!" He said, shaking his head. "I ... do ... not ... want ... to ... know. Take this," he said, handing back the offending piece of paper. "Go and talk to Jack Greenslade."

Jack Greenslade, a tall, red-faced veteran of crime reporting, was about 45. He knew most of the top underworld villains and could be heard on the phone to Jack Spot, the knife-man, or Ruby Sparkes, Burglar to the Nobility, discussing the latest dramas in their lives where once again they complained of being 'fitted' by the police for something they clearly had not done. "I hear," Jack would say, confidentially, his hand over his own mouth and the phone mouth-piece, "the Old Bill have been a bit naughty, Ruby?"

When Jack had finished his conversation I handed him my expenses sheet. "Mr. Todhunter says you should have a talk to me about this." I began explaining the trips on the Tube as Jack fumbled for his glasses.

"Jesus Christ!" he exclaimed, "Ten and bloody fourpence!"

"Yes, but ..."

"Look," said Jack, his hand half-covering his mouth again, "go away my boy, and add ten quid to what you've written."

"But that would be dishonest."

His face was now redder than usual. "My son, we live by our bloody exes. The paper gets a better tax deal by giving us phoney exes than it would if it gave us higher wages. Understand?"

I was incredulous. They were all dishonest; the reporters, the News Editor, the accountants ... the system.

I did as I was told, and feeling my father was leaning over my shoulder watching me, shaking his head, re-typed the expense sheet, adding three taxi trips and giving myself an out-of-town meal late at night.

Over the next months I learned to hire snow-ploughs, to dine with celebrities, to give 'drinks' to all sorts of officials — particularly hotel doormen — for information. My colleague Syd Watson, had been on a country job and he'd put down £2 10 shillings for a pair of gumboots he'd said were necessary to cover the story. But he went too far.

A grim-faced accountant, obviously trying to walk some sort of honest path in the wicked system, asked the News Editor to have Watson bring in the actual boots, as they might well be used by a reporter with the same-sized feet on another 'country job'. Syd hurried out to the nearest Army Surplus shop where pairs of gumboots, hung from hooks. He forked out £2 for a new pair, taking care to spatter mud all over them before presenting them to the News Room.

Next day he got a note from Accounts. "Next time you go out on a job, maybe you could move a little faster if you undid the string at the top."

As regular as clockwork, word went through the reporters' room that a 'purge' on expenses was on. Some audit was being done, or a new accountant, unaware of the system, had taken over.

I received a note:

"Dear Mr. Zwar,
"We have taken the opportunity of easing the claustrophobia you must be experiencing in public telephone boxes by adjusting your phone expenditure to 12 shillings. Two of your crime contacts have been sobered up to some extent by cutting your entertainment bill from ten to three pounds for the week."

Chapter 2

'We Are In The Poo'

It seemed only weeks ago—not six amazing years— since I'd nervously climbed the stairs to see the editor of the Albury Border Morning Mail. It was a day that was going to change my life.

On that day I'd found a greying, harassed-looking man, sitting taut and I thought aggressively, behind a desk. It seemed clear from the moment he sternly shook hands, that he was regretting wasting the time he'd put aside to talk to a would-be journalist. All I had was an idea that I'd like to write.

He gave me a 20-minute interview and listened patiently to the lie that I'd always wanted to be a reporter. He explained that his paper already had a full team of six newsmen, but if I really wanted to try, he would give me two weeks' trial as a cadet; an apprentice reporter. At the end of that time, if he could see I wasn't going to be God's gift to newspapers, and it was fairly apparent he already had that thought in mind, 'we would go our own separate ways'.

It was a hot Summer's day, and as I walked out of the old two-storey building in Albury's main street. I desperately hoped I didn't smell. That was the drawback with working in my father's tannery. The stink of tannin used by the factory to cure cattle hides and make them into leather, became so deeply impregnated in the pores of the skin, that I ponged whenever I perspired. This was most embarrassing at dances in the Beechworth Fire Brigade Hall on a Saturday night, when I was trying to get gum-chewing girls on the floor.

"You got this dance?"

"Sorreee."

After all, I realised I was already balding and looked years older than 19.

The provincial centre of 1950s Albury, on the day I was supposed to be going to a dentist, was a 40-deg. perspiry cauldron. It had a dull, conservative air of a big country town pretentiously calling itself a city. Shopkeepers and professional men wore suits and ties; ladies shopped in large hats. From the outlying districts 'cockey' farmers and their 'missus' arrived to shop at Mates, the department store, for crockery or curtains. The latest cotton frocks with 'the new boat neckline' were available for 73/6; and thanks to Velvet Soap — said the ads — blankets were still soft and fluffy after 22 years.

Outside in Dean Street, there were unfortunate mix-ups between shoppers from nearby Wodonga, across the State border in Victoria, which had different road laws from Albury, New South Wales, as they encountered each other at intersections. Victorians, turning right, swung left first and then right. New South Welshmen turned from the centre of the intersections and quite often the two met, denting cars like the latest Holden which was selling for an astonishing high £900.

I travelled back to Beechworth by bus, reading the day's Border Morning Mail and wondering what Dad's reaction would be. There was no doubt that he would loyally back me in whatever I chose to do in life; he had been good about my admission that I would never make a tanner like him and his father before him. But what did I want to do then? That was the problem. I'd told him I had no idea, except that it had to involve self-expression, like radio work, or writing. I was a youngster who, I was told, had grown up 'older than my years' wearing a frowning air of concern. Why? Maybe because I was even then, 'parenting' my parents. I believed they were in need of help; not always understanding one another. There was no real friction, just a lack of communication.

My mother certainly loved my father. She would have smothered him with affection had he allowed it. I'm sure that he loved her as much in return, but never, but never, demonstrably. It might have been his Teutonic genes that prevented him giving the hug and kiss she yearned for; I have a rare photograph of them posing for me together. Dad is stiff and embarrassed, hoping it would soon be over. Standing just as he must have done when his Sergeant called, "Shun!" and "Right Dress!" in the First World War, the knuckles of his right hand stretched out to my mother's shoulder. I knew their lives were dull and countrified, with little to fulfil them. I vowed that it wasn't going to happen to me. Dad's whole life was the tannery his father had founded and which he operated for decades with his two brothers. It was the lifeblood of little Beechworth, (pop. 3000) employing 140 people, and at one stage supplied electricity to the township. He worked 10-hour days, controlling several sections of the sprawling tannery, and most of the workers "worshipped the ground he walked on". (I was told by several, and promised never to tell him). He was just 50 when the tannery was sold and closed down. Suddenly, all that was left for him was to make a bet on the phone on race days, have his two whiskies at 11 o'clock in a stark, character-less pub; a sleep in his leather armchair in the afternoon and one or two whiskies before "tea." He was a diabetic and slept a lot, reading little, apart from the racing selections which he perused closely on a Saturday, phoning the illegal Starting Price bookie at one of the pubs.

He believed it was unmanly to weep, and made great efforts to stifle his feelings. When I'd drive home years later from working in Melbourne, he would stay in his big leather chair as I walked into the room, his eyes flooding with tears. He used his handkerchief to try and hide it, and would noisily blow his nose. I also longed for a closer relationship but the chance had gone. We had more to say to one another when I lived in London and we airmailed each other cassette 'talking' tapes.

As I got closer to Beechworth, I knew Mum would happily back my career decision. She was a small woman, round and kind and loving; she had curly black hair that remained that way into her 80's. She'd been born in New Zealand and still sung Maori songs at the piano in our seldom-used drawing-room. She brimmed with affection that went out to Dad and I, the various dogs and cats we owned, the neighbours and their dogs and cats.

Up until now, any real alternative to leather as my career had never even been discussed. I would spend a year at the tannery and then go to Leeds, in Britain, to a tanning school. Even if I'd had other ideas, university was out of the question; I failed to matriculate in English, which was a compulsory pass for university acceptance. I had never failed in an English exam before. But matriculation exams were held publicly, rather than internally, and I sat for the first hour in the cavernous Exhibition building, petrified by the occasion and not writing a word. Straight after Christmas that year I put on my workman's overalls and left home with Dad at 7 am for the Beechworth tannery.

My year in the sprawling leather factory is best remembered by my illicit affair with the sexiest woman I have ever met — Margrita. She was a Lithuanian migrant and one of scores from the Baltic states brought to Australia for a new life in the late 1940s. Margrita worked in the specialised leather department and wore a brown dust-coat over her perfectly-proportioned little body. She had pouting red lips and her ears were hung with huge golden earrings. In contrast to the smell of tannin, her body exuded an exotic, heady perfume. I was sent to hang treated leather with her in the close confines of the drying-room. Within minutes she had walked across and ostentatiously rubbed her little body up against mine. For a 19-year-old virgin male, fresh out of boarding-school, this was an unnerving experience, necessitating my eventual departure from the drying-room in an embarrassing crouched position.

During subsequent visits to the dryer, Margrita taught me two phrases in Lithuanian — 'Kiss Me!' and 'I love you.' She called me 'Cherie' and as we whispered together in the confines of rows of hanging hides she readily agreed to meet me at 7.30pm one night in a back street to be picked up in 'Rufus', my 1923 Dodge tourer. I was shaking with nerves by 7pm as I told my parents I was off to a mate's place to help repair his racing-bike. Right on 7.30 I drove slowly along the darkened Beechworth back street and sure enough, walking purposefully along the footpath was Margrita. She hurried across, climbed into the back seat and hid while I headed for the 5th fairway of the golf-course.

We got out, I laid a rug on the grass and we held each other close; she warm; me shaking. Patiently and expertly she taught me how to kiss — to enjoy the warm, soft and tender lips I had admired so much whenever I saw her in the tannery. We caressed and whispered to each other, but I remained chaste, though it wasn't through lack of trying. 'Cherie,' she would warn me, 'I 'ave a 'usband.' Even today I shudder at the local scandal had we ever been caught out in a liaison that went on for almost a year.

I had matured quickly in other ways, if not sexually. I had been a boarder at a private school in Melbourne from the age of 12, and at 17 suddenly given the daunting responsibility as boarding-house captain, of being in charge of 60 boys. Our Housemaster had been a prisoner-of-war in Changi, and when he returned to the Arthur Robinson House, he told me it was going to be difficult for a while. "You're going to have to do some of my job," said Faf. The role of House Captain involved reading prayers at night, holding prefects' 'courts' to judge boys' rule-breaking; and the sobering responsibility of caning for misdemeanours, seriously politically incorrect, in this day and age.

All the time I worked in the gloomy tanning pits and staining-shed at the tannery helping to make leather for car seats and handbags, I kept asking myself how could I tell Dad that it wasn't for me? Secretly, at the end of the day, I'd sit out on the verandah at home, notebook and pencil in hand, and scribble stories about the old gold-mining town that 80 years ago had been alive with prospectors, Chinese market gardeners and wild pubs. By now it had settled back into complacent obscurity, earning its living from the tannery, the mental asylum, the old peoples' home or the jail.

I'd taken my first step in journalism: a column in the local paper, the century-old Ovens and Murray Advertiser, where I wrote on cycling under the nom-de-plume 'Sprocket'. I was experiencing the beginnings of a literary 'fix', a writing urge that originally came from letters from Mum's Auckland Aunt Tui, glowing gems of feeling and description. Dad was a technician who had inherited his own father's expertise in leather. He had few interests in creativity, though he was a good artist when he was young. When I hinted one day that I might like to do something entirely different — like working in radio, he was aghast. "That's where they all wear brothel-sneakers, isn't it?" He was disappointed that I didn't see leather as a career, but understanding about my looking for an alternative, as long as it did not involve lace-less shoes.

When I arrived home from Albury, he sat back in the huge armchair, made from his own leather, and put me immediately at ease, saying he was pleased with my news of a fortnight's trial. "If that's what you want, son, do it. All I want is for you to be happy."

Two weeks later I found myself in the hot, claustrophobic Border Morning Mail reporters' room, scribbling a report in longhand, (I couldn't type) describing a fire that had destroyed a paddock of grass on the outskirts of Albury. In pitch dark at 4 o'clock next morning, I sneaked out to find the paper on the landlady's lawn and saw in print, my one-paragraph story on page two. "Fire yesterday destroyed ..."

Type-addiction gradually began to take over like the sexual lust I still had for Margrita, my eyes impatiently searching for my own words on the paper's pages; wanting more. Soon I was eagerly 'covering' everything that moved; single vehicle accidents, a tramp who told me he was starving on his pension and could I 'lend' him two bob; then, a nasty court-case, involving incest and, as usual, the daily fulminations of the Mayor. I worked in the evenings for nothing, interviewing old ladies in retirement homes. 'So your husband was in the First World War!' So was my own father, I'd forgotten that. And there, a day or two later, were my words in 10-pt. type, in a newspaper that thousands – at that very moment – must be reading.

It was at the end of the first week, when the chief subeditor and father-figure on the paper, Frank "The Colonel" Kearney, called me into his broom-cupboard office. An amiable, old-fashioned figure with black, cow-lick hair atop a long, kindly face, Frank sat at his desk stabbing at an inkwell with a steel-nibbed pen, slashing at reporters' words, scribbling headlines and at the same time carrying on conversations with whoever happened to be in his office; a reporter, his friend the local tailor, or both at the same time. It was six o'clock, and still stiflingly hot. Frank explained to me that "The Old Man", Mr. H.C. Mott, owner of The Border Morning Mail, a formidable moustachioed gentleman in a safari suit, long socks and pith helmet, had reported to him that the gipsies were in town and the paper should do something about them.

"Go over to Monument Hill and see what's going on there," said Frank. "That's a good boy, there."

I got into the office Holden with a photographer and we drove on to a paddock on private property to see a ring of battered cars, trucks and tents, in and out of which, wandered children, dogs, swarthy dark men and then the most beautiful creature I had ever laid eyes on since Margrita. She wore huge hoop earrings and a once-white cotton dress that billowed in the breeze. She stared across at me with massive brown eyes that made me go weak at the knees. Her name, she whispered to the photographer was Donna. She was 16. From inside a nearby tent a guitar quietly began strumming; and Donna, never taking her eyes from mine, slowly danced, her brown bare feet twisting and turning in the grass, long brown fingers clicking to the beat, her barely covered little breasts rising and falling as she undulated for the camera.

As instantly in love with Donna as I was, the photographer went on clicking as fast as the guitar strummed. We shared a drink with her brothers and chatted about life on the road, the history of the gipsies; about happiness. I went back to the office and wrote a besmitten article that took up half a page next morning below a row of Charlie's pictures. And to my astonishment the romantic story of 'the Romanies coming to town' appeared under my own name! "The Romance of the Wanderers". By Desmond Zwar, Staff Reporter. I had my first by-line. I had arrived.

Next morning all hell broke loose. The Colonel had been called in early and after a phone call I quickly followed. I found Frank at his desk stabbing at his inkwell. He wore, as always, his black, pin-striped trousers and an ancient, ink-stained brown suit jacket. His kindly face, with the forelock of Hitler-style hair, was scrunched in pain.

"Sonny, we are in the poo." The Colonel never swore. When crises hit, as every night they did, the extreme measure was for Frank to take out yet another Bex headache powder, mix it into a glass of water and swallow it; offering one through a wall-hatch to Des, the print foreman, to get him over his own stress. "Poo" meant that the trouble was serious.

It appeared that there had been an unfortunate mix-up of signals between The Old Man and The Colonel. The gipsies were in fact Mr. Mott's dire enemies. He was incensed at their presence in Albury and wished his paper to do something to get rid of them. To make it worse, they were camped on his land. The headline stared up at the Colonel and I above my precious by-line. "The Romance ..."

Frank said, despairingly, "You try and do the right thing, there, sonny, and you are wrong, there." The Colonel had something else to worry about. The previous evening Australian United Press, the wire service that covered Federal and State politics and capital city events for provincial newspapers, had missed a crucial Canberra story. Frank stabbed at the inkwell. "You know, sonny, if the Good Lord Himself walked down Collins Street, AUP would probably miss it."

As the lowliest cadet reporter, my duty each evening was to watch over the advertising front counter which had a door on to the main street of Albury. From 7.30 until 8.30 the citizens of Albury brought in their Birth and Death Notices; for sale classifieds and announcements of lamington drives. My job was to decipher what they had written and to take the money. I sat in front of an ancient telephone switchboard and pushed in pegs to give lines to reporters who shouted for them from the adjacent Reporters' Room; a job handled efficiently during the day by the Front Office Girl, but to me still a mechanical mystery.

One reporter, to my 19-year-old innocent eyes, had appeared to be somehow different from the others. He was tall, fat and strikingly well-groomed. And he—this in the days before after-shave—positively reeked of perfume. Unaware from a sheltered boarding-school life that some men were not like others, I pushed the thought aside; life was too exciting to be bothered about it.

Having weathered the gipsy fiasco and with still four days' trial left, I manfully plugged and pushed at the phone pegs, commiserated with the bearers of Death Notices and in between times, pecked with two fingers at a typewriter. There was a sudden roar from the Reporters' Room. "Line please! Give us a line!" I recognised the voice of the perfumed Hilary. I plugged him into Line 2. Seconds later I had the impression of someone standing behind me. As three or four people on the other side of the counter scribbled away at their classifieds I felt hands on my shoulders. And I smelled the scent. "Thank you for the line," purred Hilary, softly rubbing my shoulders with fat paws.

Some feeling inside of me churned and said this was wrong. I got up and faced the large man saying, "Don't do that." He smiled sweetly and persisted, reaching towards me again. I reached back, swung my fist and smashed him in the nose which exploded with blood. It couldn't have been me doing it, was the one thought rushing through my mind. Whoever had done it, Hilary was now sprawled on his back across the desk. Women screamed and ran into the street. There was a thunder of feet as someone raced down the wooden stairs from the floor above; and at the same time, two reporters burst in to find Hilary blood-stained and lying like a stranded beetle, shouting up at me. What had I done!

The owner of the feet on the stairs was the Advertising Manager, who also happened to be the Old Man's son. He and the printing department foreman met at the final stair, the foreman bearing a page of metal type locked into a frame that was to be a full-page stock and station ad. for next day's paper and needed approval. The force of their impact released the hundreds of pieces of lead which flew about the floor, some of it lying in Hilary's blood.

My career in journalism was surely now at an end. It had lasted 10 days. I could almost smell the leather of my Father's tannery again back in Beechworth. By 9pm it would be all over when the second cadet task of the night was to take the office car to Albury railway station where the guard from the Spirit of Progress from Melbourne, would hand over that evening's Melbourne Herald. It was to be rushed back to The Border Morning Mail where The Colonel would hack out great chunks from its pages to print in his own paper, pausing only to change the headlines.

Feeling ill, I tapped on The Editor's door to ask for the keys to the Holden and surely be handed my dismissal.

He rose from his chair, reached out and shook my hand. It wasn't goodbye. He was smiling. "Desmond," he said, "for reasons I will not go into, we have been trying for almost a year to get Hilary to leave. There have been serious court charges, but because a witness failed to appear, we could never dismiss him. He could have sued us.

"He resigned tonight. He said if I didn't get rid of you he would leave. I told him you would be staying."

I walked out of the office on air, past The Colonel's ever-open office door. "There you go, there," he said to the Printer. "The Violent Youth." He had christened our New Zealand reporter "The Haka", and George Gaertner, "The Little German". I was "The Violent Youth" until I finally left the paper.

I pedalled my bike down the hill from my rented room in East Albury letting the sun beat down on my head; I was rapidly losing my hair and the latest baldness treatment I was using, specifically advocated airing the follicles. I'd boiled up a stinking sulphur compound and rubbed it into my scalp the night before in the garage, trusting the assurance on the bottle that the hairs coming away on my fingers were, as the label said, 'a good sign.' It hurt deeply when two colleagues I passed, shouted out: "Hey! Baldy!" I'd been taught not to let feelings show.

I had no idea whether the day would bring a bush-fire, a Petty Sessions court case, or a chat with 'Tiny', the police contact whose confession rate was not presumably, unconnected with criminal suspects accidentally falling down the stairs from the CIB room where they were being questioned. If that failed, there was always the persuasiveness of his smoker colleague who was reputed to use a glowing cigarette-end between the toes with remarkable effect. Certainly, I knew, as I propped my bike against the wall in the laneway, that there would be no more reports on gipsies. The Colonel and I had learned our lesson.

Albury was a prosperous town in the 1950s, and without serious social problems. There were a few drunks on the streets, but drugs were unheard of. The city had a respected and efficient Mayor, Alderman Cleaver Bunton, who seemed to have been there for as long as anyone could remember, and was a reliable father figure. I met him often because the paper had a system of 'rounds' with a reporter calling on the Mayor in the morning, then the police, the fire brigade and the hospital to ask if there was anything "doing".

Alderman Bunton seemed to have several jobs; one of the best-known was his job broadcasting the news on the local ABC radio station. It was not unusual to hear him read in dry, rather plodding tones: "Here is the news, read by Cleaver Bunton. The Mayor of Albury, Alderman Cleaver Bunton, said yesterday that ..."

Alderman Bunton tirelessly opened flower shows, displays of works, launched the new fire engine and spoke at Rotary. Whatever he 'opened', he had a set speech, which saved us writing it down in shorthand. "It is pleasing indeed to be present on this auspicious occasion and it augers well for the City of Albury that this state of affairs has come about ..." It applied to everything. When we met for the first time, he mentioned that he would like to inform me about something 'rather important' later, as he knew my father; obviously he was unwilling to discuss whatever it was in front of the reporter introducing me.

I called on him on 'rounds' later that week and his long, bloodhound face was serious. Cleaver said there was a person on the Border Mail, who he felt he might perhaps warn me about. I asked if it was Hilary? Embarrassed, he said well yes, it was. I said there had been an unfortunate altercation some days before and that Hilary had decided to leave the paper. I spared him the details and he seemed relieved.

My wage was £3 10 shillings a week; out of that had to come £2 to pay for full board to a widow landlady who had made her hot little fibro cottage into a boarding house for young men, and there was an aged gardener who rented her garage. I shared board with a stock and station agent and a dentist, all of us derided by Mrs. Watkins as 'rotten curses' for the way we left our bedrooms and the bathroom. In her converted garage 'Daddy" Ryan, a huge, mad Irishman, could be heard talking loudly to himself. Whenever he got to the breakfast table first he would carry on alarming conversations with himself, saying "And do you remember that?" Yes, was the answer, of course he did. Daddy took an instant dislike to me. When I sleepily sat down at breakfast he would pause from eating his Weeties, his huge, calloused hand poised half-way to his mouth and demand in a booming voice: "Are you better?"

Mrs. Watkins would wipe her hands on her apron and say: "But Mr. Ryan, Desmond hasn't been ill."

"Oi only hoped," growled Daddy, glaring across at me.

I often worked until late at night and tried to sleep past 7am, but it was impossible. Mrs. Watkins would have her radio on full blast with Cleaver Bunton's news-reading vibrating the fibro walls; she brushed aside my pleas to turn the volume down. Then one night when I came home on my bike, I had a brilliant idea. I stood on a chair in the darkened kitchen and removed one of the old-fashioned radio's valves, hiding it in my drawer. Next morning: blissful silence.

"That rotten radio has broken down," said Mrs. Watkins when I got up at 8 o'clock. I obligingly offered to fix it and slipped the missing valve back in its place, earning huge gratitude from the old girl for my technical brilliance and an extra egg with my bacon. I had to 'fix' the radio many times after that; but there was nothing I could do to tone down Daddy Ryan. "You've got a wonderful memory," he was telling himself down in the garage.

There were six town councils in the Border Mail's circulation area and it was my task to cover their monthly meetings. They were dull affairs with farmer-councillors urging that their side-roads be fixed or cursing the complaints of ratepayers who, sometimes with good reason, felt they were being forgotten. As the chamber clock crept around to midday, meetings gathered a little pace, for it was tradition that a fine lunch was to be enjoyed. A little hurry would come into the proceedings.

"Just before we get up for the break," Councillor Jones of Beechworth Shire Council requested. "I think we should vote on the Engineer's idea for a pagoda on the lake to help in the beautification scheme. I'd like to move that we do it."

"I'll second that," said Councillor Wilson, "but I reckon we should get two and breed from 'em."

Every night when I brought The Herald back from the station for The Colonel to hack to pieces, I would read the best stories before they were sliced from the page and pushed through the hatch to the linotype operators to copy. There were bank hold-ups, political brawls, murders; the real stuff of life. My interview that day with the grower of the Best Cucumbers at the Albury Show paled into insignificance. Melbourne beckoned ...

I decided to take the plunge. I wrote to The Editor of The Herald and asked for an interview. A note on stiff parchment came back by return. Sir Keith Murdoch, the Managing Director, would himself see me. I took the Spirit of Progress train to Melbourne on the morning of my day off and, heart-in-mouth three hours later, walked the several blocks to the great grey building in Flinders Street that housed The Herald, The Sun News-Pictorial, The Sporting Globe and The Weekly Times. Clutching my book of cuttings from The Border Morning Mail, I was ushered into the Great Man's presence. Greying, with massive eyebrows over startlingly dark brown eyes, he sat at the end of a board-room table where, judging by the coffee-cups, there had just been a meeting. He told me to sit down while he glanced through Ald. Cleaver Bunton's utterances and my interviews with nursing-home matrons. The chocolate eyes then fixed themselves on me. "Good bush reporting," he grunted. "We'll give you a try.

"Now go," he said, motioning towards the next office, "and see Williams [the General Manager] and he'll work out the details."

I emerged from the lift, heart thumping, with a third-year cadetship on The Herald, starting in three weeks' time.

Many years on, glancing through my file of precious cuttings, I again feel the excitement of being a young reporter on what was then Australia's greatest newspaper. Arguably the best evening newspaper in the world.

* * *

I find myself 4,000 feet up on icy Mount Donna Buang where a search is going on for two hikers lost somewhere below in the snow. I weep, even now, at the memory of being beside Scots-born radio technician Alex Hubbard, sent by his company to use a new-fangled 'walkie-talkie' radio to help co-ordinate the search which has been going on fruitlessly for three days, with hope fading for two young lives.

'Tower calling Mike. Tower calling Mike. Come in Mike.' But there are only crackles and hisses as Alex tries to plot the positions of search-parties Mike 1 and Mike 2.

Then: 'Mike 2 to Tower. Mike 2 to Tower. We have found the missing persons!'

Huddled in his sodden overcoat in a small touring car that had to be pushed the last few yards in the snow, Alex Hubbard grabs the microphone, bumping his head on the dashboard as he leans down to decipher the muffled call. It comes through again.

'We have found the missing persons. THEY ARE ALIVE. Repeat. They are alive. They are suffering from frost-bite and shock. But they are alive.'

Twelve miles down the mountainside, the parents of Jennifer Laycock and Kirk McLeod, in the lobby of the Warburton Hotel, had almost given up hope. Mrs. McLeod was called into a phone-box and half-a-minute later she burst out of it, tears streaming down her cheeks. 'They've found them!'

Back I go to St.Vincent's Hospital where I'm allowed

to work as an orderly in the Casualty ward for the night. A drunk is brought in by ambulance-men. 'This one's a bottle job,' a driver explains to a nurse as they roll the old man from stretcher to trolley. The man's face is covered in blood, his hair matted with it. 'Oh what a beautiful morning!' he is singing.

I live for three days in a cave 100 ft. below ground, having climbed down a terrifyingly narrow steel ladder from what appeared to be a small hole in the paddock we'd driven to ... .a world, illuminated by our torches, of stalactites, drips of lime frozen over hundreds of years into rocky fingers pointing downwards.

There I am in a paddock off the Geelong road, spying on members of the Victorian Gun Club blazing away at pigeons and starlings sprung from traps, shattering their bodies with bursts of gun-fire; some birds still alive but then torn apart by children or dogs; wounded pigeons fluttering about on the ground, then grabbed by the head and their bodies whirled about to strangle them. Emerging at last from my hiding-place I confront the red-faced committee with questions: 'Don't you think what you're doing is cruel? What about the birds still lying somewhere, wounded?'

The man elected as spokesman, remembers for me: 'Last year we shot 7,600 pigeons, 8,700 starlings and 1,800 sparrows. It's not really that bad, you know. You must have a weak stomach.'

Next day I attend the morning press conference given by the Premier of Victoria, Mr. Henry Bolte, who, I have discovered, is a live bird shooter. The Premier has become used to a tame chat with parliamentary reporters who have got to know him too well. Standing in that day for The Herald's man, I wait until the end and ask him: 'Is it true, Mr. Bolte, that you are a live bird shooter?'

'You bastard!' he says. And closes the conference. I telephone the story of the confrontation to The Herald's copy-takers. It does not appear in the paper. Melbourne — like Albury — isn't such a big town.

* * *

The week I began on The Herald, Melbourne was in upheaval amid wildcat industrial strikes. Communist takeover of leadership in the unions was leading to ugliness at meetings with fights breaking out and bashings of those members not willing to follow the party line. The Tramway Trackworkers' Union was at the time led by a loud-mouth bully who could, at a whim, close down the city's tram system.

The Herald, was staunchly anti-communist. After publishing a particularly tough editorial about communists holding the population to ransom, there was a march on its Flinders Street. building ending with booted workers standing on reporters' desks haranguing the staff before being escorted off the premises by police.

It was in this charged atmosphere one morning, that I noticed a man in overalls sitting at the Chief of Staff's desk, in earnest conversation. Ron Hobbs, the COS, a suave character who looked and spoke like Humphrey Bogart, called me in and introduced me. 'This is Bill, he's a right-winger in the Tramways Union and he's opposed to the Commos. He tells me that the members of the union are being steamrolled by the Communist leadership and they don't like it. Many of the members are Italian migrants who aren't being told the real truth about what's going on and they vote the way they're told. Bill will give you his union card so you can get into this morning's meeting so you can hear what goes on. And when you go down there, don't look any different than a tramways worker.'

I quickly drove home and put on a tattered pair of overalls and a battered gardening hat belonging to the next-door neighbour. Over the top I wore a ragged gabardine overcoat, cutting out the pockets so my hands were free to write notes on a small notebook underneath.

Back in the city I caught the tram to the union hall and flashing Bill's union card to the burly doorman, got inside, and made my way to a seat right next to the wall so I could remain unnoticed. The hall quickly filled up. Noisy workers laughed and argued as they took their seats on long wooden forms. I noticed space was becoming limited and men were squeezing in; to my concern the crush was pushing my neighbour, a burly, unshaven fellow, closer to me.

When the hall was full, the union secretary climbed on to the stage and began talking about how he and his comrades were going to force the fight for better wages by shutting down the tram services. Surreptitiously I started taking shorthand, scribbling a page at a time in the little notebook. By now, my neighbour and I were jammed in so tightly that he felt every move of my hands. He'd turn and cast a glance at me and I'd stop writing. Up on the platform the rabble-rousing was gaining new heights and again I started to get it all down.

This time the big fellow next to me turned and stared at me, long and hard. Then he shouted in my ear: "Stop fucking playing with yourself. Listen to what Jack is saying."

That afternoon the front page of The Herald headlined my first-person 'inside story' of the bullying tactics of the tramways union, leading to another march on the paper. Amid all the desk-top haranguing Ron Hobbs called me in, grinning. "Good effort. But listen, Cock," he said. (he called everyone Cock) "What's this I hear about you giving it a little touch-up?"

As a humble reporter I was getting £20 a week in the days when Sir Keith Murdoch dropped by the desk to ask: "And what are you driving these days?"

"Still the Morris Minor, Sir Keith."

Well, how about £40 a week? Not from the frugal Sir Keith, I stress, but the sleek, new, you-beaut PR industry. Former newspaper colleagues were doing it. And they all had new suits and went for coffee at ten and were dragging in a massive £2,000 a year. How long had this been going on?

Public Relations, said the American book I opened in the library, was a person's or a company's relations with its various publics; a company these days had to be taught to be gracious to its employees, the people with whom it had contracts, and most importantly, the media. A lot of executives and their companies in Melbourne 40 years ago, were being unkind to their various publics and that was why they had strikes and their profits remained stagnant. Now this smart American group had come to Australia to fix all that; to make people sit up and take notice of clients and their products; to influence thinking and decision-making and to create press interest and offer to talk, if need be, to governments. PR consultants, on their part, had to be: 'E'r ready (as Shakespeare put it) to crook the pregnant hinges of the knee, where thrift may follow fawning ..."

Eric White Associates, pioneers of PR in Australia, had recently opened and had started a recruiting drive for journalists who could write interesting press releases newsworthy enough to make the business pages. It snapped up young men with the ability to make something out of nothing on a dull day using their innate creativity, to dash out a hard-hitting newsletter for an office equipment monthly, extolling the virtues of silent-closing steel filing cabinets and the efficiency of plastic in-trays. There was also the need to persuade their old papers to publish important puff-pars about a new Sales Manager's appointment at H.L. Bloggs and Co..

When the whisper came to me on Ext.226 at The Herald I was ready for it. Yes, of course I would be free on Tuesday to lunch with Mr. Laurie Kerr, the legendary ex-footballer who controlled the Eric White company downstairs in a Collins Street, Melbourne basement. Deep

Throat warned me: "He doesn't drink. Remember that."

We went, of course, to Menzies Hotel and at the bar the bronzed ex-footy star asked me what I'd like to drink. "Oh, orange juice, thank you, Mr. Kerr." His eyes lit up, cheeks crinkled in a grin. Well he'd have an orange juice too!

We went into lunch and he handed me the wine list. What would I like to choose? "Well could I perhaps stick to orange juice? I don't really er ... drink." I was in grave danger of being kissed at Table 6. The rest was a formality. I would, of course, be joining EWA at double the salary The Herald was paying me. "Now," he said, leaning forward. "The matter of clients." I would, he explained, "be starting as an Account Executive." There were a couple of exciting accounts he knew I'd be fascinated by: Brownbuilt the builders of grey steel office cupboards, filing cabinets and the revolutionary sliding system, Compactus. And then there was the Spastic Society. He had specially earmarked the unfortunates of birth for me. I tried hard to keep looking enthusiastic.

Finally, after the third, power-packed orange juice, he said he would like to talk about The Big One. Making sure the waiter wasn't listening, Laurie lowered his voice to say he was offering me the PR company's biggest account, a service Eric White's was being paid £10,000 a year to operate. (probably $250,000 in today's terms) It was United Distillers, producers of Corio Whisky and Vickers Gin.

Was there not some hidden mystery here? I had never worked in PR, knew nothing about it apart from what I'd read and also heard on the grape-vine; and I was being offered The Big One.

"Come," said Laurie, paying the £4 luncheon bill with a flourish. "Let's go down to the office and meet some of your old colleagues. They'll welcome you aboard."

Familiar faces who — not so many weeks before had sat

in dreary magistrates' courts in the morning and bashed out missing cat stories in the afternoon — were now sipping real coffee and nibbling sweet biscuits at three in the afternoon. When Laurie went back to his office they gathered around. Was I coming over? What accounts had he spoken about?

I listed Brownbuilt and the Spastics, which didn't seem to raise much interest. And then I said he'd offered me United Distillers. There was a short silence. Then Vic Cohen asked: "What did you drink with lunch?" I told him orange juice. I hardly touched alcohol.

As one, they fell about, clutching each other. Laurie had found that rare gem! The seemingly impossible; a teetotal journalist! Tears rolled down smooth-shaven cheeks. (Was there something I was missing?)

John Sholl, son of a distinguished judge, wiped his eyes and explained for me. The Client, United Distillers, owned by the massive UK Distillers Company Limited, had recently accepted the grand, expensive PR proposal from Eric White Associates to enhance their products' reputation and rid its whisky of the embarrassing bar-slang tag 'COR-TEN' — COR being the Commonwealth Oil Refinery. And EWA had assigned one of their top, bright young men as Account Executive responsible to work these wonders. The banns were out and a cocktail party arranged for the Client's Board to meet the PR people and to happily salute the marriage.

It was late afternoon and the young ex-sportswriter turned PR shining light, had finished a long day. With the Client's team expectantly clutching their Vickers gins and Corio whiskies, the bright young PR man in the new, tailored suit, moved forward, hand outstretched to meet the Board Chairman.

As the grand man also walked forward to shake hands, Laurie's account executive, by now well into the UDL products and feeling no pain, was suddenly ill; all over the Chairman's blue suede shoes. Eric White and Associates' most lucrative account could have been still-born at that moment, but somehow survived.

My friend Lorna and I sat on the grass in front of Melbourne's Shrine of Remembrance. It was evening and summer and the birds were becoming quiet.

"But why do you want to leave?" said the little blonde. "Well, it's over there and ... different." I replied, waving my hand towards St. Kilda and the sea. I was sailing the next day and had already said goodbye to my parents, my newspaper friends and my dear old Citroen car; perhaps the hardest goodbye of all.

I had decided to make, what I had been warned was precarious, the 12,000-mile leap from The Border Morning Mail, via The Herald, Melbourne, and PR, to London's famous "Street of Adventure" — Fleet Street.

The decision involved saving the £150 fare, giving notice and packing a cabin trunk my Mother had used when she came across from New Zealand.

Six weeks on a ship with no worries, lots of girls, good food and exciting exotic ports. That was the immediate reality. England was out there in the misty distance.

Chapter 3

'That Hess Was Just A Scamp!'

The day I found myself sitting on the upper deck of a red bus passing through Piccadilly Circus, with my nose still buried in a newspaper, I knew I was 'home' in London. It was a feeling of belonging; so much so that when a couple of loud Australians sat behind me and started criticising 'the Poms' to each other, I slumped down in my seat hoping they would shut up.

I awoke one chilly winter's morning, burrowing further under the blankets, summoning the courage to make a dash from warm bed to hot shower when the phone jangled.

"Desmond? Neil Hawkes here." The chief of the London bureau of the Melbourne Herald my old paper; a pedantic man, as always taking his time to explain himself while I'm now freezing in my pyjamas by my desk. I silently urge him to get to the point.

He said he had been working through the night, and there had come on the teleprinter an odd message from one of The Herald group's stable, the Australasian Post. A request he obviously felt was probably a time-waster, but grudgingly he would pay me to check it out anyway.

"I'm not enthusiastic about the end result." (Yes, yes. Get on with it!).

I knew, as he did, that the Post was a notorious 'tits and bums' magazine devoted to sex, Australiana, odd-ball stories and sport. It tended to run pictures of out-back toilets and dogs with two heads. By no stretch of the imagination had it ever touched on matters intellectual and to my knowledge had rarely shown an interest in what was going on anywhere outside Australia.

That was why the London man was so puzzled, he ruminated. The Post's Editor desired an interview with the celebrated artist, Dame Laura Knight, the only living female Royal Academician. "He's said something in the cable about Dame Laura painting nudes on horseback. He'll want pictures."

The penny dropped! Nudes and horses. Together! I said I'd go and see the old lady. It helped pay the rent. I dashed off to the shower. Working at the time for a lowly wage on the Daily Mail, I had to grasp at freelance crumbs in a thin week.

Dame Laura lived alone in St. John's Wood, and when I phoned, she charmingly invited me to 'take tea' with her at 3 o'clock the next afternoon. I took a tube train to the nearest station and walked along a beautiful terrace of houses and buzzed the doorbell. She came to the door: a small, greying woman in her late 70s, and greeted me with a firm handshake and led the way upstairs to her huge, airy studio. Cuttings in the Mail newspaper library had said she was a painter of world rank, and that made my task more embarrassing. How was I going to ask her about ... naked ladies riding horses? And then arrange to have the paintings photographed for the salacious readers of the Post?

A Royal Doulton tea service sat ready on a tray with a plate of tiny cucumber sandwiches. "But before we sit down, let me show you my studio." Dame Laura said.

She led me on a tour of her paintings of ballet dancers, clowns and, I noticed, circus horses.

The old lady must have been stunningly attractive when she was young. She wore her hair in a plait that was wound round her head; her eyes twinkling with merriment, raising her hands in girlish joy when she laughed. In the middle of the barn-like room, gazing at a sketch of one of her ballerinas I took the plunge. "Dame Laura, I hope you won't be offended by this, but I have been asked if you would show me your paintings of ... er ... naked girls on horseback."

She looked puzzled for a brief second, then she laughed. "Oh my boy! I am sorry to disappoint you. I paint nudes as you see and all my life I have been fascinated by circuses and have painted circus people and their horses. But never together. Have I disappointed you?"

I assured her, red-faced, that she had not. Only some prurient fellow back in Melbourne might be frustrated. We settled down to enjoy our China tea. From my place on the sofa I glanced across the studio and tried to remember where I'd seen a particularly large painting that dominated the room. Then the penny descended in the foggy brain for the second time. It was the courtroom dock scene at the Nuremberg Trials; the line-up of the notorious accused: Hess, Goering, Von Ribbentrop, Speer. Dame Laura's eyes were twinkling again. "You recognise it?" I assured her, yes of course I did. She was the official war artist at Nuremberg. This was one of the world's most famous paintings. "That was my working painting," she explained. "The original is in the Imperial War Museum." Nudes on horseback. I felt ill.

I explained, on the second cup of tea, that I was interested in German history. As a small boy, with a German name, I had been the butt of taunts and bashings at school. "Nazi! Nazi". I'd never forgotten the shame.

We walked across to the painting. "Look at poor

Goering," she said. "He had a terrible cold while I was painting him." Then, as we returned to the sofa she said. "You must forget about interviewing me. There is a great friend of mine who was at Nuremberg, and was ever so much more important. When he comes to London he takes tea with me and sits where you are sitting now. Colonel Burton Andrus was the Director of Nuremberg Prison, the building next to the court where the trials were going on. His job was to keep those terrible men in their cells; to prevent people getting them out; or even murdering them; and that was a real possibility. He has never told anybody his story. Why don't you let me put you in touch with him?"

She always had her 'nap' at four o'clock. Why didn't I wait in the studio for her, and in the meantime, read the air-letters she had written from the court-room to her husband Harold, in London? They would probably give me an idea of what the Nuremberg Trials were like. She went downstairs and returned with a bundle of the blue letters in a box. "There," she said. "That will help you understand."

I had in my hands a pile of letters that were a daily diary. It described in vivid, intimate detail what she had observed from her tiny observation box high up on one of the court-room walls. And indeed, there at the top of one letter was her pen-picture of Goering: "He fidgets, sniffles, wipes his nose constantly. He looks miserable," she had told Harold. And on the left-hand corner of the page there was a thumb-nail sketch of the fat, hated man, nose dripping.

By the time she came back I had already made up my mind: I would contact Colonel Andrus in Tacoma, Washington, and ask him if I might discuss writing about his Nuremberg life. The security of the Daily Mail had to be put to one side. Sure, the outlay of time and money would be considerable; but if he was prepared to talk for the first time about what went on in Nuremberg prison, it would be a world scoop. The old boy sounded a character, but a formidable one. I wondered if he'd break his silence after all these years, and why he hadn't by now?

I finally met Burton C. Andrus, the ex-commandant of Nuremberg Prison, and was greeted by a stern, crew-cut, greying man with a fierce expression on a leathery face. He was a no-nonsense Army man, short and squat and authoritative. He picked me up at the Tacoma bus station at the end of my 24 hours travelling from London in the air and on the road. There had been an air-strike over the Atlantic effecting all direct British flights to the US, so I'd had to fly from Heathrow to Amsterdam, then backtrack to Toronto in Canada, and finally get a bus down to Tacoma in the United States. I was exhausted. The Colonel said he'd booked me into the visiting professorial quarters at the nearby university at which he taught. ('Thank God! I can sleep!').

"But in the meantime, I've arranged dinner at my club." I sighed inwardly. Bed would have been perfect.

For months after my visit to Dame Laura, there had been a sporadic, mostly one-sided correspondence between the Colonel and I, which seemed to be destined to go nowhere. "Maybe ..." he had written of my proposal to write a book with him. Just maybe … it was only when I pointed out in another letter that he was 75 and 'history might die' with him that I got a phone call at three o'clock in the morning.

"Mr.Zwar, Andrus here. When you comin' over?"

I now sat at the Elks Club dining-table, bleary-eyed from the long trip, and tentatively broached the subject of diaries. I hoped, I said, he'd still have the notes and diaries he had kept at Nuremberg? "Hell no. I never kept diaries," he said. My stomach sank. Next question. How, then, would he remember what actually went on? There had been *nothing* in my London newspaper archives about

the prison itself; there were cabinets full of cuttings about
the trial and a whole row of books that had been written
about the proceedings and the fate of the accused Nazis.
But the news blackout on the prison adjacent to where
the trial was taking place, and the cells that incarcerated
the Nazi leaders, had been coldly efficient. "Yeah. I operated a tight ship," shrugged the nuggety Andrus. "I tried
to make sure nothin' got out." Obviously, nothing had.

That was why I was there, I said. I now wanted —
through him — to tell the world what it was like incarcer-
ating Hitler's most notorious colleagues.

What sources were available for my research? Didn't
he have files? Instructions? Letters? I had a sinking feeling that the whole project was turning into a fiasco.

He grinned as he finished his chocolate dessert. "Waaal
there's a whole lot of stuff up in my loft in tin trunks at
home. But you wouldn't want to go up there in the dust.
You told me in one of your letters you get hay fever."

It was hard to know when Colonel Andrus was serious or joking. He had an immobile face and one eye that
just stared at you, the other hardly moving, leaving you
to make up your own mind. I said if it was OK with him,
I would go up into the attic the next morning and look at
the 'stuff'. And risk the hay fever.

Next day I climbed the ladder.

Lying against one side of the loft were three dusty
trunks he had brought back from Nuremberg in 1946. I
carefully opened each one and pulled out orderly files of
documents, letters and stapled reports. As I opened them
I saw 'Classified' 'Top Secret', and 'Eyes Only' across the
majority of the folders. The Colonel had kept letters from
Goering asking why he wasn't allowed a batman in his
cell; even suicide notes. There were also invitations from
the judges to cocktail parties. It seemed that in 18 months
as Commandant he had thrown nothing away.

I spent the first of many hours sneezing from the dust

of 20 years and the next day, began reading the documents onto a tape-recorder. I had been billeted at the University of Puget Sound, where Colonel Andrus taught geography. As he and I both needed to lose weight, we swam daily in the university pool and lunched frugally on liquid Chocolate Metrecal, which was supposed to replace food. (I'd spoil it all in the evening at the commissary where I'd pile my plate with flapjacks, ice-cream and marshmallows).

I spent the next two days feeling I was at last inside Nuremberg jail, I could almost hear the clanging of steel cell doors and smell the disinfectant. But I realised there was still a huge obstacle to using the material Andrus had filed. The printed pages and scrawled notes I was opening in the trunks were dynamite. But the most sensational were stamped in stencil: **Classified. Not to be Released. Eyes Only**. The Colonel and I were, if we used material from these files for our book, surely breaking a most sobering law which could land both of us in serious trouble. At any time he was obviously going to say to me, "I'm sorry. I should have told you. We can't access any of this stuff." And this time he would not have been joking. I could see £300 in air-fares and two weeks' work going uselessly down the drain.

Over coffee on the Monday morning I knew I had to take the plunge.

"Colonel, we have a bit of a problem with our book."

"Yeah? What sort of a praablem?"

"The files I am taking all these episodes from are, well, classified."

His eye focussed on me hard. "Mr. Zwar," (he always stuck to the formal) "in your country (he was referring to Britain) things are maybe different. A classification board over there has to sit and classify, or de-classify, sensitive material.

"In my country, the man on the spot classifies and the

man on the spot de-classifies." His eye was twinkling. "I de-classified all that stuff this morning."

I went back to work, head spinning. We either had an incredible book of never-before-revealed secrets, or we'd have a banned book and possibly share Metrecal in a cell.

My small, lonely room in the University's professorial guest quarters was claustrophobic and bare of any decoration. Some afternoons, for light relief, and the only fulfilment I could get for my ever-present sex-drive, was to catch the bus into Tacoma to visit the downtown 'burlesque palace'. The star was a celebrated stripper called Big Julie, the proud possessor of unbelievable bosoms, who performed daily. Julie always ended her act the same way, massive breasts jutting out at the front row of staring voyeurs, her legs apart, a small V of cloth kept tantalisingly in place over her crotch, staying there, no matter how loudly the punters begged. Then one day, possibly her last on stage, she relented and tugged it off, her pink femininity exposed to all. "Suffer, you bastarrds, suffer!" she shouted. And we did. After that I went back to the dreary job of studying the lives of the jailed Nazis.

One question kept nagging me as I went through the Andrus files. How was it possible for Hermann Goering to commit suicide in the world's highest-security prison?

The 'tight ship' Andrus had so efficiently managed, had somehow manifestly failed and obviously so had hard-man Colonel Andrus. Goering, hours before his scheduled execution by hanging, had taken poison, defeating the hangman's noose. His act had dismayed the world and seriously embarrassed his jailers, not least the American Commandant. I knew I'd have to tackle him about that sensitive question.

After our swim I asked Burton Andrus what had happened? How could a prisoner, under such close observation 24 hours a day, and searched several times a day, take poison under the noses of his guards? Goering had been searched with the others before every court session and after it, as he changed back from grey Nazi uniform to prison fatigues. Even while he sat all day in the dock, his cell was minutely gone over. How was it possible for him to hide a vial of cyanide? Where had he got it from? How long had he had it?

"For the last 20 years since Goering's death," I said. "Books have been written claiming that the cyanide capsule had been planted inside his Meerschaum pipe when it was sent out for repair. Or claiming his wife, Emmy, had passed it to him when she had kissed him for the last time. Surely Colonel Andrus, you must have read what Goering himself had written in his suicide note?"

He looked at me sternly, clearly still hurt by the memory; and the question. "I have no idea," he said. "I ran to Goering's cell and was there two minutes after the warder raised the alarm. But by then Goering was dead. The blankets had been dragged back from his huge body and I saw he had on black, silk pyjama trousers. His toes had begun to curl downwards towards the soles of his feet. He had on a pale-coloured pyjama jacket, with blue spots, and one arm hung down from his bunk. One of the guards, or Chaplain Gerecke, who arrived there about the same time as me, handed me a single, folded piece of paper which had been on Goering's bunk blanket.

"It was addressed to me. I ... did ... not ... read ... it."

I could hardly believe him. Surely he had. Here was Goering explaining what he had done and how he had done it on the Colonel's own 'patch'. And the Colonel hadn't read it. But by now I knew this upright character well enough to trust his honesty. He went on, "I took the paper along the passage to the Quadripartite Commission in charge of the trials office and they began their investigation. I was never told what he had written."

"Colonel, knowing what was in that note is vital to

our book. Can I start writing off to the Commission, if it still exists? To the Imperial War Museum Archives ... to anybody who might know? Will you sign the letters?" He shrugged. It was OK, if I wanted to take all that trouble. But I wasn't going to get anywhere. "It was 20 years ago, y'know."

* * *

When I had finished the interviews in Tacoma and arrived back in London, a letter awaited me from the General Services Administration, National Archives and Records Service, Washington.

It enclosed a photo-copy of 'Exhibit AM', from the Report of the Board's Proceedings in the Case of Hermann Goering (Suicide).

It had never before been made public.

It was Goering's unread note to Andrus and a translation was attached.

"To the Commandant. I have always had the capsule of poison with me from the time that I became a prisoner. When taken to Mondorf [the interrogation centre] I had three capsules. The first, I left in my clothes so it would be found when a search was made. The second, I placed under the clothes rack on undressing and took it to me again on dressing. I hid this in Mondorf and here in the cell so well, that despite the frequent and thorough searches, it could not be found.

"During the court sessions I hid it on my person and in my high riding boots. The third capsule is still in my small suitcase in the round box of skin cream. I could have taken this to me twice in Mondorf if I had needed it. None of those charged with searching is to be blamed, for it was practically impossible to find the capsule. It would have been pure accident.

"Dr. Gilbert (psychologist) informed me that the Control Board has refused the petition to change the method of execution to shooting."

It was signed: Hermann Goering.

The Report of Proceedings went on: "Goering admitted in other notes (found later) that he had secreted the vial of cyanide at times in his anus, at times under the rim of his cell toilet bowl, and at times in his navel. He had switched it from one hiding-place to another and into his boot during the court proceedings without ever being seen. No blame could be attached to any prison official."

Colonel Andrus remembered Goering's dead eyes staring glassily up at the ceiling, his big mouth gaped open. "He was already turning green."

The sentinel had been watching him through the peephole, knowing that in hours he would be hung. He had reported seeing the fat man make his way ponderously to the half-hidden toilet, his arms and legs visible, enjoying the only privacy allowed in his waking or sleeping life. He lumbered back to his bunk and lay there, his arms resting outside the blankets, conforming to regulations. He had in fact taken something from the toilet pan, or from his anus, accomplishing his last terrible act on earth. In his cheek now nestled a tiny glass bulb vial. At 10.45 pm, his mouth held shut and his eyes meeting those of the man at the peephole, he bit on the glass with a sudden clamp of massive jaws. The potassium cyanide rushed into his mouth. There was a quick convulsion that caused him to loudly gurgle, causing the guard to yell at others along the corridor and burst into the white-painted cell, hurling the door aside.

But the Reich marshal was already dead.

Chapter 4

The Hess Riddle

There was a name that kept coming up in the yellowing files in the trunk that intrigued me more than Goering, Von Ribbentrop and the rest of Hitler's henchmen. It was Rudolf Hess, Hitler's deputy; a man whose sudden and incredible flight to Britain in 1941 had astonished the world. Why had he done it? To try and make peace with the British? To escape Hitler?

There had been many theories over the years, but nobody knew the real truth. Hess had been imprisoned in the Tower of London and other secure establishments; he was questioned by experts, his mind probed by a team of psychiatrists who found him at least dangerously eccentric, if not mad. He spoke to only one war minister who emerged from the interview still mystified. Hess was an enigma. If he ever talked, it would be an astounding revelation. By now Nuremberg had been closed down and Hess was now imprisoned in Spandau, Berlin. He was said to be 'a loner', still eccentric, maybe mad.

I had read that his son, Wolf-Rudiger, who he had last seen when the boy was just four, had spent his adult life travelling the world urging governments to make some move to get his father released from prison. 'By his flight to Scotland,' Wolf would tell anyone who would listen, 'my father staked his all in an effort to make peace a possibility. Not only peace with Britain, but with the Soviet Union. It was not a mission of crack-brained naivety.'

Rudolf Hess, Hitler's steadfastly loyal deputy, who had served a sentence with Hitler, in Lansberg jail helping him write 'Mein Kampf', had flown to Scotland with one thought in mind, his son insisted and that was to achieve peace. Wolf, a renowned architect in Germany, had to live with the embarrassment that his old father was considered mad. With no access allowed to his father by himself or his mother since his imprisonment, there was no way to prove otherwise.

I asked Colonel Andrus how he assessed Hess, his prisoner.

"When Hess arrived at Nurnberg from England," grunted Andrus, (he always used the German pronunciation of the city), "he was taken straight to the search room where his clothes and his person (even his anus) were gone over minutely for suicide weapons. On the way to the interview room I was walking with Hess and his guard, when I noticed Goering being brought along the corridor.

"Hess immediately recognised Goering, who he hadn't seen for years, stopped in his tracks and threw up his arm in the Nazi salute. Goering looked surprised, but did not return the salute, which had been banned in the prison.

"I told Hess, 'Do not salute like that again! It will not be tolerated. In this prison it is a vulgar gesture.'"

Burton Andrus, when angry, was himself a fearsome sight. One of his eyes never seemed to move, (I often wondered if it was artificial) and the other seemed to widen when he was upset. Hess, he said, had stared back at him with his own deep-set, almost black eyes, and said, 'The Nazi salute is not vulgar.'

"I told him," said the white-haired, crew-cut Colonel, sipping his first coffee of the day, "that it was I who decided the nature of greetings in Nurnberg prison and whether they constituted vulgarity or not."

He had continued along the passage-way and had taken Hess into his office. Here, at last, was the most talked-about of all living Nazis standing before him, wearing the same leather flying jacket, overcoat and flying boots he had on when he landed in Scotland on May 6, 1941.

"I sat down at my desk with Hess remaining standing, fixing me with a cold, glassy-eyed stare. I turned to my interpreter and said, 'We will outline the prison rules to the prisoner ...' Hess broke in. 'We don't need an interpreter; I can understand. I speak English.'

"'Nevertheless, Hess,' I told him, 'we are going to use an interpreter. I don't want you claiming you didn't understand an order.'

"Hess kept staring at me. He then said, in German, 'They have taken some chocolates away from me in the search room. I want them back. I want to keep them ... they are poisoned. It is one of the efforts the British made to poison me. I want them for my future defence ...'"

Did he seem mad?

Colonel Andrus said, "Many Allied doctors and officers thought he was. I looked at his eyes half-hidden by his bushy eyebrows and his cadaverous body and realised he was an intense and emotional man. But the moment he began talking about the chocolate—which turned out to be wrapped just as it had left the factory—I made up my mind that his 'madness' was a sham. He was, as I expressed in my written reports, a total fake.

"He was," concluded Hess's ex-jailer, "a scamp."

Hess was questioned years later at Spandau Prison, Berlin, by American psychiatrist, Dr. Maurice Walsh, in the presence of prison officers and with the aid of interpreters. Walsh asked Hess: "Was the idea of your flight your own, or was it planned in conjunction with others?" Hess replied, "It was my own idea. It was not discussed with anyone."

"Then," said Walsh. "Hess expanded on the answer saying he had 'often been informed by the Fuhrer' that any effort to prevent loss of life was justified and that he (Hess) had interpreted this as justifying his flight."

Dr. Walsh wrote, when the interview had ended, and Hess had returned to Cell 23: 'With considerable dignity and with great emphasis he stated in a very formal manner that he regarded his present imprisonment as dishonourable and unjust.' Walsh said Hess was not at the time psychotic; there was no evidence of hallucinatory delusion and his mood seemed normal at the time of the interview. There was no evidence of paranoia and Hess's intelligence was 'obviously superior'. He had not given the psychiatrist the impression of being grandiose or of over-estimating his own importance; rather, there had been an impression of some humility.

In summary, he reported, the impression was gained that Hess 'is an individual of superior intelligence with schizoid personality traits. There would appear to be adequate evidence that he has experienced at least two episodes of hysterical amnesia and depression with suicidal attempts. There was no doubt of the basically psychotic nature of his psychiatric illness, or that he had experienced recurrent psychotic episodes for several years past.'

Dr. Walsh handed his report to his superiors and was dismayed to be told that he should 'doctor' it. He kept the professional insult to himself for 16 years. Then he decided to reveal what had happened. He wrote in the Archives of General Psychiatry in October, 1964 that 'it was thus a matter of concern for me when the surgeon of the Berlin Garrison informed me that I should omit any reference to mental disease from my report of Hess, stating that the political situation between the United States Government and the Russian Government was tense, and that war could break out at any moment. It was difficult to see why a frank report on Hess would contribute to this result, but I was informed that the Russians would react unfavourably to a report attributing Hess's behaviour to a mental disease, since they wished to believe that he and the other leaders of the Third Reich in captivity could, and should, be held fully responsible for the crimes committed while they were in power.

'I wish only to comment on the fact that a serious distortion of historical fact can result if the psychiatrist who had submitted an altered report on the psychiatric examination of a public figure does not correct his report after the emergency has passed and where no violation of human rights or of the privacy and dignity of the individual can exist.'

Dr. Walsh's concern was hardly known outside the readership of the Journal; a year later however, he found reason to repeat his charges of report 'doctoring' to a Californian newspaper. I contacted him and he then mentioned an old colleague, Dr. Rees, who he said was still practising in London at the age of 77 and had been also ordered,- during the war, to falsify his assessment of Hess's mind. If what Dr. Walsh was claiming was true, it meant Churchill himself had connived in a falsification, which had changed the course of history.

When I flew back to London I went to the newspaper files and discovered that Dr. J.R. Rees was certainly one of the psychiatric team that had first examined Hess after his arrival at the Tower of London where he was briefly held. Feeling there wasn't much chance of finding Dr. Rees alive, I opened the L-Z London phone directory. There he was, apparently still practising, just off Baker Street. I phoned and checked that it was the same man. It was; and his receptionist made me an appointment.

Hardly daring to believe Dr. Rees would agree to be interviewed, I took a taxi to the former Brigadier's rooms to ask him about the significance of Dr. Walsh's allegations. In the next room was the very man who all those years before, had questioned Rudolf Hess day after day.

He asked me into his surgery, and he was puffing a cigarette and in shirtsleeves; a small, intense man with arresting eyes.

I showed him what his colleague, Dr. Walsh had said in his statement. Could it be true?

Dr. Rees read it and then he said, "Not only was Dr. Walsh forced to 'fudge' his findings. So was I!"

Dr. Rees said he had been a consultant psychiatrist with the British Army and had seen Hess two weeks after he parachuted into Scotland. "He had been under the care of Dr. Gibson Graham, physician in charge of Drymen Hospital, which was near where he landed. I was asked to go to Mytchett Court at Aldershot, an old house the Army had taken over. Hess and I were alone together. I had no German but he had adequate English. I was with him, for the first time, for about an hour and a half.

"After this examination, followed by others, I made it known that I was going to put out my report to the Army Medical Service that Hess was mentally ill. I was going to report: 'In my opinion Hess is a man of unstable mentality and has almost certainly been like that since adolescence. In technical language I should, on my present acquaintanceship, diagnose him as a psychopathic personality of the schizophrenic type, i.e. a tendency to a splitting of his personality.

"He is—as many of these people are—suggestible and liable to hysterical symptom formation. Because of his constitutional make-up and the kind of life he has led of recent years, he is at present in some danger of a more marked depressive reaction now that he feels frustrated.'

"However," Dr. Rees told me. "Just before I was to

make my official report, the Prime Minister, Winston Churchill passed word down that 'we would not refer to Hess's mental illness, but stress other aspects of the matter.' Churchill made it known that he wanted me to stress his amnesia and the fact that Hess was 'open to suggestion and quaint ideas'. He was ordering me to fake my report. But there was schizophrenia. It was real enough. And if anybody was schizophrenic they could have been repatriable under the rules of war. If Hess was termed insane he would have had to be sent back to Germany. That wasn't good politics. He would have gone back a hero. If I had sent my report in saying he was schizophrenic he would have been put in a mental asylum.

"I did not feel it was a good plan, medically speaking, and certainly not politically speaking. There was also a technical problem with Hess's prisoner status; it had not been decided whether he was a prisoner of war or a prisoner of State. So I took out the word 'schizophrenic'. I only referred to his personality as being 'psychopathic'. Churchill hoped Hess might know a lot more about Hitler's plans than he had revealed. They had Intelligence fellows with him all the time trying to find out. Bits of Hess's condition were an act; there was an hysterical element in it. But his amnesia was hysterical and quite genuine. We predicted that he would recover from this amnesia when he got to court, which in fact he did."

Dr. Rees went on to say that he was deeply concerned that the recent release from Spandau of Albert Speer and Baldur Von Schirach, had left Rudolf Hess in solitary confinement. "It will have a frightful effect on his mind. For any unstable man to be in solitary confinement is wrong by every known principle."

I went back to my flat and transcribed the interview from the tape I had made, then crossed the road to Sloane Square Post Office and posted it to Dr. Rees for checking. I asked him to initial any alteration he wished to make and to sign each page as being a true and correct version of what he had told me. He was an old man and some years had passed. Would he perhaps have second thoughts when he read the tape transcript?

Nothing happened for two weeks and I suspected the worst. He had got cold feet. I made a phone call to his elderly receptionist. Had Dr. Rees received my letter? He came to the phone. "I am seriously disturbed, by what you have written." He said.

"But Dr. Rees! What I sent you is a verbatim record of what you said!" Was he going to pull the carpet away?

"Oh," he replied. "That part is alright. It's just that you have me smoking and in shirtsleeves. I don't want people to think I attend my patients like that. Seeing you, was different than seeing a patient; I hope you make that clear. The rest is true. It is what happened. I have signed it and will send it back to you. But please do not give the impression that how you saw me is how I generally greet my patients."

The book I was writing in Colonel Andrus's name was called 'The Infamous of Nuremberg'. I had reached the last editing stage when the Colonel flew in to see me in London to meet the publishers. Chatting in my flat he said, "There is one thing missing. I would still like to go and see my old prisoner."

I realised he was probably the only outsider in the world who might still have the right to actually visit Rudolf Hess, incarcerated for life, in his Spandau cell. What a final chapter it would be for our book.

I made several phone calls to Berlin and at last got on to Colonel Eugene K. Bird, the American director of Spandau, whose country shared the running of the prison with the British, French and Russians on a month-by-month basis. He said he would be *delighted* to meet Colonel Andrus. And yes, he believed he could take him in to meet Prisoner No.7. I put down the phone and the old Colonel and I enthusiastically shook hands.

Two days later I drove him to the airport and he took off for Berlin. I waited all afternoon and the next day for his phone call. When it came it was a shock. He had arrived in Berlin, only to be told by Colonel Bird's driver, sent to pick him up, that lunch with the Directors had been arranged in the Mess adjacent to the prison; but the Russians had vetoed a visit by him to see Hess in his cell. Andrus had turned on his heel and caught the next flight back to the United States.

I was shattered but there was a tiny chink of hope; maybe not for our book, but another. I had Colonel Eugene Bird's private phone number. Would he be interested in me writing the story of Hess' imprisonment over the past 22 years? I wondered.

I called him at home that night and he said he was puzzled and disappointed that Colonel Andrus had so impetuously caught the flight out of Tempelhof. "The other Directors were all keen to meet him; to hear what it was like caging the Nazis at Nurnberg."

"Colonel," I said, "the book I have written with Col. Andrus's collaboration will be of world interest. But you must know that your own prisoner, Hess, is of enormous interest to history. Nobody has published a word he has uttered since he flew out of Germany in 1941. You are in a unique position to talk to him, as his jailer. What a book you could write!"

Certainly aware that his phone like so many others in Berlin was probably being bugged by his own country and the Soviets, he said stiffly, "Mr. Zwar, what you are saying is highly irregular. I do not wish to continue this conversation on the telephone." And hung up. It was a risk calling him and I hoped I had not turned him off.

I left it for a week and then I called him again. I said I was coming to Berlin for the long weekend and would he be interested in seeing me? He was brief. "Yes, I would."

I had a foot in the door.

The next Saturday, I flew into the grey, divided city of Berlin for my meeting with Gene Bird and his German-born wife, Donna. It was to be the beginning of a gut-wrenching five precarious years: for Colonel Bird, who put his trust in me when his most sensitive job was on the line; for me, financially, as I dared not go to a publisher for an advance on royalties. And for relations between the United States and the other three Powers: France, Britain and the Soviet Union if a word of what he was doing got out. The Directors' Headquarters at Spandau Prison was a sensitive meeting-place for the West and the Soviets and any scandal involving the participants would have had international repercussions.

I found Colonel Bird a nervy, somewhat excitable and overweight man in his late 40s. Gene was fluent in German. He had been retired from the US Army at 41 and then been given the awesome (as he put it) appointment as US Director of Spandau. He was the man in charge of Hess, Baldur Von Schirach and Albert Speer every fourth month. In the darkest days of the Cold War he said he had to deal on a daily basis with the Russians who had only one other foothold in the West – the Soviet War Memorial ceremoniously guarded by a handful of its soldiers. Both the Soviets and the Americans knew that the prison, manned by spies from both sides of the Iron Curtain, was crucial as a contact point; a channel for trusted messages when things looked like getting out of hand; its Directors' Mess a dedicated Allied listening post during the Berlin blockade, when actual war between the Soviets and the West seemed possible.

Gene in his Colonel's great-coat was a bulky figure with boyish dark hair, a twitchy manner and sudden swings of mood between confidence and fear about what we were discussing. He took me that weekend, to talk among the tall pines in a forest where we knew we could not be bugged; summing me up, giving little away in case this stranger could not be trusted. We dined at the Berlin Hilton, drinking a lot of wine. We visited a golf course and then he took me to inspect a gruesome dungeon where the Nazis had suspended prisoners from its walls by hooks; these hooks remained there as evidence. We talked of my record as a journalist; of the dangers to himself and his wife if any hint of a proposed collaboration ever leaked out. And over and over again he wanted to know, almost like a small boy, "Just how thick would the book be?"

It was in Treptower Forest, among the pines, where he said he had finally made up his mind about the project: it was too dangerous. "I've to think of my family and my career. Donna is ill and, as you know, confined to a wheelchair." His two daughters had their lives ahead of them. He had too much to lose.

Exhausted by the negotiations, of trying to sell myself and my integrity, I was almost relieved to agree with him. OK, it was hopeless. I asked him to drive me to the airport on the Monday.

During the weekend he had taken time off to introduce me to an elderly relative, Frau Kardosh, a widow who lived in splendid style in a mansion almost next to the newspaper magnate, Herr Axel Springer. Frau Kardosh had her own swimming-pool, priceless Greek icons, wall-to-wall fashion clothes in her bedroom. She was obviously extremely rich. Gene explained: "She is a seer. She appears regularly on German television forecasting the lives of the famous. The President of the world's biggest manufacturer of lingerie, Triumph, makes no business decision without consulting her."

Frau Kardosh, greeted us: a charming, bejewelled little woman who spoke no English. Gene translated their conversation for me and as he did, I understood enough German to realise they were, for some reason, talking about my mother in Australia. And his translation hadn't mentioned that.

"Gene, what is Frau Kardosh saying about my mother?"

He was embarrassed. "Oh nothing. Just pleasant-ries."

"I think she said my mother was ill."

He hesitated. "Well, she says she has had a heart attack and is in hospital."

I couldn't believe it. "I had an airletter from her this morning that was sent on from London. She is very well."

"That's fine then. It's OK."

I called Beechworth, Australia that evening — 9 am their time, and got no answer from my mother's flat, where she lived alone. I called her sister-in-law. "Dear, Lin is in Beechworth Hospital. She has had a heart attack. But she is over it. You can ring her there. I promise you she is now OK. We didn't know where to reach you ..."

* * *

Now Gene had delivered his decision, all I could feel was relief. The strain was over. He said he would now drive me to Tempelhof Airport.

We were on our way down a poplar-lined street when he suddenly braked his Mercedes and reached across to me with his hand outstretched. "I want to do it," he said. "You and I have a deal."

Chapter 5

The Most Dangerous Step

I now had a beautiful young Australian wife, Delphine, whom I had met in London and after years of searching for someone I could always care for, here was a girl offering me uncomplicated love. She was from Sydney, a slim ex-nurse with long auburn hair, delicate features and lively brown eyes. She was 10 years younger than me. We had met on a blind date, just four days before I went off to work on an overseas assignment that would keep us apart for almost a year. We had gone with mutual friends to a restaurant and shyly held hands under the table. Something quite scary had happened for both of us. We had three days of bliss together in my Chelsea flat — 'the Little Red Nest' Del called it. Then I departed and we began writing to one another, exchanging long tapes, getting to know each other's minds better than if we had been together. "I have never been happier," she wrote to her mother. "I can see a happy future at last." Del was a girl with bubbling enthusiasm: for travel, the arts, good food and people. And fortunately she admitted falling for this 36-year-old bachelor. And she was as eager for adventure as I was when I said I wanted to dedicate the next year, maybe more, into a secret book which could be dashed within weeks by the death of Hess or by the discovery of Colonel Bird's secret collaboration; or by the Colonel again changing his mind.

The scandal — particularly for the United States — would have been enormous if Bird and I were found out. Nevertheless, sometimes in the still of the night, doubts would take over. I now had someone else to look after than just myself. Why gamble? Wouldn't it be safer to stay in London in a salaried job on a newspaper, with a real future? Then I would remind myself that 150 years before, my German ancestors sailed out from their village, not far from Berlin, to an unknown land: Australia. They were Wends, a deeply-religious ultra-orthodox Lutheran group who gambled their lives on a family decision to leave German persecution. In comparison with what they had done, my hunch was of little consequence, and now I had a loving wife to share the adventure.

We packed the Volkswagen for the wintry drive into Europe, slipping and sliding on the icy roads, laughing and revelling in our new love.

Berlin was in the depths of bitter winter when we drove through Germany to begin working with Gene Bird, almost certainly (he had warned me) under the watchful eyes of Russia's KGB. It would have been an inefficient spy network that took no notice of a British-registered, right-hand drive car parked daily outside the Spandau American Director's residence.

By the time we reached our Berlin gasthof and settled in, only the stooped Hess was left in the Spandau prison, his two fellow inmates, Von Shirach and Speer had ended their sentences and been released. Hess slept in Cell 23 in the grim high-walled Spandau, only a few kilometres away from our hotel room in the divided city and he was said to be a 'loner', refusing to converse with his jailers.

Christmas was approaching and it was now snowing heavily. We had to dig our VW out of drifts each morning and shivering, jump into the car, revving it to operate the heater which was no match for snow-covered Berlin. I had to stop every few kilometres to rub Delphine's feet, which she told me, almost weeping with the pain, were freezing.

We had only been there a few days when Delphine caught a virulent strain of flu that was raging in the freezing city. It was snowing now even more heavily. Our room was gloomy, though spacious. Her flu worsened, and she obviously had a high fever. I alerted the gasthof manager who called a woman doctor whose receptionist said would be some time arriving because of the epidemic. We waited several anxious hours, with Delphine now slipping into delirium. A knock on the door and the lady doctor came into the room with an elderly assistant whom she began ordering around in staccato German. The good doctor wore a black diamond mink coat and she kept it on during her visit. Delphine said after she had gone, "I watched mesmerised as its long fur wafted around as she moved. It almost hypnotised me."

Muttering orders to her assistant taking notes, the doctor made a quick examination, prescribed antibiotics and homeopathic medicines then handed me a hefty bill. I paid and drove out into the snow searching for a pharmacist.

Alone now, Delphine began to drift into a haze. "I saw myself on a stretcher in my red velvet Laura Ashley dressing gown being carried feet first through a golden light. I came back to consciousness saying to myself I'm not going to die in this horrible cold place." The strange combination of medicines worked and she recovered. When she was well enough, Colonel Bird invited us to his pleasant, Fischottersteig home.

He had already shown me he could quickly learn his role as a co-author. Now he sat beside me on a couch and told me to switch on my recorder, describing Hess's cell. "It's painted dark green and cream, measuring 8 ft. 10 in. long and 7 ft. 5 in wide. It has a black floor and curved ceiling painted white. The lone prisoner sleeps on a simple iron army bed which has a wooden base beneath the mattress, tilted to help his posture. Above his head is a barred window overlooking the tops of trees where birds flutter about in weak sunshine. When he goes out into the garden he sits on a bench and feeds them crumbs."

From where he lay on his bunk, he continued, Hess could see his toilet and the cell door which had a square, iron-meshed peephole through which his guards could keep watch on him. Beside the bed stood a hard, upright wooden chair and a rough-hewn table on which lay his books, medicines and old photographs of his toddler son and his wife, which he'd brought from Nuremberg Prison. In the cell and the echoing corridors, which rang with the clash of steel, there was a constant smell of disinfectant.

That cell and another, which used to be the chapel, were his home from 18 July 1947; the day Spandau's heavy doors swung open to admit the remnants of the Hitler regime who had escaped the hangman's noose.

"Tomorrow I'll have a list of what the old man is reading. That should be interesting for you."

Gene Bird and I arranged to get together at ten the next day. But he suddenly had an alarm call at home. Hess, he said, had been found screaming in pain, clutching his stomach and had to be rushed into the prison hospital for examination. "They say it's a blockage of the intestines. It could be cancer." said the worried Director when I met him later. "They've taken him under escort to the British Military Hospital. It's the first time the old man has been out of a prison in 23 years.

"He looks pale and haggard. When I saw him he had his knees drawn up to his chin and his hands clasped around them. He was shaking. He refused to talk to any-body but me. When I got to him he grabbed my hand and said: 'Will you visit me every day at the hospital? I'm afraid. I have only a few days to live on this earth. I'm at my end now.'

"Then he had started to sob. 'Why don't they release me? Why must I suffer so? I alone tried to bring about peace in the world and for this I must stay here the long-est. It is not right. It is not just.'"

Hess had been carried down the 22 steps from the jail hospital to the courtyard on a stretcher and in a light fall of snow, placed in the waiting ambulance. He was wheeled into the British Military Hospital X-ray depart-ment where it was found there was an accumulation of gas present under both sides of the diaphragm. He had a duodenal ulcer which the doctors said might have already perforated and closed itself.

Fate had, in an odd way, come to help our collabora-tion. Gene Bird could see Hess every night in hospital. Alone. A British soldier, with a sub-machine gun at his feet, sat on the outside of a glass partition, with armed police and dogs patrolling the hospital perimeter out-side. What Hess had to say to Bird, if anything, would remain private.

It was vital now for me to quickly teach Gene Bird the soldier, to be Gene Bird, reporter. He had to be my eyes and ears. From the moment he entered the ward each night until he left the hospital he had to unobtru-sively note how the prisoner appeared, what he said: his moods, his fears. I wrote out six questions which Colonel Bird took into Hess every night; the man had never said a word that had reached the outside world since he flew to Scotland in 1941.

While I sat outside in the Colonel's Mercedes, the engine running so it could remain heated, soldiers and police stamped about in the snow, talking into hand-held radios, some of them glancing over at the car now and again no doubt wondering why a passenger sat in it, engine running, for an hour or more. But nobody approached me.

Bird emerged in his uniform and greatcoat and drove the car around the block. "Switch on the tape-recorder." He had, almost overnight, become an expert newsman. "As I walked into his room, Hess lay half-upright in blue-and-white striped pyjamas, a tube running into his left nostril. He saw me and said: 'Good evening Colonel. There is something to be said for modern medicine after all.' He had for most of his life shunned modern medicine for homeopathic and natural remedies. 'You will be surprised,' he said. 'That this thing (the tube) doesn't hurt at all.'" With Hess in hospital the prison cells were empty, but Spandau was guarded nevertheless. The three Western Powers urged withdrawal of the tower guards who were being filmed on television broadcast around the world. But the Soviets, whose month it was, stubbornly said no. Their soldiers remained stiffly on duty in the ugly towers.

* * *

It was New Year's Day and Gene invited us for lunch with his family in the Directors' Mess, a building outside the actual prison. It was windy and cold as we arrived, and once inside the warm dining-room where the Directors usually ate, we began formally toasting each other in schnapps. The luncheon wore on, the wine flowed, and then I pointed to the high walls outside. I said, almost ironically, to Gene Bird, "If I'm going to write a book about what goes on in there, I should have experience of what it's actually like inside." He had told me several times that no non-military person, to his knowledge, had ever been inside the prison and there was no way he could ever get me past the gate. This afternoon, however, we were both feeling little pain from a lunch of fine vintage wine and cognacs. He suddenly stood up and said, "Grab your coat." And in seconds we were off across a snowy path.

The guard at the first door challenged the Colonel and he said briskly, "This gentleman is an architect. We are discussing the new cell-block plans." Once allowed inside, our footsteps echoed as we hurried down the corridor. (I couldn't believe this was happening to me. I was inside Spandau Prison, the first reporter in history to get in.)

I caught sight of the food trolley, grabbed it and pushed it along to hear what it sounded like as it was trundled down to his cell. Bird by now had Cell 23 opened by a sentinel and I made for Hess's bed and lay on it as the old man had done for the past 22 years. I was trying to concentrate — through the haze of fine wine — at my extraordinary surroundings, all the time wondering at the lack of compassion involved in keeping this frail, eccentric, but surely harmless old man in such a place. I sat on his toilet and in his exuberance, Gene Bird flushed it to show me how quiet it was. (My overcoat got soaked.)

The patient Hess was finally returned in an escorted ambulance to prison and his cell, the doctors saying he had been cured of his ulcer. Gene Bird and I began working quickly in case he died, smuggling tapes and photographs in and out of the century-old prison, often under the noses of the Russians standing guard in the high towers. Hess had given our undertaking his own wary co-operation and as I finished writing each chapter Gene took it in and gave it to him to check. Shrewdly, the old man, realising his cell would be searched in his absence, stuffed the pages in his underpants so he could read them at leisure in the garden while he fed his birds.

Bird was tape-recording talks with Hess in his cell and also, out in the garden, and had taken pictures, at first Polaroid stills and then sound-on-film movie footage. We chronicled the old man's day-to-day existence; what he read (philosophy), what he ate (he enjoyed dumplings), how he felt (he always complained of stomach pains and the inflexibility of the Soviets), what he thought about (injustice, once wondering about what would have happened if his peace overtures had succeeded: 'Would I have got the Nobel Prize, like Willi Brandt, instead of now being in prison?').

Reading the chapters I had written, Hess would show annoyance that we had also recorded his tantrums and his childlike hoarding of food scraps (which he alleged would be shown to contain poison). He scrawled 'NEIN!' beside the offending paragraphs.

His son, Wolf-Rudiger, a Munich construction engineer, had visited many countries, vigorously campaigning for his father's release, urging that he be allowed to end his days at the old home in Hindelang, in Bavaria. His room had been left as it was the day he flew out to Scotland on May 10, 1941.

Bird and I decided it was time we should tell the son of our collaboration with his father and arranged to meet Wolf-Rudiger in Munich, at an exclusive restaurant. I found Hess Jnr. polite, pleasant, but obviously suspicious. He had come to trust nobody, he said bluntly. "I have often been let down by journalists." A quietly-spoken man, then in his early 30s, his father's reputation had been a massive influence on his life. Wolf said he seriously believed there was a sinister reason behind what he saw as a lack of real effort by the British to force the Russians to change their minds and release his father. He said there were papers he had repeatedly been refused access to, in the secret service departments of the British Government. They were to remain unopened until 2017, which is far beyond the 30-year rule applying to wartime secrets. "They must contain matters highly embarrassing to somebody; more embarrassing to the British Government than the German Government," he asserted.

When his father took off from Germany in a prototype Messerschmitt 110, 'Buzz', his son, was four years old. It was to be the last time Hess would see him, or his wife, Ilse, for 28 years. "It is a long time," said Wolf quietly, his high-domed forehead perspiring.

I was unable to tell Hess Jnr. at that stage, that before his father's return to his prison cell, Eugene Bird had brought up the subject of a visit from his wife and son, whom the old man had steadfastly refused for so many years — "While I am in the indignity of wrongful imprisonment".

"This is a different situation, Mr. Hess," Bird had told No.7. "You are not in prison now. You are in a hospital bed outside."

At last, sitting propped up on three pillows and wearing his blue-and-white hospital pyjamas, Hess had given in. Eyes glowing, he agreed that a visit in the hospital would not mean his obstinate rule had actually been broken. "I have brought myself to a decision," he told Bird on December 8, 1969, as I sat in a car waiting outside. "I will see them on Christmas Day."

This became instant world news, the historic meeting had leaked to the press, possibly by a hospital attendant. But what went on between the Hess family and how the meeting had been arranged, would be kept exclusively to Bird and I and later in a revealing chapter in our book; a positive milestone in what so far was really only a story of a grim prison life.

Gene Bird and the other three directors arrived at the heavily-guarded hospital to witness the first meeting of Hess with his wife and tall son in more than a quarter of a century. Hess sat nervously at a table, dressed in pyjamas. His wife and son were told they were forbidden to approach the prisoner or touch or embrace him. Hess, when he saw his wife walk into the room half stood up and said brokenly, "I kiss your hand, Ilse." Anxiously

Wolf-Rudiger cautioned his mother, "Mutti, don't give him your hand." She stared over at her husband sitting at the table. "I kiss your hand, Father." It had been 28 years and 6 months and 25 days since the morning her husband had taken off from Augsburg. And she had never seen him again.

Frau Hess had on a brown fur coat and a scarf about her head. She stared at her husband as father and son talked across the table where Hess had his feet resting on a pillow on his bed steps, his face aglow with anticipation. "But Father," asked Wolf, concerned. "Your health?"

Hess smiled at him. "I want to make it clear I am receiving excellent treatment; excellent medical care. I am responding well."

"How did it all happen, Papi?"

"The day just came when I could not swallow, or take any food whatsoever. The pains continued and then got worse and that is probably when the ulcer broke open. I have had a three-litre blood transfusion. It came from English soldiers so this makes me half-English now! As a result," he chuckled. "I now speak much better English."

Frau Hess said: "It's a long time since I have flown in an aircraft (she came from Hindelang in Bavaria that day). The last time was with you."

"Yes," replied Hess. "Times have changed. And you have changed."

"And you too!" she laughed. "You have changed. Your voice is much different now to how I remember it."

"How do you mean?" asked Hess, puzzled.

"Your voice is deeper. Much deeper than before."

"Oh, you mean it is more manly?" They both laughed. The directors gave a signal. The visit was at an end.

After Hess was taken from the hospital back to Spandau prison, Gene Bird made a point of visiting him daily, asking him about the past, about Hitler; his flight. He took Polaroid shots of him in his cell and in the garden feeding his birds; lying on his bunk; watching television for the first time on a set the Soviets had reluctantly allowed him to have in the hospital and which had been brought with him to the prison.

Each day he would methodically start a ritual in his cell at 6.45 am. Wearing blue-and-white striped pyjamas he would place his hands on his hips and do his squatting and jumping exercises, breathing deeply and stretching. Removing his dentures on the way to the bathroom he would clean them; then shave, using a Braun electric razor, running it across his gaunt cheeks and over the dark stubble on his wide upper lip. He would then blow out the razor and replace it in his locker. Then he would strip to the waist and wash.

One day, Gene Bird found him in a reflective mood, happy to discuss his relationship with Adolf Hitler. "There was," Hess told Bird, "only a certain point of familiarity you could reach with Hitler, you know. Beyond that point you could not go. There were times I felt close to him, but they were very seldom. He never revealed much warmth. He kept himself aloof. I think he felt superior to the people around him and to the common folk."

"If you had your time over again," said Bird. "Would you again serve a man like Hitler?" Hess, in crumpled denims and his shirt hanging out under his braces, looked at him. "What do you mean? Yes. I believe I would travel the same route; end up here again in Spandau Prison. I wanted to give Germany back its old pride and its old fame."

"And you would again serve under a man like Hitler?"

He looked at his questioner over his spectacles. "I would not have wanted to miss the opportunity of serving Adolf Hitler as his deputy. I was a dedicated man."

* * *

It was getting close to the time to leave Berlin. We had accumulated many hours of interview with Hess on recording tape.

I'd noticed that every night, when Colonel Bird and I came back from the hospital, I stepped out of his car in the garage, almost stumbling over a cardboard carton. Gene said, "We'd better open that before you go back. A librarian gave it to me. I think she said it contained some old books from Nuremberg."

On my last night I carried the carton inside to the centrally-heated house and opened it up. It contained thick manila folders and hundreds of pages of foolscap covered in spidery writing.

Donna, Gene's German-born wife, started reading.

"Gene!" she almost shouted. "These are all Rudolf Hess's writings! They are in his hand, and all the type-written pages have been typed on a capitals machine. They are his as well."

She immediately began translating, "He says he believed he would one day leave Nuremberg as a free man and that with the full co-operation of the Allies he was to become 'the new Fuhrer of Germany.'"

Hess's manifesto, which nobody had ever bothered to read until now, began with bulletins that would be published under his 'direction' giving specific orders about food distribution, labour, and co-operation with the occupying powers. "I have," Hess pecked out on the typewriter, "with the agreement of the Western Occupation Forces, taken over the leadership of the German Government in the area of the Western Zones of Germany, taken over the leadership of the destiny of the German people in a situation that could not be imagined to be more desperate. But a salvation is possible."

He had made specific arrangements regarding the type of official cars Government leaders would have: Hess's would be a limousine, larger than the others; but he specified all cars must be German. His tailor would be instructed to make uniforms with the capacity for waist enlargement, as former prisoners would soon be eating better than they had in camps.

He would need temporary headquarters in the Nuremberg jail where he could receive telegrams and "a great many long-distance telephone calls. I would like Reichminister Speer (whose cell was just along from his as he typed) "to be assigned the job of lessening the crisis that exists in Germany. He must be given all the help necessary to set up feeding stations and transportation, to issue blankets and field kitchens. At every large railway station there should be a kitchen to give food to soldiers who are on their way home."

Hess had turned his mind to the treatment of Jews. "If Jews ask or plead or request to save themselves from the rage of the German population and wish to go into protective camps, this should be fulfilled. In this way, everything should be done to save the Jews from acts of violence and also from unauthorised persons from entering the camps."

The old beer carton's contents—now spilled out on the lounge-room floor of the Bird residence—were page after page of curious history that had been saved from destruction by a lady librarian who had realised its worth. Now it had to be taken out of Berlin for safekeeping in the event of Gene Bird's 'other' occupation as a secret author being discovered.

Because Berlin was surrounded by Soviet-controlled East Germany, the smuggling operation had to be by air. There was no way I could drive my VW from Berlin, through the Russian-occupied sector to Hanover on the Allied-occupied border, with Hess's tapes and writings. It was decided that Delphine would be the courier and I would drive through the East 'clean'.

As departure time drew near my fears grew. Delphine

would carry the Hess papers, photographs and tapes in an attaché-case on her knees on the plane. Allowing it to go in the baggage department was out of the question. What if the case was examined before she took off? And what would happen to me en-route to the West by road, when every KGB man worth his salt, would have been aware of my British-registered car parked outside the US Director's residence day after day?

I set off at 4am in pitch dark, three hours before Colonel Bird was to drive Delphine and the papers to Tempelhof. It was windy and bitterly cold. Worse, the roads had turned to ice and I was driving before the snow-ploughs moved in to clear it. Between Berlin and Magdeburg the wind had reached gale-force and my car was being pushed from one side of the road to the other as though I was driving on a skating-rink. My stomach was empty and churning. I feared the worst as I headed for the Eastern Sector border. Would the Russians and East Germans have decided that was where I was to be grabbed?

I reached the border guard gate and it was snowing heavily. I drove through to the end of a queue of cars slowly moving forward as armed guards slid mirrors beneath them looking for people hoping to be smuggled out of the Soviet sector to freedom. Car boots were opened, even back seats torn out for inspection. Then they got to me. A gruff character in a long great-coat came up to my driving window and pointed left. "Aus!" he said. "Aus!" He was motioning for me to leave the queue and park by a large shed.

I had been caught!

I parked and shakily got out. "Nicht verstanden?" I tried. "I don't understand".

"Kommen-sie," he said. I had to follow him inside. There was a bespectacled official behind a window. Hands trembling, I offered him my passport, showing him my visa. He glanced at it and stuck out his chin.

"Nein!" Then he spoke in English. "Your papers are in order. Your car was in the wrong queue. You were in the US Army vehicle queue. Drive to the right one." I had merely driven behind the last car, not noticing its distinctive coloured number plate that designated it as US Forces.

A guard shoved his mirror under my VW, stood up and grinned at me. "Ist gut." he said, and waved me through to the American check-point.

Delphine was waiting for me at the airport, rugged up and smiling; Hess documents and pictures intact. We went to the restaurant, opened a bottle of French champagne and hugged each other.

Our manuscript was, by now, a thick book and it had been secretly shown by our literary agent, under signed contract of confidentiality, to several leading publishers. At the same time, (without informing me) Gene Bird had his mind on another outlet for the Hess prison saga: television. In great confidentiality he flew to London and was introduced to a director of Independent Television News and given a crash course in operating a hand-held, sound-on-film camera. He smuggled it into Spandau and interviewed Hess for 18 minutes, flying back to ITN in London with camera and film.

On his return to Tempelhof Airport, Berlin, while publishers were still considering our manuscript, Colonel Bird discovered his suitcase was missing. He drove to his home to find guards surrounding the house. As he stepped from his Mercedes, he was told he had been placed under house arrest.

After five years of secrecy, we had been found out.

Gene Bird was flown to Washington from where he phoned me in distress and not a little fearful for the future. He had been under intense questioning and then ordered to sign the US Secrets Act which he had never had to sign previously, effective retrospectively. His massive file of papers and photographs had been seized from his house in Fischottersteig and he was sacked as a Spandau director.

He pleaded with me on the phone: "Send everything you have, the manuscript of our book, the photographs, everything, to the State Department. We are both in bad trouble. The Soviets have gone crazy about the way this thing happened under their noses. If you don't do so they will lean on you from your nearest capital city." Assuming his call was either supervised or tapped I refused. "I am not a US citizen and the State Department had no rights to anything I have written, Colonel. I will write the book under my own name and will not even mention you." And put down the phone. I did not have to think too hard about who 'they' were.

Then a weird thing happened in Cairns, Queensland—many thousands of miles from the US State Department—where we had gone back to Australia to live. I was publishing a weekly free newspaper to provide us with a living while I was writing The Loneliest Man in the World, and one day Delphine phoned me at my office. She said she had walked into our large, dingy, cellar under the house on a mountainside at Stratford, a fairly remote spot, 8kms from the city and she had found two men there; one was wearing mirror sunglasses and who spoke to her in an American accent.

For years I had kept all the Hess word-tapes, his handwritten and typewritten manifesto and diaries, and all Bird's Polaroid photographs hidden in a row of hollow cement wall-bricks that I had covered over with mortar. Delphine, bravely, asked the men what they were doing there. They said they were looking for our pool. They wanted to give us a quote to put a pebble substance on the rough pool surrounds. One thrust a business-card at my wife. She firmly asked them to leave.

When I got home she was still shaken by the experi-

ence. I immediately called the Cairns distributor for the
product on the business-card and asked if the two men
really worked as representatives for him. "Yes," he said.
"Nice blokes. They've only been with me for a few days.
Very enthusiastic. They went and got their own business-
cards printed."

I remembered what Gene Bird had said: 'They' would
be sent from our nearest capital city. He could only have
meant the CIA. On the Sunday morning I telephoned the
US Consul at his home in Brisbane and said I was the co-
author of a book on Hess with Colonel Eugene Bird and
that I had recently had a visit from two men I believed
were Secret Service operatives. He said he knew nothing
about it.

I said: "Of course. But please write this down. Please
tell the people in Washington that I am going ahead with
publishing the book, but that it will not even mention
Gene Bird. It will come out under my own name."

A few days later I had a phone call from Gene which
this time was obviously not supervised. He seemed far
more relaxed. A US publisher who had a copy of our
manuscript had been telephoned by the Berlin Desk of
the CIA and told to 'let things simmer down'. A show
of indignation by the Americans was being put on for
the Soviets. We could publish later, in the form the book
was now in. 'Please make sure Zwar doesn't change anything.'

'The Loneliest Man in the World' was published in 12
countries and serialised in newspapers and magazines.
But it did not result in Hess's release, despite the sympathy it aroused world-wide. The Russians refused to
budge.

There was still one moral task left that we owed to
Rudolf Hess. I had kept his diaries and his manifesto
pecked out by him on an old typewriter in Nuremberg
prison. To make sure they would not be seized if ever

we were found out, Eugene Bird had entrusted me with them; they had remained behind the false bricks in my workshop gathering dust, for 14 years.

Now it was time to return them to the family.

I extracted them from my workshop brickwork and flew back with them in a hand-held briefcase to Munich. Gene Bird met me and we took a taxi out to Wolf-Rudiger's home, handing him the 500 pages of Hess's handwritten diary, giving the authentic insight into the mind of the world's strangest old man. Wolf Hess was close to tears when he opened the package. So were Eugene Bird and I, but for a different reason. A collector of Nazi memorabilia hearing we had the archive, had offered us $US250,000 for it a few days earlier. We turned him down.

Chapter 6

The Old Prisoner 'Murdered'

In 1987 Hess, blind in one eye, shuffling around with the aid of a stick, and in pain from an enlarged prostate, had hidden himself from the eyes of sentries in the prison towers, wrapped an electric flex round his neck, pulled it tight and hung himself.

That was the official suicide story. But Bird who still had close ties to prison officials who were there during his command and after he left told me on the phone, that he believed Hess was murdered.

"He walked with a cane, dragging his right foot behind him, because he had suffered a slight stroke. He was blind in the right eye and could see very little out of the left eye. Whenever he walked in the garden, he had to have a man on each side, in case he stumbled and fell. Hess could not tie his own shoes, his hands suffered so badly from arthritis. He could not get his fingers and thumbs apart, they had to literally insert a spoon into his hand so he could eat.

"Most significant about whether he suicided or not is the fact that he could not raise his arms above shoulder level. To hang yourself, you have to be able to do that.

Yet, with all these disabilities, a 93-year-old man, a prisoner watched more closely than any other in history, at a massive cost each year, was said to have entered the garden hut alone, tied an electric flex round his neck, looped it over a hatch just 1m 30cms from the floor — not high enough to hang a cat — and strangled himself!

"The flex of the standard lamp actually remained in the wall socket."

Col. Bird said that Hess's male nurse, Mr. Abdallah Melaouhi, had pushed his way to the death scene 'despite strenuous efforts to keep him away. "He got to the scene within minutes. He says he saw a black American guard, excited, sweating and with his tie awry, shouting: The pig is finished!' That guard has avoided all attempts to interview him. When a television crew approached him to talk he ran away."

Gene Bird said there were two other people in American uniforms at the scene whom Abdallah had never seen before. Abdallah gave Hess mouth-to-mouth resuscitation, and when that failed, raced to grab the resuscitation equipment which he had personally checked and signed as being in good order just hours before. He discovered the oxygen tank empty and the breathing tubes full of holes.

Abdallah, said Bird, had made a report and sent it himself to Scotland Yard in London. "He has since had death threats and is a scared man."

But who could have wanted Hess murdered? "If that man was murdered," said Bird, "it would have had to be a decision taken at the highest level. I will say no more than that."

I called Abdallah Melaouhi at his home in Berlin where he had just returned from hospital duty. He said to me: "Yes, I believe Mr. Hess was murdered. But please, not on the telephone. You come to Berlin to see me."

Several weeks after our phone conversation, Abdallah

Melaouhi, made a sworn statement to an official inquiry.

'I do solemnly and sincerely declare as follows: I worked as a male nurse caring for Rudolf Hess from 1 August 1982 until his death on 17 August 1987 at the Allied Military Prison in Spandau. From 1967 to 1970 I trained as a technical medical assistant in tropical diseases at the Institute of Tropical Medicine in Hamburg. From 1970, I continued my training as a qualified male nurse until 1973 when I received a Diploma Certificate in Nursing. In 1974 I moved to Berlin and worked at Hohengatow Hospital in the intensive care unit until 1976. I then attended the specialist medical school, Gauschule, Wedding, at the recommendation of the Department of Health at the Berlin Senate until 1977 and upon completing that training I received a Diploma in anaesthesia and the intensive care of sick people.

'I was then promoted to Superior Male Nurse and went to work at Spandau Hospital (Krankenhaus, Spandau) in the intensive care unit until 1st August 1982 when I went to work in the Allied Military Prison in Spandau as Male Nurse for Rudolf Hess.

'On the day of Mr Hess' death, 17 August 1987, I commenced my duties, which involved caring for Mr Hess, as usual at 6.45 a.m. I assisted him, as was usual, with showering and dressing, and was present when he ate a meal at 10.30 a.m. At no time did he give any indication that his state of mind was disturbed or that he was unduly depressed.

'Shortly after the meal, he asked me to go to the nearby town of Spandau to purchase a ceramic pot to replace one which was defective. Mr Hess would not have made such a request merely to ensure my absence, since I was always absent in any event from midday, during my noon break.

'At 2 p.m. I was called to the prison from my flat which

was located outside, but in the immediate vicinity of, the prison (to which I had gone on my return from the town of Spandau). After some delay I reached the summerhouse in the prison garden where I was told that there had been an incident. The small door at the front of the summerhouse was closed.

'When I entered the summerhouse, the scene was like a wrestling match had taken place; the entire place was in confusion. The straw tiled mat which covered the floor was in disarray, although only the day before I had cleaned the floor and had left the straw tiled mat carefully arranged in its usual place. A tall lamp had fallen over, but I clearly remember that the cable attached to the lamp was still connected to the main socket. It was this lamp cable which the authorities later said that Mr Hess had used to hang himself. A round table and Mr Hess's armchair had also been overturned. In summary, none of the furniture or equipment was in its usual place, and there is no question in my mind but that a struggle had taken place in the summerhouse.

'The body of Mr Hess was lying on the floor of the summerhouse, apparently lifeless. Near to his body stood two soldiers dressed in US Army uniforms. I had never seen either soldier before. I also saw an American guard, whom I knew as a Mr Tony Jordan. There was no cable anywhere near the body of Mr Hess; as I have said, the only cable was attached to the fallen lamp which was still plugged into the wall.

'I immediately proceeded to examine Mr Hess. I could not detect any, pulse or heartbeat. I estimated that death had occurred 30 to 40 minutes earlier. The guard whom I knew as Jordan stood near Mr Hess's feet and appeared overwrought. He was sweating heavily, his shirt was saturated with sweat and he was not wearing a tie. I said to Jordan: "What have you done with him?" He replied: "The pig is finished, you won't have to work a night shift any longer." I told him to bring the emergency case (which contained a first aid kit) and the oxygen appliance, while I commenced artificial respiration. When Jordan returned with the equipment, I noticed that he had first taken the opportunity to change his clothes. The equipment which he brought had clearly been interfered with. The seal on the emergency case had been broken open and its contents were in a state of disorder. The incubation instrument set had no battery and the tube was perforated. Further, the oxygen appliance had no oxygen in it. Yet when I had checked the emergency case and the oxygen appliance that same morning, as part of my normal duties, I am certain that both had been in full working order.

'Since I did not have any of the necessary equipment I did the best I could which was to perform mouth to mouth resuscitation on Mr Hess and I asked one of the soldiers in American uniform to conduct a heart massage on him. This was at approximately 3.20 pm. These efforts had no discernable effect. A doctor and a medical orderly whom I did not recognise arrived from the English Military Hospital in an ambulance. They brought a heart-lung machine into the summerhouse. I tried to operate the machine but it did not appear to function. Mr Hess was taken to hospital. I accompanied him and made further unsuccessful attempts to resuscitate him in the ambulance. There were final unsuccessful attempts to resuscitate him by the doctors at the hospital. He was pronounced dead at the hospital at 16.10 hours.

'During the five years in which I daily cared for Mr Hess, I was able to obtain a clear and accurate impression of his physical capabilities. I do not consider, given his physical condition, that it would have been possible for Mr Hess to have committed suicide in the manner later published by the Allied powers. He had neither the strength nor the mobility to place an electric flex around his neck, knot it and either hang or strangle himself. Mr Hess was so weak that he needed a special chair to help him stand up. He walked bent over with a cane and was almost blind. If ever he fell to the ground he could not get up again. Most significantly, his hands were crippled with arthritis; he was not able, for example, to tie his shoelaces. I consider that he was incapable of the degree of manual dexterity necessary to manipulate the electric flex as suggested.

'Further, he was not capable of lifting his arms above his shoulders; it is therefore in my view not possible that he was able to attach the electric flex to the window catch from which he is alleged to have suspended himself. Having regard to first Mr Hess' physical condition; second, the scene which I discovered in the summerhouse, in particular the location of the electric flex; and third, the surrounding circumstances as I have described them, I am firmly of the view that Mr Hess could not possibly have committed suicide as has been claimed. In my view, it is clear that he met his death by strangulation, at the hands of a third party.'

This had all happened in the 1987. Years later, whether Hess was murdered or had taken his own life didn't seem likely to bother anybody but the neo-Nazis publishing their mad ideas on the Internet; or Colonel Eugene Bird, if he was still with us, a dedicated soldier who had his own theories about which country would have wanted Hess dead all those years ago. (I had tried hard to trace the colonel over the years, but he seemed to have disappeared or passed on.)

Then on New Year's Day 2003, I had a strange phone message. Would I please call Mr. Serge Morozov of Russian Channel Six TV in London? Urgently. It was about Rudolf Hess.

I called Serge Morozov. He told me, "As of today all the files of 30 years ago have been de-classified and there are some sensational documents released by the Public Record Office regarding the book you and Colonel Bird wrote about the imprisonment of Rudolf Hess. The papers reveal the panic the American and British governments experienced when they were told that Hess was collaborating with you and Mr. Bird." Serge told me he was preparing a long television program on the de-classified papers and wished to interview me on tape and Colonel Bird, if he could find him. He would email me the documents.

Slowly they appeared on my computer screen, in no sequential order. CONFIDENTIAL. British Embassy, Washington. 16 May 1972 to FCO [Foreign Office in London].

'Bird is now in Florida ...' (he had been arrested in Berlin and flown to the US) ' there is some doubt whether he can be prosecuted, but the general feeling is that it is problematical and would be counterproductive, in that it would produce unwelcome publicity. The fact that Bird has not published anything makes it difficult to prove any offence.

'Bird claims to have got back all manuscripts and tapes from Greenfield (of John Farquharson Ltd, our London literary agent) and Zwar and to have rubbed out the tapes. Skoug (of German Affairs) was inclined to believe that Greenfield had come clean if only because of Farquharson's reputation, but was more doubtful about Zwar. Zwar apparently said that he had returned everything … another letter has gone to him asking for "everything tout suite".'

[Rubbish! I had not sent anything back to the State Department — as requested on the phone by a panicked Gene Bird. I had said to him that he could tell the State Department I was not an American subject and would publish the book in my own name, not his, and would not even mention his name. What Hess had to say was the salient point.]

The British Embassy message went on saying that 'Bird was not to be trusted ... though it could be reasonably hoped that he would not do anything until Hess had died.' After that, reasoned the Embassy, any damage publication might do, would be limited.

By now Mr. Basil Hall, MC, TD, Deputy Treasury Solicitor in Whitehall, had been contacted by the Foreign Office for an expert opinion. What could be done to stop the book's publication under the Official Secrets Act, he was asked? Not a lot, he had replied (to Mr. Rodney Batstone, Legal Advisers Department in the Foreign Office). It seemed 'impractical' to rely on section 2 of the 1911 Act, he said, because:

'1. It seemed doubtful whether Spandau Prison could be a "prohibited place" as defined by section 3 of the Act. It was difficult to argue that it belonged to or was occupied by or on behalf of Her Majesty.

'2. Even if Spandau prison were a prohibited place, the section does not apply to Colonel Bird who committed no offence in any part of Her Majesty's dominions and is not a British officer or subject.

'3. There is nothing which one can at present do to Greenfield or John Farquharson Ltd. They have not attempted to communicate the information.

'We discussed whether there would be any point in writing to the publishers saying that publication might contravene the Official Secrets Acts. I think we both hold the view that this might well prove an embarrassment, because there was no reason why the publishers should not make it public that they had received this message; even if we thought that a court might hold that there was a breach, which I for one do not; to write might be inadvisable.'

Rodney Batstone of the FO wrote back: 'Dear Basil, Many thanks for your letter. I am grateful for your help over this.

'In the light of our discussion we have suggested that the Americans be advised to work on Bird who might be able to withdraw the copy from Greenfield. We must hope that this produces results.'

By now the problem was becoming urgent. Confidential telegrams were being sent between Washington, London and Berlin, copied to Bonn, Moscow and Paris embassies, but 'not passed to the French'.

Colonel Bird, under house arrest in Berlin, was reported to be 'reasonably cooperative, but not 100% so. US Mission have recommended that he should be allowed to resign and return at an early date to Florida where his wife was and also very ill. [The] manuscript has not been fully checked by US Mission here [Berlin] yet. But it is known to discuss death arrangements and appears to draw on Quadripartite and Tripartite classified documents. (Interview with Hess) tapes are stated by Bird to be not in Berlin but in possession of Greenfield and Zwar. (Latter incidentally is said to live in Queensland and to be the author of 'The Infamous of Nuremberg' in co-operation with an earlier US Colonel.)

'Hess appears to have happily co-operated on the basis that he was putting his historical record straight.

'US Mission claims that knowledge of this case is very closely restricted to a few people in Berlin and Washington, i.e. at present to no-one in their London Embassy.'

In the meantime what should the Americans do to Colonel Bird?

There were considerable bureaucratic complications in Washington, the telegrams reveal. And the British Embassy was aware of the situation.

'US officials,' said one of their messages, '[are] reportedly divided between those who want to bring him home for the purpose of punishing him, and those who want to keep him in Berlin for the purpose of getting to the bottom of the whole story and neutralising the damage done. At present the latter view is prevailing. The Soviet Governor of Spandau is showing increasing interest in Bird's welfare and whereabouts. We have privately informed the Americans here that Major Yefremov had already appeared to be suspicious of Bird and had asked the British Governor a week or two earlier whether he thought Bird was helping Hess to write his memoirs.

'US Mission have also received information that the Australian named Zwar also operated under the name of "Zwar Features" from an address at 65 Cadogan Gardens, SW3.'

Then, weeks later, the British Embassy in Washington was reporting that Colonel Bird [now in Washington] had summoned up enough courage 'to return to the charge over the publication of his manuscript on Hess.

'Having first approached the Pentagon, he was interviewed in the State Department the other day. Bird was asking for permission to publish. Exactly what he would publish was left obscure, since he maintains that he returned his only manuscript to the US authorities. He did not ask for it back ...'

[True. But as co-author of the book, I had my copy of the manuscript hidden in the brickwork of my Cairns, Queensland workshop, ready for publication.]

Col. Bird was informed, said the Embassy, that 'under current circumstances' there could be no question of his receiving permission to publish; although if Hess should die or Spandau Prison be closed down, he could make formal application. It was felt better to leave him with the hope of eventual permission. The reasoning behind this was that without such a hope he might feel sufficiently frustrated to go ahead and publish now.'

M.L.H. Hope of the Embassy's Western European Department went on, 'Although Bird denies having a manuscript, he claims to be able to rewrite the book from memory. He nevertheless gave every assurance that he would not publish now. Whether or not he is being honest in saying he did not keep a copy of the manuscript (which one is entitled to doubt) it seems pretty certain that Zwar, his collaborator in Australia, has one. Zwar has also written asking for permission to publish, claiming that he, too, could rewrite the book from memory if the manuscript were not returned.' [Again, rubbish. I had never claimed the capacity of remembering 200,000 words.]

Mr. Hope went on: 'Since Zwar is only a ghost-writer and has no personal knowledge or access to Hess this is even less plausible than Bird's claim.'

No access to Hess? I had by now five years of access to Hess through my trained reporter, Colonel Bird. He had been airmailing three or four cassette tapes every week, cleared by HM Customs in Cairns, with Rudolf Hess's answers to the questions I was asking. I would send back by return mail, the chapters written from that information and Bird would take them into the prison for Hess to check. If the old man wished to work on them in the garden he would stuff the pages into his underpants and make his way to the garden seat where, under the noses of the sentinels in the guard towers, he would write his comments in the margins.

I can only look back at this operation by the State Department and Foreign Office investigators as clumsy and inept.

By now the intrepid Serge Morozov had found Gene Bird. He was still in Berlin. When he came on the phone to me in Australia it was the same excitable, enthusiastic Gene I had worked with secretly 30 years before. And he told me an incredible story …

'When you and I were hard at work writing our book, I had a visit from a US official called Russell. He came to Spandau and told me in the strictest confidence, that Henry Kissinger, then Secretary of State, had sent him over to collaborate with me to write a book on Rudolf Hess. I told him I would have no part of it. He was out of order.

'When I was arrested and flown to Washington to appear before 12 of the Top Brass, there at the table was Russell. I said: "I know you, don't I, Mr. Russell?"

He looked at me and said: "I have never seen you before."

Chapter 7

King Of The Con-men

The air fares between Cairns and London might have been crippling, but the lure of Fleet Street and the greatest city in the world, enticed us back. The Hess book was ready to be published and I had been away from the Daily Mail for three years. Would I be accepted on staff again?

'Yes,' was the answer. And on the first night, as I passed the "Back Bench" the decision-makers, the top sub-editors of the paper, one looked up, recognised me. "Oh, hello Old Boy. Been on hols have you?"

Next morning I caught a No.6 bus that swung through the early morning traffic and found myself assigned to the press box at Marlborough Street Magistrates Court.

"Call Stanley Lowe!"

The raucous call reverberated around the passages as several chatting policemen at the doorway of Court One parted to allow a distinguished gentleman through. He is wearing a pale brown British Warm overcoat that reaches to his striped-trousered knees; his ankles are clad in spats. He carries a bowler in his left hand and a silver-topped cane in the right, as he apologetically makes his dignified way through the crush to the dock.

"Stanley Lowe?" queries the court usher.

"Yes. M'Lud," the gentleman replies, nodding up at the magistrate who stiffens with pride at his elevation from humble police court bench man to the highest judiciary in the land.

"Lowe," says the clerk-of-courts, obviously without reverence. "You are charged with being in illegal possession of a Scots Guard's walking-out uniform, to-whit a crimson overcoat. How do you plead?"

"Not guilty, M'Lud," says the thick-spectacled Stanley, flicking an imaginary piece of fluff off an elegant sleeve.

Who would be representing the defendant? "I am, M'Lud, appearing for myself." And in a loud whisper that even M'Lud could hear, "It's a diabolical bloody liberty!"

To the uninitiated like this Australian newsman, there appears to be some terrible mistake. An English gentleman of such style and bearing, charged with such a sordid offence said to have taken place outside, of all places, a seedy Soho strip club.

Could this be the Stanley Lowe? The evening before being sent to cover the case I had gone to the reference library and extracted his cuttings files. Four brown cardboard folders spilled out more than 100 cuttings. Newspaper articles, many of them yellowing, told of an extraordinary life; of one Stanley Lowe masquerading as a Harley Street surgeon; the Bolivian Ambassador (when there wasn't one); an Air Vice-Marshall and a London stockbroker. The list went on. A Sunday newspaper three-part series, fell out of the most recent clips: "Stanley Lowe — King of the Con Men".

Now standing in the dock, balding, plump, bespectacled and clutching the bowler, the gentleman asked politely if a piece of paper he had in his hand could be passed across to the arresting constable. Was it not, asked Mr. Lowe, giving the clerk time to ponderously cross the body of the court, a receipt? A receipt given by a reputable clothing establishment in Charing Cross Road for ... a Scots Guards Walking Out Uniform?

Mutterings from the Bench; incredulous glares from the arresting police.

Case dismissed.

Swinging his cane Mr. Lowe meets The Press out on the steps. He is indignant, even angry. "A diabolical liberty!" he repeats.

A press conference would, he said, be conducted at the site of the alleged offence: Green's Cabaret, a 'Striperama'. Members only and in a laneway off Old Compton Street, Soho. At the head of the posse of reporters and cameramen, swinging his cane as if leading a military parade, Stanley assures us as we go with the lights, that drinks and entertainment would be available.

Strip-tease in those days was quietly emerging as a popular gentlemen's entertainment in London's 'naughty square mile'. It was possible — by paying a few shillings and waiting 10 minutes for a bogus board meeting to assess your application — to become a 'member' of various clubs. Once in, and having complied with the law, you could settle down to watch a tiny stage on which a naked girl sat in a chair in front of a single-bar radiator. When she got stiff and the audience wearied of looking at one particular side of her, the curtain would come down and when it rose again, she had moved, facing the other direction.

On this morning, as Fleet Street's finest settled around an illegal gaming table in the centre of the dingy room to listen to Stanley, a bored blonde with enormous breasts sat staring numbly into the half-dark.

We all of course agreed with Mr. Lowe, as the liquor flowed, that the charge had been 'preposterous', 'unbelievable', and yes, a diabolical liberty that such an accusation had been made against his honesty. As one, we promised that the Not Guilty verdict would indeed be splashed across our pages. There may even be, somebody wide-eyed with gin suggested, a leading article about false accusations by police remaining unpunished.

Having partaken of Stanley's sandwiches, his malt whisky, and the backdrop of distracting nakedness, I felt I had arrived back in London. Certainly, I said as I stumbled out into the daylight, I would give serious consideration to his offer of shares in the Sydney Harbour Bridge. How kind of him to put me on 'the inside running', when we had only just been introduced.

Stanley and I ran into each other sporadically over the ensuing years. When a publisher commissioned me to write a series of articles to accompany character photographs that would reveal the real 'naughty' Soho, I sought out Stanley for his advice.

We met at his new place of employment a 'naughty' book shop in Old Compton Street where punters could browse in the front section over copies of 'Health and Beauty' and nudist periodicals. After making his mind up that the customer was not in fact a police spy ready to confiscate stock, Stanley would enquire if Sir might like to see something 'a little stronger' at the rear of the establishment? If Sir agreed, curtains would be parted and a surprising scene would meet his tired eyes: blow-up dolls, dildos, whips, handcuffs, chains, and photographs on the covers of foreign magazines of people doing extraordinary things to one another.

At closing time Stanley accompanied photographer Roy Dickens and I to a restaurant to help plan our exposure of The Soho Village, and over several bottles of Algerian red, he was to tell us something of the truth of his life.

He was born, he insisted then and always has done, the illegitimate son of a wayward Lord. His Cockney accent, a foggy sort of growl, could easily revert to that of a toff from the shires, or genuine plummy Mayfair, giving some credence to his background.

Why, I wondered, had he ... er ... turned to crime? He had been the guest of Her Majesty several times, said the library cuttings, and after one embarrassing incident in New York, involving the distribution of US dollars manufactured by Freddy The Writer in Islington, he had once found himself incarcerated in Sing Sing. There had even been concern for some time that preventative detention would be considered by the British courts if Stanley strayed again from the path of righteousness. "Well, they would have thrown away the bloody key," he agreed, puffing at his cigarette.

Was it all worth it?

"Weeel," said Stanley, his eyes magnified by the pebble glasses he wore. "I guess I like people. They seem to like listening to me. And there's an old adage: the richer you are, the greedier you are. Greedy people tend to lend themselves to the con."

How, I wondered, on the second bottle of red, did Australian con-men stack up in the order of ... excellence?

"I would hope," said Stanley, toying with his glass, "that you will not take offence at this, Desmond, but your people do not really have the couth to be successful on their own. As assistants yes, but not as independent operators. I will tell you a story ..."

By now he had the whole restaurant as an audience. Tables had been quietly pushed closer to ours. Conversation was hushed. It was admittedly a small room, but the magnetism of the man was obvious.

"I was doing this little job in Paris," recalled Stan. "because it had come to my attention that some of the richest oil-men in America were in residence at the Hotel Georges Cinq.

"On a Sunday morning, I entered the private bar to find one of them there, Stetson on his head, cameras around his neck, sipping bourbon and dry. I was dressed in black jacket and striped trousers and had a bowler. As I entered the bar, a 'French man', obviously intoxicated, in fact my Australian helper, sat on a stool on the American's right; I sat on his left.

"I ordered from the barman, a single malt whisky. As it was being placed before me, I could see in the mirror in front of me that the drunken Frenchman was lurching into the American, spilling his drink. I allowed this to go on for a few minutes and then, with resigned dignity, I arose and berated the drunk in impeccable French. He staggered out of the private bar and disappeared.

"My American oilman friend was ecstatic. I had done 'a very wonderful thing'. In fact he would like to show his gratitude by buying me a drink.

"I am terribly sorry," Stanley told the oilman, in a plummy Eton accent, "but I must say no. I have a very busy day tomorrow."

"Oh," said the American. "You are here on business in Paris, France?"

Stanley had looked over his right shoulder, then his left and said confidentially, "I'm afraid it's all terribly hush-hush. You see, it involves all those elegant shops on the Champs d'Elysees. All independently owned, until next week, when a consortium will be launched on the Paris Stock Exchange, on Wall Street, and on the London Stock Exchange. I am handling the float."

He remembered, he said, the American almost breaking his wrist getting his travellers' cheques out, making ready to sign $10,000 worth to 'get in on the ground floor.' Then he asked if Stanley could see his way clear to taking a personal cheque for a further $10,000 worth of shares?

"I had to decline," said Stan, toying with his glasses. "I said, 'I don't really know you, do I?'"

* * *

A regular, morbid task on every newspaper was to bring the obituaries of the famous up-to-date; writing the actual 'death' headline and having it printed ready to slot into the page the moment the sad news came through, even though at the time of writing, the 'subject' was still very much alive. To achieve this, reporters were required to call the homes or staff of the Great to ask the whereabouts of their employers at that very moment. I had to do it and was informed, "Sir Winston is at home in Hyde Park Gate tonight." And the poster would be readied: "CHURCHILL DEAD — Dies Peacefully in Hyde Park, London flat."

Sir Winston, still in his robust 80s and far from dead, had in fact been in King Edward VII Hospital for a hip operation. On this particular evening, on the eve of his birthday, he was being brought home, and reporters, photographers and television camera crews were packing the footpaths. I was sent to Hyde Park Gate to watch the ambulance arrive and see the great man carried inside.

Daily Mail photographer George Little, a diminutive Cockney, had been chosen to take the 'pool' photograph of Sir Winston being settled upstairs in his drawing-room and having a glass of champagne; there was no room for a horde of newsmen, so one photographer would take the picture to be distributed to papers and agencies all over Britain and around the world.

As the ambulance slowly made its way down the narrow roadway and came to a halt, a cheer went up. The rear doors were opened and there, inside, was the great man seated in a chair wearing a grey suit and spotted bow-tie. I noticed one of the officers hand him a large cigar and adjust his homburg, and (sadly), turn his head for him. As the old man was carried in the chair to the pavement, he made the V sign with his right hand, his left clutching a stick. As police kept the media and onlookers at bay he was carried inside, George Little following.

I hung about for George to emerge after everyone else had departed. "What did he say to you, George?"

"Well ... it was a bit embarrassing really. I took quite a lot of pictures and when it was time to go, I wished him a happy birthday. I said, 'I 'ope I'll be 'ere for your 90th birthday, Sir Winston.' And he said: 'I can't see any reason why you won't, my boy. You look well enough to me.'"

But it wasn't to be. Churchill died. I found myself soon after, sitting in a First Class seat of a British Airways 747, sharing a bottle of French champagne with an undertaker. For a practising coward this was an unfortunate situation.

As the undertaker and I took off, we had each stared straight ahead as the plane climbed to 30,000 feet. (Well, he was British and we had not been introduced.) Finally, with the champagne and sense of awe at my circumstances (I was on a 'freebie') overcoming my shyness I extended my right hand. "By the way, I am Desmond Zwar. Where are you flying to?"

The immaculately-groomed gentleman in the Savile Row suit took my hand and said: "How extraordinary. My name is Desmond too. I'm getting off at the next stop. I have to ... er ... embalm somebody. I'm an undertaker." It needed another courtesy glass of Moet.

English Desmond then disclosed that he worked for Britain's most famous undertaking establishment and that he kept his passport and travellers' cheques by his bedside at all times, 'waiting for a call'. His job was to fly out at a moment's notice to preserve the bodies of heads of state, or a VIP whose funeral might be some time ahead; maybe requiring to be flown to another country for burial, as was the case of the airline manager who had just passed away.

Desmond revealed that he had embalmed many heads of state, including the Shah of Iran; and, he said, Sir Winston Churchill.

"At the end of his life his doctors had said Sir Winston mustn't smoke cigars, and that was something that really upset him.

"When I was taken into his bedroom to do what was necessary and the family had departed, there was a cigar butt under the bed. I noticed it was still smouldering."

Chapter 8

That 'Rubbish' Cost Megabucks!

I t is Sunday, according to the 'San Francisco Examiner' as I arrived on the West Coast after a 'freebie' ride from London to New York on Concorde, sitting up on the flight-deck as the pilot lowered the nose-cone as we came in to land.

Jetlagged, I look down from the 22nd. story window of my hotel near Market Street, and there are a lot of police down there. A siren pierces the quarter-inch plate glass and drowns the air-conditioning. It's the Lesbian/Gay Freedom Day Parade on its way Downtown.

To the coffee-shop first for flapjacks and coffee.

"To go or havin' it here? Okay, havaniceday." The night before, at 11.15 pm the hot chocolate lady had told me to make sure I "havaniceday".

Across from my table sits a fat Nazi S.S.man. Black leather Rommel peaked cap, leather chaps over the jeans with the crotch and bottom cut out of the leather, a three-inch wide spiked dog-collar uncomfortably buckled round his neck; black leather jacket and gloves, aviator's sunglasses and heavy black bovver-boots with steel toes. "In the parade, Hank?" asks a waitress. "Yessir, Ma'am."

Out on Market Street they're lining the sidewalks. The curious; the gay. The drunk; the doped. The pink-wealthy and the grubby poor. Two hundred thousand spectators will see the parade. It's now 18 years since the Stonewall riots, when gays made a deliberate move in the US to fight their tormentors and 'break out and seek liberation'. This parade, which will urge more money for AIDS research, is one more step out of the closet. I take my place by the kerb. Beside me are two young men with dyed hair, arms around each other, now and again fondling each other's behinds, oblivious of the crowd. Are they faithful? I wonder. Or enjoying Russian-roulette promiscuity?

A whistle blows and suddenly there's a roar of dozens of motor-cycle engines throbbing into life. The traditional parade leaders — Dykes on Bikes — move into formation. Each motorbike is mounted by two girls. Black leather breeches and open waistcoats; several sets of bare breasts turning a little blue in the chilly breeze. Short-cropped hair, determined, confident, hard faces driving the bikes, and a few pale, even bewildered passengers trying to look contemptuous of the jeers and the whistles, though smiling at the cheers.

Behind them 'cowboys' in the full theatre of a western movie set, arm-in-arm, smiling, proud. Lined up in immaculate formation, follow gorgeously uniformed 'majorettes', twirling batons. Then come a clutch of 'nuns', purple-and-green-haired dancers, jazz bands, more cowboys driving a stage-coach pulled by four horses, a float of arm-linked 'lawyers for individual freedom', a rumble of females wearing T-shirts with the message 'Lesbian Breeders'.

The bands are strident, the whistles and shouts of encouragement shrill. Then down the street trundles an elegant old cable-car and there's a hush about where I'm standing. It has placards asking for support for AIDS research and carries four AIDS victims; two fairly obviously dying. Two men are standing, the sick two sitting.

One wears an immaculate white linen suit on his frail body, and a white straw hat. He has a cane beside him and on his knee he clutches a teddy bear. He has a half bemused smile on his face, the other expression it switches to, appears to be fear. The lovers beside me stop their groping for an instant and say nothing until he goes past.

There are 10,000 marchers who, the police report later, take three hours to pass one point. One of the procession, David Hummel, an AIDS sufferer, is pushed along the route in a wheelchair fastened with an oxygen tank. Hummel carries a placard: 'THANK GOD I'M GAY.'

"People want to have fun," says a marcher as the parade comes to a halt to allow traffic to cross. "You can't go around crying all the time." His garb places him somewhere between a painted bag-lady and a nun and he is applauded for his comment by a three-feet tall Storm trooper dwarf wearing a moustache.

Behind Market Street I find a cab that bears a sign: 'IF YOU FEEL GOOD, PLEASE NOTIFY YOUR FACE.' The driver leans back and informs me, "No way I'd mix it with one of them dykes. Fight? My God! Give me a gay fare anytime." I see him examining me carefully in his rear-vision mirror.

I need a respite from the march and head for a different scene: the San Francisco Museum of Modern Art. Cadillac and Jaguar showrooms are its neighbours and it has soaring ceilings, a lot of marble, and in contrast to the last two hours, is hushed. The museum is presenting a 'Quiet Revolution' of British sculpture. The Burns Security man, a young, crew-cut negro, spots my tiny tape-recorder and whispers: "No pictures, Suh." I explain what I have is a tape-recorder and he comes to ease, telling me he is ex-Navy and has been to Australia. Standing for six hours at a time gazing at people gazing at sculpture you learn to relax your body with your knees he says. "My job is to prevent damage, Suh."

Upstairs I walk into a salon that is highlighted by a metre-wide, 30 metres long stretch of broken slate. A young lady is explaining that this sculpture has been meticulously put together by the artist so that the slate is piled on layers. "He has put down the biggest pieces first, then the next biggest on top of them, then the next biggest and so on." She went on: "You get a feeling of awe as you walk along." I wonder to her how the slate got into this pristine, upstairs room, imagining bulldozers and heavy earth-moving equipment. "No it comes packed in crates, big wooden crates. The artist took the slate from the crates and piled it up himself." The Museum has purchased this work of art, so it will be permanent until it is inartistically stowed in some cellar. Was it, er ... expensive? I politely ask, my voice echoing embarrassingly around the walls. An elderly lady glares at me from behind her pince-nez as the guide utters just one word. "Megabucks."

We move on to an adjacent salon where stands a pile of pieces of white rubble. Before us, the guide explains, is an incredibly costly art purchase and they are in fact pieces of the white cliffs of Dover.

I am about to ask about the vandalism at Dover when I am warned, "Please don't get too close. That chalk is terribly fragile. It is placed in a circle, with the biggest pieces of chalk first, then ..." I turn off the tape-recorder and don't ask the obvious question, the answer to which I know will be megabucks. Instead, I begin telling the lady in the pince-nez, just to soften her up, about the man who gave his pet chimpanzee a set of paints, let him loose and sold the result to the Museum of Modern Art ...

"Shhhh!" somebody hisses.

We move on; past four sheets of rusted, corrugated iron arranged in a fan shape amidst a scatter of plastic toys, a toothbrush and a broken toy car. And a thong. This is by Mr. Tony Cragg, one of the draw cards of the exhibition. A Burns Security trusty is watching over it to avoid damage.

Next door stands a table, an ancient and broken set of drawers, a chair, a packing-case and half a barrel. It features an empty Budweiser beer bottle, a newspaper, some rusted car parts and a light-bulb. I try and get closer to read the newspaper headline and the guide hisses again. However the art label was decipherable and it said that the artist, 'using bits of contemporary consumer culture' was commenting on the urban landscape and its relationship to the unnatural, pointing out the objects integral to the 'physical, intellectual and emotional lives of modern industrial society.' I emerge confused, three dollars lighter and blinking into the afternoon sunlight. I have a beguiling choice of afternoon entertainment ahead, a psychic fair, the Aswan Dancers from Cairo, a tour of two cafes in a Cafe Walk, a reading by Miss Susie Bright at the Modern Times Bookstore titled 'Deep Inside the Porn Industry', There is a Mr. Gary Sick on Iran and Must the Past Be Repeated? or Dr Bob Goulding on Redecision Therapy. Instead I ask directions back to Market Street from a gentleman outside the Jaguar showroom.

San Franciscans are polite, high on happy nervous energy and a few other things ("Man, have you done the small, brown mushroom? They don't burn you out as much."), and 'into' the psyche. Fortune-tellers and soothsayers make ... well ... a fortune. A black came reeling towards me as I walked back to Market Street to see the end of the parade. "I'm sorry, Man, I ain't got time to shake yo' hand, I sho' wish I did. Just give me a dime for a cup of cawfee." A dozen hairy-chested gentlemen in feather boas, slashes of lipstick and strapless dresses (one bearing a sign 'Stand By Your Man'),are queuing for the Port-o-let marked MEN. The parade had come to an end.

That night I arrive back in London, open our door in Cadogan Gardens, SW3, and a small red-headed boy and a loving wife come out to hug me. It is reality again.

Chapter 9

The Man Who Found Tutankahmen

Eight years before email and voice-mail, our London apartment was connected to a nearby Chelsea answering service. If we had gone out for a time, a polite lady answered the phone on the third ring, giving callers the impression she was there in the flat.

By now I was working from a tape-recorder perched on my desk, linked to the back of the telephone-handset by a suction microphone. It was forbidden under the Post Office Act to record a phone conversation, but the law had never been tested in court. There was no sinister reason behind my breaking the rules; it was because my shorthand was appalling and note-taking careless, my mind racing ahead to ask the next question.

When I finished recording an interview I still had to transcribe what the interviewee said, using a foot pedal control that stopped and started the tape. It took time, but the system gave me an accurate, verbatim record of every word spoken, an important requirement for a freelance writer: one mistake in Fleet Street and you were out. Not banned by just one newspaper, but by all of them. Word of any unreliability, or accusations of misquoting somebody spread fast.

The Daily Mail had been happy to take my articles for its weekday feature pages and now I intended to tap into a lucrative new market offered by popular Sunday papers like The People and News of the World, which paid thousands of pounds for three and four-part series.

I was therefore suitably alarmed to be accused of falsification just three weeks into my decision to go freelance.

The allegation that I had faked an article was serious, for it came from a firm of lawyers. They had complained about a feature I'd written for the Daily Mail that week and I was summoned to see the Managing Editor.

A news item in The Times, some days earlier had reported that nurses earning a miserable £7 a week in public hospitals were quitting their jobs, signing up with a London nursing agency and then returning to the same wards to be paid double the amount by a hospital system blackmailed by a starvation of staff. The nursing agency The Times named, was just one of several enthusiastically cashing in on the situation. I thought there might be an article in it for the Daily Mail, and the Features Editor agreed.

From home I phoned the Secretary/Manager at one Agency, identified myself, and asked if she could tell me how the agency system worked. I had the suction microphone sucking and the tape turning as we spoke.

Mary, a chatty Scot, said she was only too happy to help. What a lovely day it was outside. Her cat was perched on the window-sill in front of her, preening itself in the sun, and she was sorry to be inside.

She obligingly explained the nursing situation and the number of nurses she had on her books. And, she said, there were scores of low-paid hospital nurses on salary, just waiting to be signed on and jump ship; to quit a ward and then go back to their original jobs at twice the pay. Mary was a talker and the interview went on for 35 minutes. When we had finished, I phoned the Manager of a

London teaching hospital who confirmed the frustrating accuracy of what I'd been told. He said he was terribly worried by the potential damage to his hospital budget.

I laboriously transcribed the tapes and wrote the article which appeared next day in the Daily Mail to be read by millions; some writing to the Editor to say how appalling they found the vicious circle.

Next day my phone rang; the Managing Editor on the line and that meant trouble. Managing Editors rarely called freelance journalists, or any journalist. Dealing with problems was usually a task left to executives much lower in the pecking order.

Mr. Bill Matthewman was blunt and to the point. The Nursing Agency was not only denying the truth of my article; but it was also denying that its Secretary Manager had ever spoken to me! The Agency was owned by a partnership of wealthy and important solicitors and they wanted a retraction. Would I like to come into the office to explain?

I asked for an appointment that afternoon and having prepared myself, caught the Tube into the office, my stomach sickening. Was this the end of Desmond Zwar Features?

Bill Matthewman, a tall, kindly fellow, made it clear when I sat down that if what the solicitors had said was true, the paper and I were in trouble.

I opened my briefcase and handed him 18 closely-typed pages and a tape cassette which began with the words: "This is Desmond Zwar, I write for the Daily Mail and would like to interview you about ... and then switched to the chatterer, Mary describing the loveliness of the weather, the antics of the cat and the salary situation of nurses joining her agency. A relieved smile passed over Bill Matthewman's face. "Is that the way you always do it?" I said I did, and it was done precisely to guard myself against accusations like these. Here was firm evidence that would stand up in court to prove the allegations of faking, blatantly untrue. What the Post Office did about the taping if it got to court was another matter.

It would have been sweet to hear the reaction from the dodgy solicitors when confronted with the evidence, but being the professional he was, the Managing Editor kept the affair to himself. They had 'tried it on', was all he said, and in doing so, were obviously quite unconcerned about destroying a career.

Being obstinately right has always been important to me—in everyday life as well as journalism—and over many years the taped interview has always been utterly reliable. The nursing agency incident was a boost to my career: I was given delicate investigative assignments by the paper because I knew how to use a tape-recorder. Other reporters were soon buying the same tiny Fi-Cord, made in Switzerland, replacing the only alternative of cumbersome reel-to-reel machines used by the BBC, requiring heavy battery power and were far too bulky.

Desmond Zwar Features began to make serious money, selling several three-part series to Sunday newspapers for as much as £10,000 for as many words.

The operation came to a halt briefly, when I was offered the task of editing the Mail's gossip column: Tanfield's Diary, a page of tittle-tattle about the country's rich and famous. I didn't have to look far for my first column: the charming secretary of 'Diary' sitting by my elbow, became famous herself when she married author Nicholas Monsarrat, who had written his bestseller The Cruel Sea. She invited me to the wedding and I had a few minutes at the bar with the groom. He warned me that an author had to actually experience events to write about them well (he had been a district officer in Africa and used the experience to write The Tribe That Lost Its Head); and, he said, one should show loyalty to people who were loyal to you 'on the way up'. He indicated an elderly lady across the room. "She's my literary agent, always has been and always will be. I wrote The Cruel Sea at sea, on any bits of paper I could lay my hands on. Backs of orders. Anything. She had it all typed up and took the manuscript to 10 different publishers, who each turned it down. But she persisted. The 11th. took it and the rest is history. I have had lots of people want to represent me since then, but I have said no."

In the eccentricity that operates on newspapers, I was then asked if I'd like to move into the Daily Mail's features room, as Acting Deputy for the Features Editor.

I had been getting up at 6 am, buying six daily papers from Johnnie, the Cockney news-vendor in Sloane Square, breakfasting, and then marking possible feature ideas on the pages from news items.

'Bognor Vicar Tells of Death Cell Interviews' was a news item in the Financial Times (of all papers) that recorded a vicar's address to a luncheon. I contacted The Reverend who said proudly that he had been in the death cell comforting 22 convicted murderers and wartime spies before they were "topped" (hung). We collaborated in gloomy Bognor on a Sunday series: 'Death Cell Vicar' which earned us about £3,000 each.

Most of my ideas were aimed at the Daily Mail and having culled the best three or four, I'd take the Underground into the office and present them. One or more might be chosen. Or none. Now, if I took up this new offer, all my ideas would be exclusive to the Daily Mail and I would be paid a salary to compensate.

It was at the end of a day in Room 8, just before Christmas, and we were wrapping up the pages for the first edition. If anything happened during the night to cause sub-editors to change an article that was somebody else's problem.

I was about to leave when there was a call on the secretary's phone; she had gone home, so I took it. The

Security man downstairs had a Mr. Adamson wishing to see somebody who might be able to help him. It was about some photographs. I have no idea why I did it, but I asked Security to send him up. He arrived from the lift, a small, 70-ish man in threadbare black suit meekly clutching his hat. He didn't want to be a bother, but he had just come from being with Prince Charles and ... he'd said the magic word! I ushered in Richard Adamson to a chair beside mine in the paper-strewn features room and he said he didn't want to take up a lot of time, but he had been in Luxor, Egypt, in 1922 with British Egyptologist Howard Carter. Carter had been picking over the last area he was to dig in Egypt's Valley of the Kings; searching for Tutankhamen's tomb. Adamson, then a 23-year-old, had been a policeman in Cairo, he said, well ... more than a policeman really; he was a spy. He had been involved in 'security work' in Cairo, infiltrating the Wafdist Party which at the time was attempting to overthrow British rule in Egypt. (The story was getting more and more intriguing!)

"I had passed on certain information which led to the arrest of 28 Egyptians — four sentenced to death and the rest jailed," he said matter-of-factly. "I was a marked man, and it was deemed advisable to send me away from Cairo." He had been sent to join Howard Carter and his wealthy patron, Lord Carnarvon, in the Valley; and Carter, knowing of Adamson's 'trouble', had insisted that his identity and background be kept secret, employing the young policeman to type up his work notes on the daily dig, making sure that he (Adamson) wasn't mentioned.

My colleague, putting on his coat behind Adamson's back, on his way home, mouthed the word: 'Nutter.'

I ignored him as Adamson told me he had just come from a private audience with Prince Charles who had been so fascinated by what he told him of Egyptology that he had extended a scheduled one hour's chat to four hours, keeping a royal detective cooling his heels outside the Prince's rooms. And now, as one of the few witnesses left, he had been invited to take part in a film by the Egyptian Tourist Department to re-enact the discovery in the Valley of the Kings. This was why, in some desperation, he was seeking the paper's help. "I would like to get my photographs back from Cairo." There were some hundreds of his photographs the Egyptians were still keeping in the Cairo Museum; a collection officials were reluctant to acknowledge even existed.

Why did he want his old pictures? I asked him.

"One picture is historic: it is a box-camera snap I took and showed to Carter the day before he uncovered the passageway to Tutankhamen's tomb. Just after I took the photo, the Egyptian workers covered over again what was later shown to be a step I had photographed."

Was he in fact, claiming that it was his own alertness and shrewdness that led to the actual discovery? Well, he said, that step was the first leading down to the tomb, and had he not shown Carter that photograph, the deadline for the expiration of the dig licence would have passed and Carter would have departed Egypt empty-handed. Had such a claim been made public before? I asked him. "Oh no, Mr. Zwar. I would not seek to make claims that would detract from anybody else's efforts. Mr. Carter was a good man ..."

He had taken the snap on 3rd November 1922, almost the eleventh hour of the end of Carter's exclusive digging rights in Egypt. Armed with an old John Bull box camera, he was pottering about taking snapshots of the excavations, having his film developed each night by the manager of the Winter Palace Hotel in nearby Luxor. He had lent the Egyptian Museum this photograph and many others, and had not been given them back. I confirmed their existence on a visit to Cairo in 1992 and was told they were soon to be used in a 'major expo of the Tutankhamen memorabilia.'

I was now so fascinated with what Adamson was telling me that I invited him back to our flat for a drink, and he went on with his story. He sipped sherry with Delphine and I and both of us felt a shiver of excitement as he went on with his account of what happened half a century ago.

When he was pottering about with his camera, he said, he noticed three Egyptian diggers uncover what looked like a large boulder near some workmen's' huts. "I then saw them quickly cover up the boulder with rubbish they had taken from another spot, and start digging in a different direction." But before they hid what they had uncovered, the alert Adamson photographed it.

"The next morning Carter arrived on the site at the usual time and said: 'Everything all right?' I said: 'Yes, the work's going along now.' There was only a short time of the concession left."

Lord Carnarvon, Carter's wealthy mentor, had already returned to England. 'Well, there's not far to go now,' Mr. Carter said, and went on with what he was doing." (For seven backbreaking years, his health failing, Carter had tried, and he believed failed, to discover the last link in the pharaohs — the tomb of the boy king Tutankhamen (1333 B.C — 1323 B.C) which he firmly believed was somewhere in the arid Valley.)

Carter, said Adamson, had then crouched down in the sand and had drawn a line with his finger showing how far they were going to excavate. He said to Adamson: "Then we'll level all this up."

"Sir," said Adamson. "What about these funny stones?"

"What funny stones?"

"There, with all that rubbish that has been put on top of it. They are about 50 yards away — I can pinpoint them. Here, I've got photos of them." And he took the fresh prints from his pocket.

"Carter studied the photographs. He then said: 'We'll have to uncover this lot again.' He called the Arab workers over and ordered them to do it. There was a bit of an argument. The ghaffir (foreman) didn't want to do it. That, in itself, ought to have given rise to a bit of suspicion, but it didn't dawn on us then. But Carter insisted, and they uncovered the stones. Carter took his coat off, and I took off mine, and we got right down to it to examine them. It was a step I had found! There was one underneath it and one underneath that. Carter stood up. 'These are no boulders. We'll need some help.' I said: 'You'll get no more help tonight, Sir.'

"'Right,' said Carter. 'We'll carry on ourselves until it gets dark.'" Together Adamson and Carter scraped sand and rubbish away from six steps. The next morning, starting at dawn, they uncovered another ten. Facing them now was a door. "Carter was obviously excited. He said to me: 'I think we've reached what we are looking for.'"

Carter wrote later in his own account of the discovery: 'It was clear by now, beyond any question, that we actually had before us the entrance to a tomb ...' And he gave the only clue to another person being responsible for the momentous discovery: 'Hardly had I arrived next morning (November 4th) than the unusual silence, due to the stoppage of work, made me realise that something out of the ordinary had happened. I was greeted by the announcement that a step cut in the rock had been discovered underneath the very first hut to be attacked.'

This was the first and only reference—oblique as it was—ever made by Carter that another person was responsible for perhaps the world's most important archaeological find.

"We found a passage-way," Adamson went on, as Delphine, my wife, came back into the room with drinks.

"Then we came to a door. We uncovered it and found another passage, leading right. The passage was covered with plaster, but some of it was of a different texture. Somebody had been there before us. We removed this and it took about half an hour. Then we came to rubble, all boulders and wood.

"Carter then decided to cover up our entry and cable Lord Carnarvon to return to Egypt. He did, and on November 23 our party of six once more uncovered the passage-way.

"First Mr. Carter made a small hole at the top of the door and inserted a lighted candle to test the purity of the air for any foul gas. Lord Carnarvon, myself, Mr. A. R. Callender, Mr. Rex Englebach, the Chief Inspector of Antiquities, and Lady Evelyn Herbert, Lord Carnarvon's daughter, watched during a tense silence as Howard Carter picked up a torch and looked inside — it was a moment I can never forget.

"Eventually Lord Carnarvon called out: 'Can you see anything, Howard?'

"The reply was, 'Yes. Wonderful things! Wonderful things!'

"He stepped down and handed the torch to Lord Carnarvon who peered into the hole for almost a minute. Eventually the torch was handed to me. I looked inside. I don't know what I expected to see, but most certainly the sight took my breath away. As I moved the torch around, details came into view.

"There was a room, about 25ft. by 30 ft. and as I shone my torch inside, everything seemed yellow. I thought at first that the lens must have been dusty to give off this yellowish look. Then I realised what I was looking at was gold.

"Suddenly my beam picked out some objects, the like of which I've never seen before and which I'm sure I'll never see again.

"There were three large couches in the form of animals. It was uncanny. All around, in a state of haphazard confusion, were chests, vases, shrines, chariots and thrones ... everywhere the glint of gold. Gleaming eyes were picked up by the torch and they glowed frighteningly in reflection.

"The centre couch, a hippo God, had eyes that glared right back at you, about three feet from the torch. It was just as if the thing was alive, and I drew back. I think I looked for perhaps half a minute before I handed the torch back.

"One had the feeling as if we were in the presence of someone who, although dead, was alive and watching. You seemed to inherit the belief of those long-dead Egyptians; that they do not die, but live on in the spirit of their Gods and ancestors."

The sight the party was taking in had not been seen by man since 1,350 years before the birth of Christ save for a frustrated break-in by thieves, established scientifically to have taken place some 12-15 years after the funeral. Then it was time to break through to the inner chamber. It was protected by two life-size sentinels in black, overlaid with gold; upon their heads the Royal emblems of the sacred cobra and vulture. Carter took a few minutes to remove stones and make a gap large enough to squeeze through. He was confronted with two massive doors of an outer shrine, closed by bolts but otherwise unsealed. The workers prised open the ebony bolts and the double-doors fell open. Inside was the Burial Chamber ...

Adamson said he first saw a chair, studded with gold. It had a servant figure carved on it, offering the king the conventional wish of devotion: a million years of life. "A sad touch in a tomb of a king who had died at the age of 18 and there, jewelled and golden, was his throne, and on it a scene showing him seated on a chair while his young queen anointed his body with oil from a jar. There was a collection of household implements; the king's shields and spears, his great fan of ostrich feathers, sceptres, walking-sticks and trumpets made of silver."

Above the intruders' heads, a dozen boats waited as if ready to sail down the Nile as a flotilla.

It was almost a year later that in the burial chamber itself, the excavators broke through and uncovered the greatest treasure of all: four gold shrines containing a sarcophagus and a nest of three coffins, the last fashioned from solid gold.

"Because consecration liquid had been poured over the Mummy, it was stuck fast in the coffin," Adamson told me.

"Heat from primus lamps filled with paraffin had to be used before the Mummy could be removed. Over the head and shoulders was a golden mask. The Mummy was lying at an angle in the coffin, evidently it had been tilted when lowered and the consecration liquid had set and kept it in that position.

"When the wrappings on King Tutankhamen were finally removed, one could only stand and gaze, bereft of thought, action or words."

Richardson Adamson was silent for a while. "That scene has rarely been out of my mind over the years. To look upon the features of one who had lived so many centuries ago, to see him as a civilisation, long since departed had seen him, and to know you are looking on the face of an actual Pharaoh of Egypt who had ruled so vast an empire long, long ago, was incredible. Around his neck and across his breast, his wife and mourners had placed a collarets made of cornflowers, lilies and lotus. They were dead and withered, but after 3,000 years still had a trace of colour. The face appeared to be looking back at you, mockingly, eyes partly open. There was a scar on his left cheek.

"The bandages were extremely fragile and crumbled at a touch. All fingers and toes had been bandaged separately and gold sheaths placed over each one. Gold sandals were on the feet. Some resinous material had been used to plug the nostrils, partly open the eyes and pushed between the lips. The skin was a greyish colour."

Adamson was ordered, he said, to remain at the scene "for a few weeks" to guard the treasures as they were catalogued and removed from the tomb. He was to stay there in fact, for seven years.

Some time later, Delphine and I flew to Cairo and after seeing the Tutankhamen treasures in the Egyptian Museum and going to the Valley of the Kings at Luxor, I gave Egyptian authorities the record of my weeks of interviews with Richard Adamson and his claimed role in the discovery: a role never mentioned in the guide books, and unknown to Egyptologists who had devoted their lives to researching every detail of the rich heritage they were showing me.

Were Richard Adamson's photographs still held in the museum vaults?

Egypt's most famous Egyptologist, Mr. Zahi Hawass, Director-General of the Giza Plateau area for the Egyptian Antiquities Organisation, confirmed that Adamson's photos had been held by the Egyptian Museum, but said they were 'now in an archive in Britain.'

He agreed that the Egyptian Museum had once held the significant photograph of the steps Mr. Adamson had shown Howard Carter. It had been kept with dozens of Adamson photographs and there was no reason to disbelieve what Adamson had told me. Mr. Hawass, an Egyptologist for the last 25 years, was now seeking to have the Adamson archive returned once more to Cairo for an international symposium he was organising to mark the 75th. anniversary of the discovery of the tomb.

"All of us have known that the Egyptian workers found the steps. But we have always believed that they (the workers) went to Howard Carter and asked him to come and have a look at the steps. Mr. Carter had always believed Tutankhamen's Tomb was somewhere there. It was just a matter of time needed to discover it."

From what he had been told of the Adamson Archive he believed that the photograph would prove what Adamson had claimed. Had the workers deliberately tried to conceal the discovery from Carter?

"Yes. I believe that."

Richard Adamson, in less guarded moments, had told me he had been conveniently 'forgotten' by Howard Carter, even though he had spent years helping Carter collate and index the treasures in the tomb.

Each evening, he said, when the day's digging was over and Carter and his team had gone back across the Nile to Luxor, the 27shillings-a-week corporal would get out his folding camp bed, his sheets and two blankets, and settle down for the night.

"There really wasn't a need to take the army bed down into the tomb," he smiled. "There were already 12 or 15 similar beds down below. They might have been 3,000 years old, but they were in excellent condition. Their design was no more crude than the bed I was using."

Adamson would settle down in the eerie tomb, reading by a light from a generator and playing his gramophone. Accompanying the hum of the generator at ground level, the strains of "Aida" echoed through chambers dug almost forty centuries before. "A single red lamp lit the burial chamber. It was kept on all night, but shaded so I could sleep.

"I was never scared. I had a direct field telephone link with Carter and I could get through to him immediately in an emergency. But it was odd; I was a single British soldier guarding the most valuable and incredible treasure the world had ever seen.

"There was also a series of trip-alarms, bells and wires which would have awakened the whole of Luxor if there had been an attempt by thieves. They probably believed the tomb was guarded by a whole regiment!"

Once an alarm bell did shrill loudly in the night. Adamson immediately awakened and grabbed his revolver. "Who is it?" he called out, his voice reverberating through the chamber.

"It was Carter, he couldn't sleep and had come over for a chat. Earlier that day he'd asked me if I wanted someone with me, because the Mummy had just been opened. I think he came to see if I was alright."

Around the archaeologist and the soldier stood golden chariots, funerary furnishings, beds, chairs and household ornaments their jewels burning in the light like flames. "One bed was hinged and folded like a camp cot; others were massive gilded affairs, decorated with animal gods to protect the sleeper. There were handsome chests and caskets made of oak and inlaid with gold, gemmed with fine stones and filled with the Pharaoh's clothing, his household linen and personal treasures. There were chairs with lion feet and with curved backs; folding stools with legs shaped like the necks and heads of geese.

"There were daggers with sheaths that were works of art, headrests and writing material. A small pair of linen gloves was found that could be worn today; each finger was outlined in tiny golden stitches."

Adamson remembered that Carter and his team had become so familiar with the objects and their owner that 3,000 years melted away and they found themselves speaking in the present.

"'Be careful with that bowl he's been using,'" he'd tell his workers. "Put it over there where he's got his chairs.'"

Mr. Adamson said he thought nothing of tucking into 3,000-year-old bread with Egyptian cheese for supper at night. "They'd had it restored in the testing laboratory and it tasted just like normal, unleavened bread."

One day he sneaked a taste of a reconstituted sediment found in a gold and alabaster drinking cup, discovering it was wine.

"We dipped a feather into it and it tasted like mead."

I asked Richard Adamson if it didn't seem ungrateful that he was never mentioned other than being referred to as 'a European in the party'?

"Oh no. I was a nobody there," he said. "The Egyptians were suspicious about me and I was worried they'd know who I was. There were still a few days left of the concession and Carter might well have found the steps himself. He was at the time very downhearted and very depressed. "I lay no claim to discovering the tomb. There were other people in the team who did far more than I did, and Carter did not allude to them in any way.

"Because the Egyptian team were the same diggers that had been used by other expeditions for this work, they knew this was something different. As they were going towards the exit of the tomb they were deliberately covering it all up. There were only two more days to go, and Carter could never have gone back; but the Egyptians would have come back.

"I asked Mr. Carter, Do you think they knew what that stone was, Sir? And he said, 'Yes. Those diggers are no fools. They knew what they'd found.'"

When he was 80, and having lost his legs to diabetes, Richard Adamson returned to Egypt – –wheelchair bound – to re-visit the tomb.

"Right there," he told his companions, "is where I had my bed."

Chapter 10

Back To The Past

When Winter began to close in on London, the windows in our century-old flat began to rattle with icy blasts, and we got the urge for sunshine and the beach. But this time it was serious.

Delphine had been injured in a fall from a horse. Until now she had been happy trotting through Hyde Park on a little Welsh pony called, 'Garnet' but when she decided to ride at a Western-style riding school one weekend, while I played golf, disaster struck. She was thrown by her mount on to a sawn-off tree stump and suffered a crushed vertebrae. She had taken weeks to recover, both in hospital and later in our apartment, where I nursed her. On his final visit, our doctor stood warming his back on the radiator and said, "I don't think it would help for her to stay here in London and face another winter …"

We had gone home to Australia before, but this next move was going to be longer and necessary if she was to have a full recovery. Making up our minds about leaving, underlined the two choices we always had in our lives and they were an expensive 12,000 miles apart. We could be mentally stimulated and rather physically stagnant, living in London; or be physically alive and mentally less stimulated and live back in Australia. That evening, we had a good dinner of Scotch beef from the Sloane Square specialist butcher, several glasses of red and chose the sunshine.

I arrived back in Melbourne and reluctantly went to see the Editor of The Herald. He sat behind his large desk sporting a tennis shade, (just like he'd seen fellow editors wearing in the movie The Front Page), and tightened his lips at my suggestion of a salary somewhat higher than the one I'd enjoyed before I left his paper. Experience gained in Fleet Street meant little to him. Or was it jealousy?

"We would have preferred you to have stayed here and learned our ways," he said, bristling at my polite suggestion that there might be some newspapers that The Herald might learn something from. No doubt, he also recalled my joyful resignation and farewell in The Phoenix pub across the road, when I made a beery reference to what I saw as a creeping complacency that was dumbing down a once-great evening paper.

Pride swallowed, I was back once more in the criminal courts staring at murderers, confidence tricksters and stand-over men. I covered district cricket matches on Saturdays, and wrote human interest pieces about tramps and, latterly, alcoholics. Melbourne seemed as dull and satisfied with itself as it had always been.

It was then that Alcoholics Anonymous, a casual writing assignment, gave me my first insight into true Christianity.

I'd been asked to write an article on this American-founded organisation which for many was the alcoholic's last chance; it was said that AA sometimes gave instant sobriety to men and women who had been drunks for years. It sounded too good to be true.

I phoned and made an appointment. Jim, a tall, fortyish man who was the focal point of the alcoholics' network, met me in his office. Jim had one leg, and when I got to know him better, told me how he had lost it — he'd fallen drunk into a pig pen. And the pigs had started to eat him.

Could I go to an AA meeting? I asked. He said sorry, but no. AA meetings were only open to problem drinkers and they wouldn't be happy to have a reporter there, listening to what went on.

Well, what <u>did</u> go on? Was there some secret religious experience involved? I had seen the Lilian Roth story in the film, "I'll Cry Tomorrow", but I was still sceptical that a simple gathering of fellow alcoholics could suddenly change the life of somebody who had been a slave to drink for years. "It happens," said Jim through a puff of smoke. "But more often than not it's after a failing or two. I'll tell you what I'll do. I go to an AA meeting three or four nights a week. I'll ask at the one I'm going to tonight in the city, if you'd be welcome. Best I can do, mate."

Later that day he phoned. I had the OK. So long as I went with him. And kept in the background. And shut up.

I caught the tram into Collins Street and walked several blocks to the Toc-H building, where the regular Friday night AA meeting was held; there were about a dozen men and women gathered around a long table, all smoking. None of them appeared drunk; but there were pouchy eyes, purple-red cheeks; shaky hands. Jim seemed to be in charge and called the meeting to order. "OK Bill," he said, pointing to a skinny man with dark-ringed, haunted eyes. "You'll be chairman tonight. OK?"

Bill put out his cigarette and asked us to stand in a circle, holding hands, and if we felt like it, recite the AA prayer that was printed on a white banner someone had hooked on the wall. God grant me the serenity to accept the things I cannot change, to change the things I can. And the wisdom to know the difference.

We mumbled it and sat down around the table. "Harry, do you want to start?" Bill asked the man on his right.

Harry was as fat as Bill was thin. I took him to be a worried accountant. He was bald, had on an old grey suit stained on the lapels; he wore a red, badly knotted tie. He stood up and looked about him through the clouds of smoke as the members lit up again. "My name is Harry. I am an alcoholic." He told a story which most of the gathering had possibly heard a dozen times. Of years pursuing 'the geographical cure', of trying to re-locate to escape the grip of the demon drink. And how it had caught up with him every time; in Adelaide, Oodnadatta, Perth. Wherever he'd walked, or hitched a ride, or travelled by train to run away from it, the grog had reached out and got him. He'd had a family when it all started. And a job. Today? "Well," he smiled self-consciously, "I've got AA. I have been sober for a week. This mightn't seem much to you," said Harry, looking across at me. "But if you had to hide bottles of grog in every station toilet cistern between Frankston and the City, as I did, and get off and drink it on the way to work, sobriety means a lot." He sat down and Magda stood up. She was a gentle lady. She spoke quietly with an educated, rounded upper class Melbourne accent ... about losing her husband and her children to drink and by no means last, she lost her self-respect.

"Do you know what happens to a woman who has to beg in a pub for a drink?" Surely not. Not Magda. But she said a lot more and there was an awkward silence around the table.

When it was over Jim with the one leg waited behind and asked me what I thought

"It all seems a bit unbelievable," I said. "That people who have been to jail, lived such awful lives, can give up the grog ... just by coming to a meeting?"

He grinned. "I can only tell you it's like spending 20 years in a thick fog. You don't know what's going on. Then, when you come out of it, everything is beautiful. Colours are brighter than you've ever imagined, sunny days are brilliant. Every day is a new day. Don't get me wrong," he smiled, "but I've got to tell you a reformed alcoholic enjoys life a bit more than people like you, who have never had the problem. They come out into a brighter sunlight. They appreciate things a lot more."

Then he asked an odd question: "What did you notice on the way here tonight?"

I tried to think. Cars, people on the tram. Lights going out in some of the shops as they closed.

"Didn't you hear the birds?"

"What birds?"

"In the trees as you walked up Collins Street. The starlings. They were beautiful! The trees are full of them at this time of the year." I had heard nothing. Now I could understand what he meant. I had a good job, I had no financial obligations; I enjoyed wine but I didn't have a drink problem; I had never been drunk. And yet I didn't hear the birds.

Now I wanted to go back to AA. Why?

AA meetings took place every night, somewhere in Melbourne. I was allowed to attend several and by now I'd gathered enough information to write an article that Bill read and approved of. And I was told I was now welcome to go to any AA meeting at any time. But I still hadn't found the answer to the seemingly inexplicable: men and women who had been in mental hospitals and drying-out centres, some who still smelled of the Paraldehyde they'd had to take as an alcohol substitute, would suddenly — or after one or two lapses — never touch a drink again. And for some reason they had a quiet contentment I didn't have. There were of course, new drunks at the meetings who had found their way there with the assistance of a doctor or a policeman or distraught relative, but they tended to sit at the back of the hall mumbling or quietly weeping, haltingly trying to tell their stories.

Magda, the 40-ish divorcee with huge, tired eyes, who

had been sober for two years, said to me, "It's drunk helping drunk through the next 24 hours, dear. You saw Mary come in last night? Well I took her home and sat up with her all night ... to get her through until the morning without her touching a drink.

"Oh, she had a bottle of gin stashed under the bed and I guess others hidden all over the house. But together we helped get her through the night without touching it. She might well break down again today. I'll be seeing her again tonight. And I'll probably be sitting up with her again. The first 24 hours free of grog sometimes stretches to 48; and then maybe to three or four days. And you can break down and give in and lose it all and go on a terrible drunk. But as long as you know that there's someone you can call on; who understands and cares. That's what gets you through in the end. AA is not an organisation. It's people. People helping people."

After a year of going to suburban AA meetings, and the one in the city, I wrote a longer, deeply researched article which appeared as a full page in a rival newspaper, The Argus. (My own paper felt it was too stark for a "family" publication). I had written about my experiences at meetings, trying to explain AA and its role in Melbourne's life. I put a lot into it; I was 'hooked'.

Once a year AA held a public meeting in the Lower Melbourne Town Hall, to which anyone could come. It was traditionally packed with alcoholics' relatives, or the curious who wished to witness the baring of alcoholic souls. No longer were these labourers, television personalities and even judges sheltered by the anonymity of church hall meetings that only alcoholics attended. This meeting was packed, with people standing against three walls, looking up at the stage. The chairman for the night was Jack Little, a high profile personality on television's Channel Nine where he broadcast "Ringside at the Wrestling". Jack, an American, was a reformed alcoholic.

Bespectacled, immaculate in a shiny suit, Jack hushed the audience of some 500 and went to the microphone. "There are people having to stand along the walls," he said. "Would my fellow alcoholics who have seats, kindly stand up, please, and offer them to our guests?" As one, about 100 men and women got to their feet, immediately identifying themselves.

Jack opened the evening by telling his own story. "I lost my family, my career, my dignity," he said. "When I was desperate for a drink I would roll a drunk in a gutter for his money. That is how low you can get." Ladies shook their heads. "Not Jack Little …"

Half-way through the night a subdued, middle-aged man, also well-dressed and smoothly confident of what he was saying, told the story of what it was like to be a dipsomaniac — a periodic drunk. He said he knew each time it was coming and so did his wife and children. "We had an arrangement," he told the audience, pausing. "Before they left me.

"I would go with my bottles to a shed at the bottom of the garden, and drink. I would lie there drunk, day and night and my wife would pass food in to me, like a dog that had to be fed. I was unshaven, filthy and incoherent for maybe a week at a time. I had lost my job.

"One evening my wife threw in some food wrapped in the pages of a newspaper. Some time next day I was awake enough to spread it out, and read it. I'm sure her choice of paper meant nothing. It was accidental. But when I uncrumpled one of the pages it had this article in it about AA. I read it right through. And I got out into the street where I found a policeman. I asked him to get me to an AA meeting and he did.

"That was some time ago. Tonight I have my sobriety. I have my family back. I have my job back. I am well again. And I will always keep this piece of paper." He unfolded my article.

Television had arrived in Melbourne and it was greeted like the opening of a mini-Hollywood. Three TV studios: ABV2, GTV9 and HSV7, feverishly took on singers and comedians who had previously been struggling to make a living in concerts or fund-raisers. Almost overnight they became stars with their own dressing-rooms, drawing hefty pay-cheques. A former model called Panda, and a character with salacious schoolboy humour, Graham Kennedy, were hailed as celebrities, paid mind-boggling salaries and mobbed even when they went out for a cup of coffee. Technical staff had been rushed into training courses in the United States so the new-fangled wonder could go to air.

The Herald owned HSV7 and decided it would have to have a TV columnist writing on the program page. The Editor appointed me, and I had unrestricted entree to the studios, could write almost anything I liked (so long as I paid special attention to HSV7). And I could work from my South Yarra flat. The only time I needed to go into the office was to drop my copy into the sub-editors. It was bliss, hardly interfered with my tennis and gave me official carte blanche to chat up attractive dancers and glamour personalities over coffee, as a necessary means of getting gossip for my page. (Somebody had to do it). Rivalry for ratings and the advertising dollar was intense; the greatest exposure a 'star', the more shirts or spaghetti sold.

I had finished my column one afternoon and filed it when there was a call from Pat, the enthusiastic PR lady for ABC television at Ripponlea, an outer suburb. "We are rehearsing a new show and there's a man on it you just have to see. He's incredible! It's his first time on television. Can you come down at nine o'clock?" I wasn't sure. Nine o'clock was the middle of the night! Pat, though, was a sweet, underpaid enthusiast and the ABC's ratings were a dismal third behind the commercials; so I agreed.

The set at Ripponlea was a tangle of cables, glaring overhead lights and voices booming down from the glassed-in directors' booth. At the far end, stood a large bed, tilted on an angle so its inhabitant could be seen and filmed. He was an elderly fellow in a night-cap and an old-fashioned full-length nightdress half-covered by a check dressing-gown. He clutched a hot-water bottle to his chest and he was writing a letter; his quivering, lisping voice reciting what he was writing to his wife, Beryl, apparently at sea on her way to England on a Woman's Weekly packaged tour. "Dear Beryl, I'm missing you already, my dear. Things are going along here at Humouresque Street; I have been watering the gladdiessss ... and Next Door have been very good inviting me in for the odd, occasional game of Five Hundred ..." A piano in the background tinkled: 'It's a Lovely Day Tomorrow'.

Sandy Stone, the gentleman in the bed, sounded as though he might have a problem surviving until Beryl eventually made it home to Moonee Ponds. His voice, (later described by its portrayer as 'high and scratchy with a sibilance caused by ill-fitting teeth') rose and fell with long pauses, often repeating words. The cameramen filming the scene with their lumbering, cumbersome equipment, were silently laughing, one had tears in his eyes as the old fellow droned on ...

"What do you think?" whispered the enthusiastic Pat.

"I think he's a genius! Who is he?" I replied.

"Barry Humphries," she said.

Barry emerged from the dressing-room, tall, pale-faced, with an anxious look and long hair dangling over his right eye. He thanked me for my enthusiasm and said he'd actually cut a gramophone record with Sandy Stone on it; if I'd like to meet him next day he'd give me one. He hoped I might find space to mention it in my column.

The 45 rpm record, now a collector's piece, was a frighteningly accurate and cruel send-up of vapid suburban lives, called: "Wildlife in Suburbia". On it, Sandy described the everyday dramas in his life: the 'strife parking the vehicle at an important football semi-final' and coming home 'to find The Herald all over the lawn', excitement at fever-pitch on a Saturday morning when he thought he'd lost Beryl in the 'Foodarama'. 'However, fortunately, she had the good sense to go back to the vehicle.'

My enthusiasm for this then unknown genius was quickly shared by thousands as the ABC-TV 'special' went to air. But there were some Melburnians stung by the realisation that he was describing the reality of their own lives, and they hated it. Others bored out of their minds by conservative old Melbourne and trying to either get out of it or make it more interesting, hailed Barry as a star. Riding high, he took off for London; later to fight what was to become a serious drink problem.

My own return to England on a ship called the Johann Van Oldenbarneveldt, almost coincided with his. And our paths crossed. When I heard Barry was to have his own show at The Establishment, a small Soho experimental theatre, I got together a group from the Australian Downunder Club so we could give him encouragement and show our enthusiasm. The "Downunder", a basement in Fulham for homesick or just lonely Australians, had a sawdust floor, with ledges along the wall for glasses, a small dance-floor and a hectic bar that served draught beer and pints of lethal cider.

Rolf Harris, shy and eyes-down, played his accordion and sang on Thursday nights to a crowd that had lost its sobriety by nine o'clock. Mine Host was Ken Warren, an actor who had starred in 'The Summer of the 17th Doll'. He was a nuggety, rugby-playing bruiser who stood no nonsense from his clientele. A reporter friend of mine was told by Warren he was 'barred' from the club until he mended his ways. "What's the charge!" bawled the tragic-eyed Wally.

"Drunkenness," replied Warren.

The enthusiasts from the Club now loyally packed the first two rows of The Establishment and clapped and cheered Sandy Stone and his satire on Melbourne. Behind us the Poms sat puzzled; they had obviously missed the point. The pathos of losing Beryl in the Foodarama flew over their heads. Barry's season was cut short.

Barry and I made an appointment for a drink next day and by now he had embraced his scripts as his own style; when we met he said it was good to see me 'after such a long period of time'. I apologised for being a few minutes late. He looked at his watch and said it was now 'approximately in the vicinity of eleven o'clock'.

Humphries' genius by now hid a strange sense of humour at variance with the stage archness of his alter-ego Dame Edna. He was known to go to incredible lengths to perpetrate jokes, the reaction to which in most cases, occurred long after he had departed the scene.

After the failure at The Establishment, he took one of his first steps to fame and fortune understudying Fagin in 'Oliver'. Over a drink or three, he revealed to me that every night after rehearsal, he would stop at Boots, the all-night chemist in Piccadilly Circus, and ask to buy 'a large bar of Lux toilet soap'. When the assistant took it down from the shelf Barry would place ninepence on the counter and then turn to walk out of the brightly-lit shop. "Sir! You have forgotten your soap!"

"Oh," Barry would gravely reply. "I only wanted to buy it." And he would continue on his way into Picca-dilly, the baffled assistant replacing the soap on the shelf. This went on for a week.

On the final night Barry actually took the soap, hav-ing paid for it. And the assistant, who had become accus-tomed to the ritual, said, surprised: "Do you actually want the soap tonight, Sir?"

"Oh how silly of me," said Barry, returning the cake of soap to the counter and walking out. He had, however, switched the real soap for a bar of lard he had enclosed in a Lux wrapper. The joke would only happen when some English person got into a shower or a bath and tried to lather themselves with a bar of Lux purchased from Boots ... He would not be there to witness the furore and could only surmise the degree of anger. Odd?

One weekend he invited me to a party at his North London home and as he was farewelling his guests his pregnant wife felt sick and vomited — all over a stack of his books placed incongruously in the middle of the hallway. He grabbed her, pushed her aside, and cried, "My books! My books!" They were first editions of some obscure author and far more urgent to save than his fainting wife.

Back again on the Daily Mail, I met him in the reporters' room at the height of his career as the Dame, when he surely needed no more publicity. He was arranging something with the Picture Editor.

The following morning, in snooty Sloane Square, a queue waiting at the bus shelter noticed a tramp in the gutter on the opposite side of Sloane Avenue. To the horror of well-dressed Sloane Rangers and dark-suited gentlemen who were Something in the City, the tramp, wearing a torn, stained overcoat, hand-mittens and battered hat, shuffled across the road to a steel rubbish receptacle bolted to the power-pole beside the people queuing. Bankers buried their noses in The Times, pretending to be oblivious of the scene, as the odious tramp rummaged in the bin. First he dragged out a wrapped ice-bucket, which had in it a frosted bottle of Moet et Chandon champagne, and a glass, which he placed in the gutter. He reached in again and hauled up a foil-wrapped parcel which he tore open revealing a roast chicken. Happy, he sat down in the gutter, sipping the champagne and tearing off pieces of chicken while the queue shuffled forward and for them, mercifully to board a double-decker bus.

The joke was how the Sloane Rangers would later talk about what they had seen on the way to their business. The photographer recording the faces and their reactions from the other side of the road had nearly wet himself. Again, Barry could only imagine the scenes at the offices ... Odd?

Perhaps his weirdest effort was the morning he boarded the District-line tube at Wimbledon, which was beginning its journey and was sparsely filled. Wearing heavy dark glasses, as though he was blind, he clutched a pianola-roll in his hands, 'reading it'. He had his right foot encased in a huge bandage, as if he had gout, and he placed a stack of large parcels on the empty seat next to him. As the train began its journey, it steadily filled with rush-hour passengers. By the time it got to Gloucester Road, there were many strap-hangers and others crammed by the doors. The 'blind man's' parcels remained beside him, taking up the empty seat; the British, forever courteous and sympathetic, said nothing and clutched straps when they found no place to sit.

Two stations on, a 'German' entered the compartment, pushing his way through to where Barry sat. He had on lederhosen, hob-nailed hiking boots and a Tyrolean hat. Under his arm he carried a copy of Die Welt. Grasping the strap over the empty seat he started muttering loudly about parcels taking up room unnecessarily. The blind Barry ignored him and went on 'reading' his Braille, lips moving.

At last the German hiker could contain himself no more. Shouting "Donner und Blitzen!" he savagely kicked the blind man's bandage-encased foot, then angrily pushed his way out of the tube train. There were cries of sympathy, people asking Humphries if he was all right. He held a shaky hand in the air and said: "Forgive him. He is German." Then he went on with his 'reading'.

By now his Dame Edna Everage had made Barry rich and famous; the fame bringing with it an increasingly serious problem with the bottle. Roy Dickens, an English freelance photographer I worked with, had become bewitched by him and became his drinking companion. It was a nerve-wracking idolatry, because the 'happier' Humphries became, the worse became his jokes. He carried with him an early-model, dark red Qantas in-flight plastic hold-all that every flight passenger was given years ago. When he got drunk, it was Dickens' job to make sure it wasn't left behind in the last pub. One afternoon as they lurched out of a taxi in Fleet Street to go to yet one more pub, Dickens, carrying Humphries' red bag walked a little way ahead. There was a shrill cry behind him. It was Humphries. "THIEF! STOP THAT THIEF! HE HAS MY BAG!"

Even sober, which was becoming a rare occasion, Barry's humour was embarrassing. He'd got the part of a wandering troubadour in a West End musical, 'Maggie May' and had given me two tickets. Dressed as a tramp in the Lionel Bart operetta, he carried a drum on his back, cymbals between his knees and a mouth-organ wired in front of his mouth. He was to open the show, and as the curtain went up there was Humphries, eyes gleaming, making a discordant racket with his one-man band. Then he spotted me and a friend in the front row. "Jeez, that's Des sitting there! How ya goin' Des?" The audience roared with laughter as I tried to lose myself in my seat.

Chapter 11

'Tie Me Kangaroo Down'

The Downunder Club in London's Fulham, was a saw-dust-strewn basement, smelling of stale beer and bodies. For lonely, homesick bachelors like me, it was a haven — a piece of Australia where no Pom could intrude.

It was owned and run by Australians and its firm rule of 'NO POMS' was enforced by Ken Warren, famous for acting in 'The Summer of the 17th Doll' in London. Noisy, airless and rough, as 'The DU' was, it was importantly a great place to pick up equally lonely Aussie girls. And who knew what might happen after a couple of pints of cider, drunk from heavy glass mugs with handles?

A couple of nights a week the owners employed a shy, bespectacled character called Rolf Harris, to play his accordion and sing. Rolf had a string of songs — both bawdy and Ocker — that had his duffle-coated, impoverished audience screaming for more.

But Harris's eyes were fixed on the floor, his curly head bowed over his piano-accordion. Only when he gained a bit of confidence, did he begin to glance at our mob standing shoulder to shoulder, parking our drinks on narrow, jutting ledges as we clapped him. He was, he told me, getting 'thirty bob for playing for three hours.' After a couple of years the DU owners grudgingly offered him a fiver.

Nobody—apart from the raucous, hard-drinking Australians—had ever heard of the lad from Perth. We were all homesick, poor dreamers who had invaded London, ready to set the world on fire; and many like me, were getting knocked back for work. But at the Australian Downunder Club you could get drunk on two pots of rough scrumpy cider at ninepence a glass, and over Harris's singing, shout at each other about how lousy life was turning out in the Old Dart. Then later, to spill out into the foggy roadway at midnight with every hope that the Fulham locals were being thrown out of their pubs at the same time and be ready for a fight.

Years later, the now millionaire Rolf, came to my home for coffee and homemade carrot cake (he ate almost the whole loaf) and talked about the agony of his early shyness.

"I was there at the 'DU' for six years on and off." he recalled. "I left after a while because I wasn't getting enough money; thirty bob for playing for three hours! Eventually, after six months, the Aussie owners said, 'Well look, we can pay you two pounds ten.' So alright, I came back. Then I was away for a couple of years and they offered me a fiver! During that time I was learning, and growing in self-confidence. But for ages, when I started at the DU, I either looked at the sawdust on the floor while I played, or faced the wall. Playing very quietly and hoping nobody'd noticed that I'd started. Gradually as the evening progressed I'd pluck up confidence and face people."

It was at this time that the thin and bearded Harris was asked to go into a recording studio to make a recording of a song called 'Kangalypso'.

It eventually became 'Tie Me Kangaroo Down, Sport,'

and 'took off'. And the rest is 'wobble board' history.

Rolf sipped at his coffee and recalled, "The DU was a glorious safety-valve for me. I'd arrived in England feeling like a little boy, ready to tug the forelock. The British accent made me feel like a total peasant, because of the way I spoke. Everyone but me was obviously high up on the social order. So to go down every week to the DU and relax and not care how you pronounced things was tremendous. I'd been told whenever I went for jobs: 'You must lose that atrocious accent, Old Boy, or you'll never work!'" He said he would have gone on being shy and awkward if he had not been taken to task by Hermione Gingold.

'Tie Me Kangaroo Down' had by now become a hit and Rolf was invited to sing and play at his first cabaret and after his performance he was introduced to the famous actress. "She said to me, 'Can I tell you something about your show? You never looked at me once.'

"I said, but I didn't even know you were in the audience!

"She said: 'No. You misunderstand me. You never looked at anybody in the room. You were working to a spot on the wall. You are throwing away 90% of your potential when you're afraid to meet peoples' eyes. When you speak to individuals in the room, by some amazing magic, everyone really thinks you are speaking just to them.'

"That," says Rolf, "was the best piece of advice I have ever been given in show-business." He said he now lived at Bray, near Maidenhead, overlooking the Thames. "The house had previously been owned by a couple who had made a lot of money with a magazine called 'Exchange & Mart' and they had put in enormous double-glazed windows, which at the time were the biggest that Pilkington's, the glass people, had ever put into a private home. The kitchen was all pale blue tiles, from floor to ceiling;

pale blue floor. It was like going into a hospital lavatory! Very scary! We changed all that, knocked down a wall, and built a greenhouse so you could walk straight out of the kitchen and into the greenhouse. We have breakfast there."

Rolf obviously enjoyed my wife, Delphine's, carrot cake, and ate most of it but he confessed he had never become 'fascinated' with haute cuisine. "I enjoy a good curry. Travellin' round the world you get tired of bland food and need something with a bit of spice in it. Cook? I do an amazing scrambled egg. Aussie beer? I have never found any real need to drink. I'm not a goody-goody, but I never found it necessary to drink to rebel against anybody. I always had so many other things I wanted to do. I don't go to parties. I don't smoke. Sound a bit of a square, don't I?

"I get a buzz doing stage shows, or live television, rather than something pre-recorded. You have that extra electricity—the adrenalin that starts to flow when you have only one chance. You can't go back and correct it. It takes you to a higher plane of performance. If there's a show where all the wrinkles are obvious, to me, it's better television. In the States where some sponsor is paying a million dollars for a TV show you get antiseptic perfection, and it takes the life out of reality. In Australia and the UK they want their stars to be just a little bit of an extension of what they, themselves are. They feel that with a little bit of luck they could be up there doing the same thing."

Chapter 12

'Wanna Buy A Brothel?'

H umphries' image of staid old Melbourne was of course dated. I found the prim old city had changed dramatically when we returned on yet another, 'England or Australia' indecision.

I noticed this small-ad. in The Age, still a grey newspaper.

'Brothels — F'hold & business $1.05m. cls city'

Brothels in 'The Age'? I called the number in the ad. And spoke to Doug Nicholas, Brothel Broker. (In conservative old Melbourne.)

As I wait at his desk, Doug finishes a gruff phone conversation and puts down the receiver. "A time-waster," he says, shaking his head. "It's the same with 40 out of the 45 calls I get on average; tyre-kicker getting his kicks. They just want to know everything that goes on inside a brothel. I tell them, if they really want to know what the deal is, they must come in and talk to me. Few of them ever do."

Doug has on a smart blue shirt with white collar, expensive blue tie, sparse hair combed forward, Napoleon-style over his forehead. I find he is the only man to talk to in Melbourne if you want to buy a brothel. "There are one or two others who talk about it; but I'm the biggest in the business."

Any punter serious about buying a freehold bordello, including the spas, round beds — and the girls — climbs to the first floor of an office-block at the grubby end of King Street in Melbourne, to talk to Doug. A cut-out policeman meets him at the top of the stairs and Doug ushers the client into his tiny conference-room. The visitor, according to Doug, anticipates salivating over brochures, photo-albums and descriptions of the pleasures of the establishments currently on the market. He is to be disappointed.

The man who knows more about Melbourne brothels than the Vice Squad, which is no longer deeply interested anyway, has no listings. Doug taps his head. "It's all in here. I don't put much on paper. I'm not a paper type."

How did it ... er happen? Doug said that about six years ago he found himself working in a suburban real estate business. He had lost all the fish in a trout farm when a pump broke down, and he had gone bankrupt. He'd been a farmer, publican and a truckie. A solicitor friend then suggested real estate.

"It was one of those shared offices and the guy sitting at the next desk was working for himself; he was selling brothels. He told me he was moving to Queensland and asked, 'Would you like to do this job?' I said: 'Mate, I'll do anything.' I'm a people kind of person who fits in. So I went and had a look at eight or ten brothels with him to sort of get a feel for them.

"When I went to the first brothel I did feel a bit uneasy. I hadn't been in a brothel before. The one thing the guy didn't explain to me was that you don't look at the scantily-clad girls as you go in; don't ogle them. You just talk to them as I'm talking to you now. And you mustn't go in with the idea that they're anything less a person than you are, because they're not. After a while I was better off going into the places on my own, more confident. I just walk in now. G'day girls, how y'a goin? Sometimes they look at you thinking you might be a customer and you have to say, 'No! No! I'm here to work.'"

Freebies? Oh no, says Doug, offended. "And I don't dance on tables at the table-top establishments I have for sale. I'm a happily married man with children and my wife knows all that goes on; I often take her with me on inspections."

His Global Estate Agents at the time had 'offers' on seven brothels in and around Melbourne ranging from $500,000 for a cosy boutique establishment, to $3m. for the glitziest, 'with spas, miles of marble and an orgy room with a round bed that can accommodate 10 people.' At one stage he was negotiating to sell Melbourne's most successful brothel for $15m. but the deal fell through. Doug might sell two or three brothels in as many months or experience a three-month 'dry' period and sell none. "But I keep in touch with all the owners in case a brothel is ready to change hands." The most expensive he's sold so far was worth $1.5m.

Doug says he likes the small, suburban establishment with its red wallpaper, fireplace and nice girls 'exhuding ambience'. "They should have a warmth about them starting at the desk where you have a nice, understanding receptionist who can put a shy man at ease. They will quietly lead him into a room, give him a cup of tea, or whatever, and then bring the girls in and introduce them, so he feels at home. It doesn't have to be 5-star to really swing." A brothel, he says, can fail for a host of reasons. A wealthy man wanting one for a purpose other than making money should forget it. Doug's computer has brothels on its files that are in the doldrums because an owner favours a particular girl and starts an off-duty relationship, or he gambles away the earnings. "There is a very big cash flow and it must be scrupulously looked after and accounted for. Brothels should be clean and tidy. The old adage that you don't look at the mantelpiece when you're stoking the fire isn't really true ..."

The biggest myths about brothels, says Doug is that they're full of drugs, are sleazy, and operated by underworld villains. "Not true. They can't afford to be sleazy; their ownership is always under careful scrutiny. You can only own one brothel and there is only an occasional one in Melbourne that I know of, has drugs." There is no violence and no bouncers at the door; the surveillance cameras at the door and not in the rooms, he hastens to point out, warn of drunks or trouble.

"Maybe there is a clip behind the ear now and then when one brothel-owner pinches another's best girls, but doesn't that happen in ordinary business? There are more crooks in the pulpit and Parliament."

Until recently the largest source of finance if you wanted to purchase a bawdy-house was a Melbourne solicitor who quickly found demand exceeded his supply of funds. "We bled him dry!" Now one of the Big Four banks has overcome its distaste for the particular line of investment and is enthusiastically lending. "Every Christmas I give a lunch for everyone involved in the year's deals; brothel-owners, finance brokers, valuers and the bank. My wife has to come in and drive me home to Torquay. Often I just advertise a brothel only as 'an investment' and there are people who ring up and when they find it's a brothel, say, 'Oh no. I'm not interested in that.' I don't blame them. To each his own. But a brothel is an excellent investment whether it's a freehold or a lease. The goodwill depends very much on its receptionist and its girls. One of the best ladies in the business is 56 years old; looks great, keeps herself trim and is in great demand. Another lady owner also works; she enjoys it so much."

He recalls one beautiful young lady, seated near Reception when he was making an early morning inspection. "She was shivering when I went in and still shivering when I was on my way out, and it was Summer. I said, for God's sake put a sweater on, luv! She wasn't wearing much. She said, 'I'm not cold. I just want a man!' She is a confessed nymphomaniac and just can't get enough of her work."

Doug had not been concentrating on brothels for all that long, when the phone rang with a woman offering to sell her adult bookshop. "She'd seen the ads. and thought I was the logical bloke. So I do that as well. And table-top dancing establishments and escort agencies for the same reason, though there's going to be a shake-up in that business before long. I think it will be more strictly policed." (Sex performed on stage was at the time easily seen in Melbourne).

A good escort agency, Doug says, can be very lucrative. "Not a lot of money to run and some of the best girls who go with the high-rollers at the Crown Casino are getting $600 an hour. Of course they have to be very beautiful; the pick of the crop.

"There are gentlemen gambling at the Casino who have to have a good-looking lady on their arm. They're charged $170 an hour as escorts, and a girl might be hired for 24 hours and taken back to his room or to a 5-star hotel. That's over $4,000 for 24 hours' work ..."

Over the years he has learned to differentiate between girls offering full sex 'don't call them prostitutes, they prefer to be known as sex-workers', the 'masseurs' who are in the 'rub n' tug' business who reject intercourse, and the table dancers whose activities in some establishments flow through the full spectrum. "Some of them do a little bit of everything."

Sex in Melbourne, muses a fit-looking Doug, who exercises with his dog along the beach, has become a boom industry. "More so in the Summer than the Winter, though. In the Summer the blokes see girls walking about in their minis and micros and get ideas. In the Winter they're covered up. It's not so good for business."

He takes me in his car to meet a gentleman whose grand brothel in an industrial estate is listed for sale. The softly-spoken, greying client apologises that the cleaners are still in, but we may look around. He is by trade a technical man (Doug had told me) whose broken business partnership left him unexpectedly part-owner of a brothel. He opens the office door and points to a security monitor carrying the scene from hidden cameras from four public areas at once. "The girls also have buttons beside the beds," says the owner, "which will turn on a flashing light in the passage-way and bring the whole staff to the room if there's trouble. Another alarm brings security, or the police and they are here within four minutes." A sign behind the receptionist warns: 'No drugs or alcohol permitted on these premises at any time. Only safe sexual practices are engaged on these premises.'

The brothel — purpose-built 11 months before — is an Italianate extravagance of marble. Marble walls, marble floors and gleaming spas, fitted with wall and ceiling mirrors. Expensive leather armchairs and footstools adorn the waiting-room where the girls dressed in 'after 5' frocks are introduced to the customer so he can make his choice. "I will not have girls running around in skimpy outfits," says the owner primly. "I don't allow tartiness."

Musak wafts through the six 'entertainment' rooms, each with its ensuite shower and toilet; cupboard shelves are stacked neatly with fleecy monogrammed towels.

He takes us into the Orgy Room, which has a spa large enough to accommodate six, with two king-size beds pushed together in the room. The churning, foaming spa, with nude statuettes on either side, and erotic paintings on the wall, is unscented, as are the soaps in the bathrooms and the girls themselves. "For obvious reasons," says the owner. "A client does not want to go home smelling of perfume. It is a nice house. I had a lady expert come and do the decor." He says hopefully. "You build a nice house, you put nice ladies in it and you should get nice clients." It is also a non-smoking establishment, probably the only one of Melbourne's 80-odd brothels then with such a rule.

His ladies' time is charged out at $200 an hour. The client hands over the money or his credit-card, at the desk and receives from the Madam a small cloth wallet in exchange. It contains lubricant, two condoms and a $100 note, which he hands to the girl. Hours are 12 midday to 2 am., Sunday to Thursday; the doors are open until 4am on Fridays and Saturdays. Doug wishes him well and assures him of several possible leads being in the pipeline.

Next stop: near-city Richmond, where the two-storey brothel has been operating for almost 20 years. The pretty young receptionist has a cultured voice and low-cut sweater revealing deep cleavage. She confesses it's her first day on the job and the phone is ringing off the wall. She explains the rates to callers: '$120 half-hour; $160 three-quarters of an hour; $200 for one hour. Two ladies at once: $200 for 30 minutes; one hour $350. Thank you for your call, darling.'

The brothel is an old house with electric fires in what were once fireplaces and shower cubicles protruding awkwardly into the rooms off a narrow passage. One of the girls, just going on a seven-hour shift, is a tiny brunette wearing bra, panties and short, black filmy negligee. Her hand shakes a little as she talks to me and applies lipstick at the mirror. She says she is cold. How does she feel when she is paraded with several other girls in the introduction room and she is turned down? "It truly doesn't bother me," she smiles demurely. "Some men are looking for tall, busty ladies, which I am obviously not!" She appears to be in her late teens or early 20s and inspires, in at least this male, more of an urge to protect than to lust over.

She turns from the mirror. "It's not all sex, you know. We are also here to listen. It is totally anonymous, so we can give understanding as well as affection. What is said in the house remains in the house." Her accent, like the receptionist's, could be private school. She smiles. "I like to stay in the one brothel. I like to give it loyalty; I don't move around."

Back in the car, Doug's phone blares again. Like the other calls, the man does not give his name. Doug is meant to recognise voices and does. One boomer is $200,000 short of being able to make a purchase and apologises that it's best to forget the deal. Another wonders if he can buy a $1m.+ business on deferred terms? A third is looking for 'a nice little earner' at maybe $500,000. "My philosophy in real estate," says Doug, as he heads for the beaches. "Is to tell the truth. It's harder to remember lies and you're gonna get found out in the end. That's why they keep coming back to me; there are no deals under the table."

The last brothel call for the morning is one that has the warmth and ambience Doug says is to his taste. The Madam is a late 40-ish blonde with a heavy Continental accent and a big hug and kiss for Doug. "She's an ex-worker herself and I sold her into the business," he explains when she's gone. "She was paying 15.2% bridging finance and I was able to help her save $50,000 a year; so she's grateful." The rooms are small, with green walls and thick carpets. Mirrors on the walls, ceiling and behind the spas make them seem large. One has fake Roman columns and a chandelier and there is a four-poster bed draped with old-fashioned lace and covered with red velvet. Tastefully folded towels are in the shape of flowers. Unlike the marble edifice and its 'after 5' dress-code visited earlier, the 'ladies' this morning are wearing — well, not a lot.

A powdered, friendly blonde in filmy black, her extraordinary bosom spilling precariously over her bra, sits down with a coffee to tell me how she 'looks after' a gentleman who has paid $200 for an hour of her services and finds himself 'spent' as the clock ticks over the first five minutes. She puffs at her cigarette and touches her high-coiffed hairdo. No problem, apparently. "I just lie there and talk to him; find out what he does in life and give him a massage."

The Madam, in a bright red mini-skirt joins us. "Yes. We often act as counsellors; listen to their problems. It is not unusual for a man to pay for an hour and just sit there crying. And maybe he'll take the next hour doing the same. I tell you the truth!"

The blonde leans forward confidentially and I concentrate with some difficulty on her eyes, which at midday are heavily mascarrared. "We also do fantasies. They might ask us to dress up as schoolgirls so they can be principals or just schoolboys; or we play doctors and nurses. Sometimes you look at yourself in the mirror and you have to keep a straight face!"

Bursting out of their schoolgirl tunics, Julie and the girls charge an extra $30 an hour to take on character; then there's bondage and 'Greek' (which she doesn't do) which costs more. Her Madam cuts in. "Sometimes the chentleman might like to have six girls in the Orgy Room to himself. That is $1,200 for the hour. He might also like them to … interact." Some, she assures Doug and I, through a puff of smoke, pay $200 an hour and stay there, taking one hour after another. "I have had them stay here all night, just pouring their hearts out."

Rudolf Hess reading my manuscript in his cell.

Desmond Zwar (arrow at top) watching Russian astronaut Yuri Gagarin arrive in London.

Desmond Zwar on `homeless tramp' assignment for
The Herald, Melbourne.

Desmond Zwar portrait.

Reporter Desmond Zwar listening over Sir Keith Joseph's shoulder as he gives a minesterial statement in London.

Desmond Zwar reporting for the London Daily Mail at actress Betty Hutton's press conference.

The Queen, Rupert and Me

BUCKINGHAM PALACE

Dear Mr. Zwar,

Thank you for your letter of
October 31st to Mr Heseltine, who has left
with Her Majesty for South America.

There is really very little to
tell you about The Queen's dogs, and I am
afraid there is no question of talking to the
person who looks after them, who is in fact
The Queen herself.

Her Majesty has four Corgis, three
bitches called Heather, Foxy and Tiny, and
a dog called Buzz. Foxy and Tiny, who were
born in September 1965, are Heather's puppies.

As well as The Queen's Corgis, The
Prince of Wales and Princess Anne were given
a Corgi each in 1955 called Whisky and Sherry,
who have lived in the Royal nursery ever since,
but Whisky died a month or two ago, so only
Sherry, who is a bitch, is left.

Apart from the Corgis, which move
about with the Royal Family, there are a
number of shooting dogs in the kennels at
Sandringham. Roughly speaking, The Queen and
The Duke of Edinburgh and The Prince of Wales
have two dogs each, and there are a number of

others, which vary from time to time according
to when there are puppies.

If there is any other help you want,
perhaps you could telephone me, but I do not
think there is very much else I can tell you.

Yours sincerely,

Anne Hawkins.

Asst. Press Secretary to The Queen

*Buckingham Palace replying to Desmond Zwar's letter of
inquiry about the Queen's corgis.*

Nr.7 (German) 26.4.1969

An die Direktion

In der „Frankfurter Zeitung" vom 22.IV.69 ist auf S.2 unter der Überschrift „Rudolf Heß" die Rede davon, ich hätte 1941 durch meine „Flucht nach England" Aufsehen erregt. Weiter heißt es, inzwischen seien „viele Gnadengesuche" für mich eingereicht worden.

Da die Behauptung, ich sei geflüchtet, meine Ehre verletzt und der Eindruck entstehen kann, ich hätte Gnadengesuche eingereicht oder jemanden beauftragt solche einzureichen, bitte ich zu genehmigen, daß ich meinem Rechtsanwalt Dr. Alfred Seidl, München schreibe, er möge eine Berichtigung verlangen.

Ich bitte hierzu um einen Bogen Papier.

Rudolf Heß.

27.IV.69.

*Rudolf Hess writes a letter of request to the
Spandau Prison authorities.*

162

Inside Rudolf Hess's cell. Desmond Zwar was the only reporter in the world to get into the prison and into Hess's cell. His bunk had an inflateable rubber ring for comfort.

Sir Winston Churchill come home from hospital on his birthday.

Adam Zwar, Delphine and Desmond Zwar
just weeks before Delphine died.

Chapter 13

'Don't You Worry About That!'

Sir Joh Bjelke-Petersen the most eccentric, colourful—and yet possibly most effective—Premier Queensland ever had, asked me out of the blue, to write his Life Story.

As a reporter I was familiar with his garbled 'Joh-speak' — ("You ... you, you reporters, you ... you, you just think that ... that, that you're all so ... so ... well, don't you worry about that"). He may well have sounded crazy at times, but I had always suspected that the verbally constricted Joh was far more shrewd than any of the 'chooks' taking down his ramblings in shorthand.

Soon after he lost his premiership, after 20 years in office, I had a phone-call from a friend in Townsville who was hosting a dinner party. She asked if I might be interested in collaborating with Sir Joh in writing his story. I replied that it was certainly an interesting proposal. "Right," said the caller. "I'll put Beryl Young on the phone. She's here having dinner with us."

I thought that was a bit odd but then Beryl, Sir Joh's personal pilot spoke on the phone. "I'm having dinner here and Mary has recommended you as a possibility.

Would you like to come down to Brisbane and have a chat with Sir Joh?"

I said I would, as long as he was prepared to be serious. It would be impossible if he just treated me as another one of his 'chooks' (his own term for the media who stood around taking down news morsels doled out to them whenever he needed them aired). I queried if he would be prepared to face the awkward question of how such appalling corruption had taken place under his nose, particularly that involving a 'bagman' and resulting in his knighted Police Commissioner and two of his ministers, going to jail? There was a short silence. "I'll talk to him," said Beryl.

She called the next day. It was 'go'. If I would fly down to Brisbane the following week I would meet Sir Joh, Lady Flo, Beryl the pilot, and his business adviser, Richard Lancaster.

I arrived in Sir Joh's office and he came forward to shake hands. Shrewd blue-grey eyes glinted, and without stuttering a word of the garbled Joh-speak that was the delight of impressionists, apart from 'Gee' and 'Aye' instead of 'I'; he fussed about, anxious to get cups of tea. He was, he said, prepared to tell me all about his life; his dramas and about his sacking. For my part, I tried to put him at ease by saying that if the biography project foundered half-way through, I would never divulge anything of a sensitive nature he might not want published. It was important however, that he told me everything and then later, used his right to edit; otherwise I would be working in literary handcuffs.

We had three taped sessions together and he was as good as his word: he told me the details of a long list of sagas and some of the odd enterprises he had embraced like the Hydrogen Car and Mylan Brych's 'cancer cure'; why he seriously wanted to be Prime Minister, why he banned 'Playboy'. He revealed the political alliance he

had with Andrew Peacock, the Gair Affair and the midnight wrecking of the Belle Vue Hotel.

Between sessions I went out to dinner with Beryl, his
pilot, confidante and (some said) a lady with an unusually strong influence on him. Passing a Ventolin under
the restaurant table—we both suffered from asthma
and I had left my puffer at home—I got the impression
that this wiry and wily woman was going to ferociously
guard what was said and what was to be published. I
discovered some weeks later that my instinct was right.

Next day I went back to Sir Joh's office with the tape-
recorder, then on to the Sheraton for dinner with him and
Lady Flo. I held out a chair for her as she prepared to sit
down. Sir Joh said, "Don't do that! She'll want me to do
it in future!"

"Oh Joh." sighed his wife who was then more famous
for her pumpkin scones than her own political career.

Sir Joh said he wanted to start by talking about his
religious faith.

He then read to me handwritten notes he had kept
of his sermon as a lay preacher at Kingaroy Lutheran
Church on 7.1.1940.

'Speak of whatsoever things are true, whatsoever
things are honest, whatsoever things are just, whatsoever
things are pure, whatsoever things are lovely, whatsoever things are of good report; if there be any virtue and
if there be any praise, think on these things.'

Paul speaking in Philippians 4, 8.

He gazed out the window. "Every day I read the Bible.
Every morning and every night, no matter what time it
is. I read God's word this morning at five o'clock, kneel-
ing by my bed asking His forgiveness because I know we
are all sinners. We do many wrong things.

"Jesus our Saviour is the mediator between God and
Man and can ask for us to be forgiven. Then I ask for wis-

dom and understanding for the things I am about to do. And for guidance in the things one ought to do.

"In the worst days of the electricity strike I got comfort from Isaiah. And I made those fat electricity workers climb up the stairs to see me because the strike had knocked-out the lifts."

When anger over his iron-fisted policies was at its height, Sir Joh said his family received kidnap threats.

"Threats were made against my son-in-law, my grandchildren and me. For sure, it happened many times. They were even going to blow up my house. For three years I had a policeman sitting outside my door, had all my windows in the Parliamentary Annexe blocked out so nobody could see who was inside. I even had to wear a bullet-proof vest.

"Actually it didn't affect me at all. I knew that there were a lot of people who hated me intensely; but we lived through those days."

What did he feel about loyalty, I wondered. Were his colleagues loyal to him?

"To me loyalty is one of the key traits I seek in other people and offer to them in return. There are so many people who I have worked with over the years and they stay loyal with me and I stay loyal with them. Loyalty is what you offer when things are bad for your friends. When people I count as my friends — like Kerry Packer — were facing serious allegations about tax evasion and bottom-of-the-harbour allegations, I was one of the few who stuck by them. The media would ask me, 'Are you still supporting them?' And I would say, yes of course I am.

"I will go on supporting anybody as a friend and trust them unless it is proved that I should not. I rang up [the people in trouble] regularly every week. Hold your head up I'd say. Stick with it. And they did. And nothing was ever proved against them.

"When politicians, Don Lane and Russ Hinze were named in the Fitzgerald Inquiry I called each of them in and said, of course you'll remain as a Minister. I don't let anybody down. I don't throw them overboard because I'm frightened.

"They say you're ruthless." I said.

"I'd describe myself as firm and positive rather than ruthless. You have to be strong and give a lead. That's why I don't agree with this idea of consensus.

"When the electricity strike was on, I knew there was no way in the world I would give in to them. We had to go to the courts; I wanted to move quicker than that because it all took time. Then Fred Mackay, the one man who knew how desperately serious it was, came to me and said we were operating on such a reduced capacity that only a few hospitals were getting power. The operators who were manning the power stations were exhausted, at the end of their tether. He said, 'Mr. Premier, we can't sustain it any longer. You must give in.'

"I said, I am shocked. But I am not going to accept that, Fred. He said, 'You've got to accept it. There's no alternative. The men can't work day and night.'

"All the people in the room: the industrial people, the power people, the legal people, agreed with him. Then they left the room. I sat there dumfounded.

"Just then Beryl Young, my pilot, came from her desk about 20 yards down the corridor and asked me what had happened.

"I told her and she said : 'So what! Of course you don't compromise.'

'It gave me a terrific boost. I said to myself, so what and decided on another tack. I went on television and said I hoped they would close everything down. The lot. I rang the Managing Director of Comalco and said that it looked like they'd close down his smelter at Gladstone and put 2,000 employees out of work. I said I was going to go on television to urge them to do it. He said, 'Well if they do that we'll never open again'.

"I said, the sooner they do it the strike will be over.

"I went to church on the Sunday morning and I prayed.

"Then when I got back to the office they started to approach me. A lot of their top people in the electrical trades unions rang me privately. Some of them were key operators in the power stations. They wanted to see me. I said, why should I see you? I couldn't care less what you do. But I'll tell you this, if it goes on much longer some of you fellows had better start thinking about fleeing the country. The people aren't going to cop it much more.

"Late in the afternoon, one man was particularly insistent that he should see me. So I told them to come and see me in my office on the 23rd. floor of the annexe. There are no lifts operating because of you, I said, and you've got 23 flights of stairs to walk up, as I have been doing all this time.

"They came in, puffing and panting, some of them big, overweight fellows with large stomachs. They seemed quite decent people, genuinely concerned about what was happening and wanting to get it finalised. I told them, I'm not interested in whether you will or you won't go back. Because tomorrow, you will go back. Tomorrow each of you will be given a document and if you don't go back to work you face a possible fine of $50,000 each and the union of course much more. If you think you're going back on the terms and conditions you had before, you're wrong. You'll have to forego your superannuation and you'll have to work a 40-hour week.

"They went back down the stairs very humbly and very meekly.

"Everyone was handed a legal document tied with red ribbon: the next day and strike was over.

"Ruthless? Well tough. It's the sort of situation where

somebody must be prepared to sit it out until the bitter end.

"If somebody strikes, they think they're giving you a problem. My motto was to always give them a bigger one. Confuse them. It's very simple. These people now in charge of government and new to it all, will probably get run over the top because they will try and negotiate. You can't do that with the unions, you have to be strong and positive in this ruthless age in which we live."

On Gough Whitlam and a republic: "Gough button-holed me in Canberra one day and said, 'Joh, why do you always attack me? I never attack you.' I said: It's not you, Gough. It's your jolly policies I attack.

"Whitlam told me quite seriously he was going to be first President of the Republic of Australia. 'You can start calling me Mr. President now Joh, so you can get used to it.'

"I took several premiers with me to London to tell them how determined the man was. We met with Ted Heath and Sir Alec Douglas-Home and impressed on them that we were a sovereign state and wanted to remain that way. They listened patiently and said they would take it all back to Her Majesty.

"The first time Whitlam met me after that he said, 'Joh, you might have won that round. But we'll get there. Australia will be a republic.'

On fraternisation with the Labor Party: "There has never been any social common ground between us whatsoever. I brought in a rule that we should never sit down and drink or have dinner with the Labor people. It had been happening in the Members' bars and I stopped it.

"You cannot effectively oppose people politically if you're going to bed with them all the time. If you're going to sit and laugh with them and drink and get half-full and then tell them all the things you're going to do — which is one of the problems we had with some of our boys—you're in trouble. Once you start drinking with a Labor fellow and he's maybe a bit cleverer than you are and less under the influence of the whisky than you are, he gets a lot of things out of you.

"So we kept to ourselves. If you are opposing somebody you don't sit and break bread with them."

I asked about how he would deal with Aboriginals and their obvious problems: "I was chairman of the Hopevale Lutheran Mission near Cooktown for 11 years," he said. "Cherbourg Mission is very close to where I live and I have had Aboriginals working with me on the property for many years, treated exactly the same as anyone else. So I know a bit about Aboriginals.

"Their drink problem is a serious one. Unfortunately they use too much of their money on alcohol. They get a lot of money, a lot of support, more support than white people get for their children. The average Aboriginal is a good type of person, not wanting to cause trouble. I have great respect for them. They were not permitted to drink for many years and then the do-gooders got the best of [former Queensland Premier] Frank Nicklin and they were given free access to drink. People argued: 'Otherwise when will they be able to get used to drink and be treated equally?'

"We have never reached that point. Physiologically they are unable to get used to drink. The more money they are given, the more they drink. Perhaps the answer is in their genetic make-up. All I can say is, I hope some answer to this self-destruction is found soon.

"Their most serious problem is where they've got in the land-rights agitation. The average Aboriginal doesn't think in this way. It's the handful of militant agitators, most of whom have white blood in them, who are doing it. They have been given an opportunity and have seized it. It is getting ugly. Recently a large cache of arms was found in Western Australia and I believe we are heading for bloodshed.

"In Queensland we gave Aboriginals a Deed of Grant and they have control of about 8 or 9 million acres. We have given them the land and are the only State to do so. Under 'land-rights' the land is not being utilised, it is being neutralised.

"The signs are going up everywhere: NO WHITE MAN BEYOND THIS POINT. I know, because I have been told by them, that they are out to control the coast-line right down around the Gulf of Carpentaria to the tip of Cape York. They have been buying land secretly, using false names. One of them showed me the plan they have on a map. 'We want to control who comes in and who comes out.' Some fishermen have already been blocked from coming ashore.

"This Land Rights problem is going to bite deeply into this nation. Then Fraser, Anthony and Hawke will have something serious to answer for. It's going to end up with the Aboriginal militants achieving their objective of a nation within a nation; a government within a government. They have said this openly and if they achieve it they will have the absolute right of inviting the Cubans in as they are now, in Angola, or their friends the Libyans. It's as clear as daylight that it's going to happen."

How did he feel about publicity—much of it derogatory—regarding colourful Gold Coast developer, Mike Gore and the so-called 'White Shoe Brigade'?

"When I started my push for Canberra, Mike Gore came out of the blue and said he was going to make sure I got there. He was going to play a leading part in it all and was off to raise funds; he'd get heaps of money.

"I'd known Mike for years, right back when he was involved in boat-building.

"The big money didn't eventuate. Mike got into financial trouble, but nevertheless he kept on making statements about the umpteen millions of dollars he'd put at my disposal. He's a bit like that, talks big, thinks big, and probably believed in his own mind he could raise it. So I just smiled to myself. I knew there was no $25 million there and that Mike would perhaps put in a hundred or two. His White Shoe Brigade was the figment of some journalist's imagination.

"Today it's too late for Mike Gore or any other big businessmen who bewail what the Hawke government and Keating are doing to them. There are a lot of businessmen who believed when I was on my way to Canberra, that they could just watch and go on living with the Devil. They had a spoon long enough to sup with him. Today even Hawke's big pals, like Kerry Packer, aren't feeling as relaxed and as palsy-walsy as they once did. Their price of supping is going up."

***

Sir Joh, who was aged 92 at the time of writing, blind and unable to communicate, had recently failed in his attempt to claim $353 million compensation for the damage the Fitzgerald Inquiry did to his health and bank balance.

He had talked to me about the Inquiry, and his health, on one of our tapes.

"When I was a child I contracted infantile paralysis, as it was called then; now they call it polio. My parents rigged up a device from a telephone cell and connected the wires and made my leg twitch. My mother used to massage away the pain that made me cry. I have been left with a limp. It doesn't hurt me, but sometimes if I get a bit tired I might limp a bit more and people notice it. It's because my right leg is thinner and so much shorter, nearly half an inch shorter than the left.

"In spite of polio putting me on my back for 12 months I've been most fortunate. I don't ever recall having been sick with the flu. But when I was a child and caught a cold, which was rare, we always had a warm flannel around our necks at night-time. I don't know if it was imagination or not, but it seemed to get rid of it. [the cold]

"We just grew up [at 'Bethany', near the peanut-growing centre of Queensland's Kingaroy] the natural way, running around in the open and working, and we always seemed to be pretty fit.

"And I have remained fit. These days I only have to watch my diet in the sense that I try not to eat too much. The big problem when I was Premier was that we were always given so many luncheons and dinners and functions.

"On one occasion, when we were flying around the State, we called at quite a number of places and we had eight lunches and dinners in the one day! My staff gave up long before I did, but at each one I tried to show some interest because so much preparation had gone into it, and I ate a little. That has always stuck in my mind. It was a record.

"I don't have any weight variation; it always stays about the same: 80 kilos. Generally one or two kilograms below that, but never above it. We just keep right on it. It could change if you just let yourself go and ate heaps and heaps of food all the time. I try and not eat too much butter; that can sometimes affect my gall a bit. I drink very little. No need. I generally drink water. Or tea or coffee, but only a couple of cups of each a day. I have never smoked. Never even tried it. I've never taken vitamins except perhaps a bit of Vitamin C sometimes.

"I have no ailments. Every day seems the same. I don't have regular medical check-ups. I had to when I was a pilot, every 12 months. I have only ever seen doctors for the pilot's licence. There was never any trouble; the same every time. No problems with heart or cholesterol. I am very fortunate. God's been good to me.

"I work out on the farm [at 'Bethany'] on odd days when I get time; that's my biggest trouble today; I don't get enough time to do any exercise. I have a running machine at home and we run on that every morning and every evening. Don't spend long on it, but I get on it and make it run fairly fast!

"I sleep four or five hours a night. That's all I need. I wake up when I've had about four hours. It doesn't make any difference if I go to bed early or late. I can go to bed at 10 and I'm awake at 2 in the morning; or at nine and I awaken an hour earlier.

"I generally get up and go and get the paper if I'm in Brisbane [where he spent three days a week]. When I'm home, I lie there until just on daylight and then we get up.

"Stress? Well, we get a lot of battering, and knocked from pillar to post. But by and large I have no stress. You wouldn't survive 20 years in politics as a Premier if stress affected you, would you? We've had three years of investigation [the Fitzgerald Inquiry] since I got out. It still goes on. They haven't got enough to do, so they spend their spare time on me, a tribe of them. It doesn't affect my sleep. It just annoys me to think that after you did so much for the State and left a million dollars behind they're still looking. They remind me of chooks at a husking; when they used to shell corn, the husk goes up the elevator and there were always bits of cracked corn left behind. And for the next two or three months your chooks were always scratching around the husking look-ing for some grains. It's the same sort of thing: they're still scratching around."

When Sir Joh took his Cabinet to 'show the flag' and have its formal meeting in Cairns, the National Party faithful put on a barbeque for the Premier and his minis-ters. "Now," said the lady in charge. "What would you like to have, Sir Joh? We've got prawns, barramundi, steak and vegetables."

"I'll have the steak, my dear," said the Premier.

"And what about the vegetables?"

"Oh they'll have steak too."

***

I went home and wrote three chapters of the proposed book, and the outlines and synopses of 20 more, sent them to Sir Joh, awaiting his summons to Brisbane to start serious work. Three weeks after airmailing the copies off to Sir Joh, Beryl and Richard Lancaster, I received word from Richard Lancaster that Sir Joh had read what I had written and had a feeling of 'dismay'. Would I come down for a meeting?

'Dismay'? That was a strange reaction to what was, after all, a verbatim, but grammatically re-organised version of what Sir Joh had actually said. When I entered his suite in the Qantas Building, Sir Joh was unusually shy. Beryl Young opened the conversation. "We have all read what you have written. It isn't really what we had wanted."

"But they were Sir Joh's actual words!"

"Maybe so," said Beryl. "We see the book differently. We see it as portraying Sir Joh as a white knight rejuvenating Queensland, making it one of Australia's great states."

I swallowed and glanced at Sir Joh who was studying his desk-top.

I told the three of them, with Sir Joh still busy looking at his desk, "I see the book as being two-thirds asking if corruption could go on right under Sir Joh's nose. I see the white knight thing as a single chapter ..." And I went on, sarcastically now, suggesting that if they wished to engage a safe, public-relations writer to work with Sir Joh, to take down his thoughts without question, maybe I could find them one.

"Good," said Beryl Young. "Please do that!" I went across to a phone on the other side of the room, phoned my publisher in Melbourne and asked him if he could help. He said he would put Joh in touch with someone.

As promised, I destroyed my 'sensitive' Joh Tapes and filed away some of his harmless, non-contentious thoughts which we have often discussed since, for we remained good friends.

Chapter 14

'Tahiti And Sixpence'

I was a bachelor until I was 36 and, naturally, girls were constantly on my mind. I'd read everything that had been written about Tahiti, and it was my ambition to go there one day to experience the romantically exotic. What man hasn't dreamed of living as a castaway on an island, tended by bare-breasted maidens, and eating tropical fruit plopping down from the trees?

I'd read what Somerset Maugham had written in 'The Moon and Sixpence' and English poet, Rupert Brooke, had scribbled, as he sailed away from the Tahiti he had lost his heart to: "I looked for the Southern Cross as usual, and the moon; and looked for it in vain. It had gone down below the horizon. It is still shining and wheeling for those good brown people in the islands and they're laughing and kissing and swimming and dancing beneath it.

"I reflected that there was surely nothing else like them in this world, and very probably nothing in the next, and that I was going away from gentleness and beauty and kindliness, and the smell of the lagoons, and the thrill of that dancing, and the scarlet of the flamboyants, and the white and gold of other flowers; and I was going to America, which is full of harshness and hideous sights, and ugly people. So I wept a little, and very sensibly went to bed."

Now, 40 years after Brooke closed his diary, I found myself leaning over the railing of an ocean liner as it slid into the same Papeete dockside. Mountain peaks soared behind a little town half-hidden by swaying palms. From down below on the dock came the rat-tat-tat of drumsticks on coconut husks; electric guitars strummed the urgent, sensuous beat of the tamure and in front of the band a line of smiling grass-skirted Polynesian women, 'vahines', flashed their smiles and their hips. As we got closer we could actually smell the sweet frangipani and the tiara – a perfume far more pungent than I had ever smelled from the same sort of petals in Australia.

We tied up, and girls with huge brown fathomless eyes came aboard kissing our cheeks and smilingly placed leis of the flowers over our heads while the band below continued the rhythm of the pelvis-grinding dances.

Down on the wharf I noticed a greying, thin, deeply tanned European, his vahine, long black hair crowned by a garland of yellow-and-white flowers, sobbing as she, surrounded by her bags, waited to go aboard our ship and leave him. I had written to Rupert Brooke's cousin, Peter and now he waved to me as I held up a card with my name on it.

His sad farewells over, the thin Englishman in the faded flowered shirt and brown slacks, shook hands and said in an accent straight out of public school, "Let's have coffee across the road at Cafe Vaima." We sat down and he told me through clouds of smoke that he had been in Tahiti since 1947.

"I caught the 8.40 from Guildford into the City of London one morning—for the last time!" He chuckled at the suddenness of the decision. Two vahines sitting at the next table put their hands over their mouths and laughed with him. "I was," said Brooke, sucking on his French cigarette, "fed up with commercialism and modern industrial life. I had a good job. I made good money and I knew I could plan my life until I was 80. What?" He took another drag and went on. "Everything was laid out for me in England. I knew with certainty that I could remain in my firm as a stock-broker; I knew I could be rich but, you know, riches to me are riches of the mind; riches of a way of living; riches of personality and genuineness. More and more, in England, genuineness was giving way to hypocrisy; the 11th. Commandment 'Thou shalt not get found out' was the motto of business and government and I was fed up with it. I had read a lot about Tahiti through Cook, Pierre Loti, Gauguin, Maugham, and my cousin, Rupert Brooke. They all said it was unique. They hadn't said that about Tonga. They hadn't said it about Honolulu or Samoa. Everybody I spoke to said, 'Oh it's changed now. Become very commercial, I hear ... but I was determined."

He waved across to the giggling girls who, he said, lived in his village. "It's 12 years since I landed here. And from the moment a charming vahine put a lei around my neck as I stepped on to the wharf, I discovered what they had written years before was still right." He pointed to the small, weatherboard shops and the narrow, broken footpaths. "Papeete is a dirty little town with Chinese restaurants serving awful food. You must come out with me to my village in the districts, where there is no power, no electric light, just grass huts, flowers, fishing and jig-jig on the beach, what!" The girls went into peals of laughter.

"You know, I remember standing on the wharf as I did today; the ship that brought me was departing and there was this charming girl crying because her soldier friend was leaving. Leis were thrown into the water and over the side as it drew away; and as it moved out to the open ocean this vahine turned to me and said in French that I should come with her if I had nowhere to go. It seemed a good idea to me!

"We caught Le Truck, the open-sided bus that goes around the single road and went to sit by the beach. It was about 10 o'clock at night and we were overlooking the lagoon when a party of fishermen came in using torches. They had their guitars out and were singing softly in Tahitian, and the moon was coming up. I said to the girl, 'I have no place to stay.' And she said: 'What does it matter? Come with me. Today is today and tomorrow is tomorrow. Why worry?'"

A little unsteadily, for the coffee had long ago been replaced by Hinano beer, Peter got up and walked over to his motor-bicyclette, inviting me to get on behind. We headed off through the outskirts of Papeete and on to the winding road with its hibiscus borders that went out to Faaa and Punavia, where the power supply came to an abrupt halt. His village was on the edge of a black sand beach. We parked the bicyclette by his house, a one-bedroom grass-thatched hut with sides that swung outwards and up, to be propped open to let the air and light in. A lime tree's branches dangled within arm's reach of the kitchen and Peter, saying 'time for English tea', pulled in a bunch of leaves, shoved them into a kettle and poured boiling water over them. It was delicious.

He had no shower, but said he used the bathroom in the house next door. "They borrow my bicyclette; I give them tobacco and they give me fish. Sort of a communist set-up, what? I have a little money that is sent out from England and it is enough. I am a remittance man. My family pay for me to stay away." He lit a kerosene lantern and then reached out again from the kitchen, tearing a banana off a hand of them roped to a branch of the lime-tree. That night we putt-putted back into Papeete and did a pub-crawl of the bar dances: Bar Lia, Zi-Zou's and the most famous of them all: Quinn's Tahitian Hut A guitar-thundering, beery hall where I danced with the most beautiful girls I had ever seen, heads and necks festooned with frangipani, wearing red, blue and gold flower-print cotton dresses, the tiara behind their ears; eyes shining with amore, or at least the promise of it. I was in bachelor heaven. Above the din Peter explained the morals: "If they like you they'll make love with you. It's uncomplicated with them. Like kissing cheeks."

He was right …

On the way back to his village that night, the little bicyclette coughed, and came to a sudden stop in a large pool of water a storm had dumped an hour or two before. Hair soaked, gardenia hanging bedraggled behind his ear, Peter shouted to me,

"Thank God we're British!" It seemed enormously funny at the time.

Next day I boarded the ship and sailed away from Papeete, the guitars wafting away in the breeze and just the smell of a shy girl's tiara round my neck. The petals would die, but not the memory.

I vowed that one day I'd go back. Tahiti had the same effect on me as it had on Rupert Brooke, Paul Gauguin and the thousands who had visited the Polynesian islands. The islands in those days were unspoiled paradise.

* * *

It was London in a freeze when the phone rang and the man on the other end introduced himself: Bengt Daniels-son of Kon Tiki raft fame. He was in London and some-one in Papeete had given him my name. He got to the point asking if I would I consider staying at his Tahitian residence to work with him on a book?

I had never met the bearded Bengt, but knew the story of the Kon Tiki raft and its epic journey from Peru to Tahiti. Bengt had stayed on for all those years and was living at Punavia, a few miles along the coastal road from Papeete. When the Kon Tiki balsa raft had made it to land, Danielsson, like so many before him, had fallen for the islands.

The Swedish born historian and anthropologist said he had already written several books about the voyage, about love in the South Seas, and the true story of Paul Gauguin's life in the islands.

He and his French-born wife, Marie-Therese, invited me to dinner at their rented Kensington apartment. I noticed a Volvo parked outside; it had a Tahitian number-plate. "We've got a small fare, a self-contained flat in Punavia, which you could use," said Bengt over drinks. "I have a copy of the Bounty's original log, and though most of my books are translated from Swedish into English I want this written in English."

There was now, he said, an airport in Tahiti — Faaa — where jets roared in from all over the world, an ear-splitting contrast to the arrival of ocean liners at the frangipani-strewn wharf in Papeete.

I needed little persuasion and a month later flew in to a daily ritual of swimming in the lagoon over the coral reef with Bengt's young daughter, Maruia. I had breakfast of fresh papaw and bananas with Tahitian coffee, then settled down to work with Bengt on the book.

Next door Marlon Brando had rented a house for his mistress, the exotic Tarita Tumi, a half-Chinese, half-Polynesian dancer who had a small part in the movie he had made in Tahiti, 'Mutiny on the Bounty'. Tarita was auditioned and met Brando but she had no idea who he was. She was an uncomplicated, beautiful girl who danced for tourists at night and washed dishes by day. Now she lived alone in a splendid beachside house, equipped with the latest American appliances, waiting for Marlon's sporadic visits from California.

She joined Maruia and I as we glided over the astonishing reef every morning, allowing the tide to take us about two kilometres down the coast; the girls' long hair — Maruia's blonde, Tarita's jet-black — flowing behind them. One morning as we trudged back to our houses, Tarita said, "Come in, Desmond and see my house."

She showed me her kitchen, giggling as she pointed to the huge refrigerator, its doors plastered with studio photographs of Marlon.

Next morning there was to be no swimming. Bengt said he had to drive down to Faaa to meet Emile Gauguin off the plane from Los Angeles. Emile, as I'd seen him on my first visit was a massive French-Tahitian, the illegitimate son of Paul Gauguin. He habitually squatted outside Quinn's Tahitian Hut dance bar demanding 200 Tahitian francs from tourists if they wanted to take his photograph.

"He's been in Los Angeles for 18 months," Bengt explained. "He's coming back for a holiday and I've been asked to take him to his cousin's home where he will stay for a fortnight. Then I have promised to put him back on the plane for LA."

He said that two years before, Emile had caught the attention of a Los Angeles gallery owner in Tahiti on holiday. The lady had shrewdly seized on the simple fact that there was only one person in the world with the right to sign the name Gauguin on a painting; and there he was, this huge, smiling Buddha sitting outside Quinn's, begging.

As we drove into Faaa, Bengt, told me, "She took Emile in hand and taught him to daub with paint like a child in kindergarten. And more importantly, taught him how to scrawl his name. She then persuaded him to return with her to Los Angeles and paint. Americans fell over themselves to buy the paintings no matter how childish. They were signed Gauguin, and that was enough."

Now Emile was on his way back to Tahiti first-class, but with a return ticket to make sure the lady's money-making machine went back to America. Bengt had been entrusted with meeting him — and most importantly — getting him back on the return flight to LA.

We sighted Emile as he came through Customs; no longer a Buddha figure as I'd last seen him, but a slim, smiling character in a plaid sports-jacket and straw hat with hat-band to match. He kissed Bengt and demanded the first stop: the Papeete fruit market, with Emile marching delightedly through the stalls like a celebrity, taking out his new American dentures to show to his friends. Tahitians have notoriously bad teeth, and the new dentures were a status symbol.

We drove Emile to his cousin's house and Bengt made a firm agreement with him to pick him up in two weeks' time ...

Now, on the day Emile was to fly out of Faaa: catastrophe! Bengt took a call and came away from the phone frowning. "There is a problem. Emile is in jail!"

He explained that Emile had decided he had no wish to return to the United States to daub pictures and stay on a diet. But with a return ticket and Danielsson's promise to put him on the flight, he felt trapped.

He believed there was only one solution to the problem. He couldn't hide in Tahiti. So instead, he took a willing vahine down to the beach on the waterfront and in broad daylight made love to her.

Tahiti, as easy-going as it was about love-making, always did it discreetly in the jungle or behind doors. Emile had crossed the line and was arrested. The gendarme who made the arrest explained to me later, "Not on the beach, and not at midday, M'sieu. And certainly not in front of the home of the British Consul."

Emile was delighted to be in jail. Like all prisoners on the island he was allowed to trot out the gates and down to the markets every morning and buy his tobacco, chat to the stall-holders and then make his way back to his cell. Tahiti was an island and there was no escape.

Two days later I was to fly back to London and when I got there I called the Los Angeles gallery-owner to tell her that unfortunately her protégé would not be on the flight on which she was expecting him. She couldn't believe it. "There must be some mistake," she said. "Emile was really happy painting. And his paintings were selling for an awful lot of money."

When Tahiti had dissolved into a dream, and I was happily married with no need to think about vahines, I discovered another genuine artist on an island in Queensland whose castaway dream had become reality.

Noel Wood, when I met him, had lived a Robinson Crusoe existence on his own island, Bedarra, in far North Queensland, for 40 years. I found Noel after a 90-minute drive down from Cairns to Clump Point, near Mission Beach and took an island-hopping ferry to be dropped off by its dinghy on Noel's tiny Island.

Our first sight of the castaway was on a sparkling, sunny day as our little aluminium boat, with Delphine and baby son, Adam aboard, crunched on to Wood's private beach. A tall, bearded man with flowing black hair and wearing a faded kaftan, hurried down to meet us. He was about 65, handsome, with lively brown eyes, bare calloused feet and a gentle voice. "Welcome!" he said. "Come and have a tint." (I learned later that 'a tint' covered a generous goblet of wine, a beer; or if you were a good friend, a sip of his beloved cognac).

Noel took us to his thatched cottage and told us how he had bought his third share of the little lizard-shaped island for £45. The whole island had been purchased just after World War 11 for £20 by an Englishman who had arrived 'with mirrors for the natives and his own water'. Noel, when he got there, alighted from his boat and strode across the white sand and selected a spot shaded by palms and a massive bread-fruit tree, and built his home. He did his own roof thatching by plaiting palm fronds, and put up strong walls by cementing beer and wine bottles together. He painted there, with the sun filtering through shutters he'd made from driftwood saved from the beach, lit at night by a hissing kerosene lamp.

He had hens which laid orange-yolk eggs enriched from coconut scraps. He caught fish off the rocks and he grew his own vegetables, supplemented by taro, which grew wild. Bananas, mangos and breadfruit proliferated around his property.

Friends from the mainland regularly dropped in to see him bearing meat and cognac; a boatman brought mail across from 'Oz', along with airmailed subscriptions to Time Magazine and The New Yorker. He had no telephone, no electricity and no running water. In case he became ill or had an accident he had arranged to place a large cloth signal on the beach hoping someone on the other side of the bay might see it and bring help. But the grazier who owned the large property wasn't often there.

Noel Wood's paintings were in demand and he had spent three years in Hollywood working on movie sets. As his fame and the story of his island life spread, he had been visited by the curious from all over the world; prime ministers, English dukes, dissatisfied millionaires, and of course television crews, sitting at his feet in the sand or at night by his fire, listening to him and envying his life. "Sometimes I don't even have time to go up and feed the chooks." Noel grumbled about the stream of guests.

Because cyclones were a regular fact of life in that part of the tropical world he had built his own shelter by digging into the side of a hill and storing tinned food and water. He had used it several times with screaming gales tearing down his palm trees and threatening to whisk his frail house out to sea. "The fowls get terrified and I have to admit I have been bloody scared too."

Over the years, he had several girls and mature ladies to share his life; but as he told author John Mortimer and Leo McKern (of Rumpole fame) when they made a visit. "They were artists and writers and no good with plumbing."

He had his own oyster-bed and before dinner that night — fish cooked in a stone pit — we went down to the sea at sunset and Noel, kaftan drawn up to his waist, hammered off a couple of dozen fat, succulent oysters which we had with cold Chablis.

It was only after a visit to a Cairns eye specialist in later years that he was forced to make his life a little easier by rigging up a solar system that gave him hot tank-water for his shower and more importantly, a reading lamp so he could enjoy his books and magazines at night; his eyes had already been strained by the sputtering gas-lamp.

When he decided we could be friends, Noel showed me a small cottage on the other side of his part of the island that he had built for 'guesties'. We would be welcome to rent it when the present tenants had left. Delphine, myself and toddler son, Adam, then became an irregular part of his life for a peppercorn rent of $20 a week.

At weekends we made the trip down to Clump Point. A helpful garage proprietor would come out with us to the end of the jetty where gas cylinders, cartons of wine, suitcases of food and clothes were unloaded and carried aboard the lurching 'Friendship', the little island-hopper. The garage man then reversed all the way back and stored our car for us. Each weekend, as the 'Friendship' hove to opposite Bedarra, its Kenyan-born skipper, Perry Harvey, would order the deckmate to lower the aluminium dinghy for us for the short journey to the beach. While this was being done, Perry would switch on the public address system and speak to the tourists, many of them from overseas, who were lining the rails and watching the performance as Delphine, baby Adam, suitcases and gas bottles were lowered gingerly into the bobbing dinghy. "This family, ladies and gentlemen," Perry would say, "is about to land on this small desert island. He is a writer and they intend to live here, cut off from the outside world."

"Oh my!" the American tourists would exclaim. "Isn't that terrible! And with that little baby ..."

"Yes," Perry would solemnly agree. "It's a bit of a worry." He carried out the ritual every weekend and it became the highlight of the tourist day-trip.

Once landed, we'd drag our gear up the beach, settle into our cottage hidden behind the palms, and go over to Noel's 'side' with fillets of steak and his beloved Hennessy.

Noel came over to show me the best fishing spots, plodding with his huge battered feet, straight up the almost vertical sides of a rock cliff and expecting me to follow, carrying fishing gear and bait. He appeared surprised that I was terrified of the drop below. I'd fish there, as if I had thrown a line into an aquarium, watching coral trout and red emperor glide suspiciously around my hook. When I caught a thrashing fish, Delphine and Noel would cook it that night in a red-hot rock pit, covered with banana leaves, accompanied each time by oysters prised off Noel's lease.

As the sun went down, the stars came out and the hurricane lamp hissed, we would settle down to 'tints' of cask wine and Noel's memories of New York art shows, Hollywood celebrities and what the Duke of Bedford had said when he paid him a visit the other day.

One balmy night when we'd all gone to bed, I heard a squeak that disturbed the starry silence. It went on and on and I could stand it no longer. I got up, lit the gas-lamp and discovered that a breeze had sprung up and was rubbing two limbs of a tree together. I did the only practical thing an urban male could think of: I climbed up on a ladder with an oil-can and oiled the limbs where they touched. It worked, and gained me an honoured entry in Noel's list of Nuts Who Have Visited Bedarra Island.

Our friendship with Noel and use of his cottage carried on for years. Then, one weekend, we arrived on the beach once again to be greeted by a worried, solemn figure. "I had a visit from some developers yesterday and I'm a bit concerned," said Noel. "They wanted to buy me out and gave me a lot to drink. I refused. But they said as they departed that I was a silly old prick and that they knew my daughter in Melbourne had my power-of-attorney and they would go and see her."

Noel, feeling no pain, had climbed into his aluminium dinghy and put-puttered across to Mission Beach to the phone in the pub to warn his daughter. When he came out to the bar, 'two huge, hairy Italian cane-cutters were there and asked me why I was so upset?'

He told them. The largest, Luigi, then said, "Noelly, you have been good to us and we owe you favours. Tell me those fellas' names. I go to the phone and call my friends in Melbourne and they finish."

Said Noel, "Now I'm bloody terrified that he did it ..."

Chapter 15

We Find Our Paradise

J ust when the wheel of fortune seems stuck in a rut, it often grinds into action and smoothes out the pathway. It happened when we made a seemingly mad decision to live in Cairns, a place I'd previously never heard of.

The London Sunday Times Travel Editor had phoned me in Sydney to say she wished to include Australia in a coming travel section and had heard I was back there. She commissioned me to write an in-depth travel piece on Far North Queensland to give English readers a glimpse of its exotic tropical isolation; also what sort of house 'could one buy?' And what would it cost? Could 'one' buy a decent bottle of wine? And what were the restaurants like? If readers wanted to go out and actually live there, what was the standard of education they should expect for their children?

It was then 1971, and our son, Adam was on the way; already dubbed 'the little walnut'.

Much of what I had gathered about Cairns before Delphine and I flew in, was that Leo McKern, the veteran Australian actor who was to find fame as Rumpole of the

Bailey, now lived there. He'd settled at Stratford, 8kms from downtown Cairns, after making the movie Ryan's Daughter.

Because it seemed to be an odd move for a famous star, Leo had been interviewed and written about in all the papers. 'Why on earth …'

However, my brief from the Sunday Times, a paper much more staid than it is now, was certainly not to write about personalities. When a local real estate agent suggested he might introduce me to Leo I politely told him not to bother.

We had been in Cairns for a week fact-gathering. An enthusiastic real estate agent, Monty Montefiore, was our guide and he gave us his full time, relying on the long-shot that if English would-be migrants read the article they'd get in touch with him. (I didn't say so at the time, but I felt it was a long-shot indeed.)

It was our last day, and Monty picked us up at the motel and drove us up a steep goat-track to the summit of a Stratford hill. "It's got a spectacular view," he assured us on the bumpy way up. We got out of the car and gazed down across shimmering cane-fields, over the wide Barron River, and further out — the sparkling ocean.

I turned to Monty. "I'll buy it! Where's the house?" At that moment a burly, unmistakeable figure emerged from behind a hedge of allamanda. Leo McKern greeted Monty and said he had just come back from the pub where he'd been chatting with the local cane-cutters. He waved away my embarrassment that I wasn't there to interview him. "Come in and have a drink," he said, in his Old Bailey purr.

Leo's breeze-brick and weatherboard house was perched on two-thirds of an acre. There was a pool, surrounded by lush tropical creepers and hedges. "Well," said Leo, sipping his wine, "what d'you think of Cairns?"

"We love it," Delphine said. "One day we might even come and live here."

"Well, why not buy my house? It's for sale. We've been here 18 months and we're leaving."

"Thanks, Leo," I said. "But we're nowhere near making that sort of decision. We will be staying in Sydney for a while." He poured us another drink. "I'm advertising the house nationally in 10 days' time. If you change your mind, let me know."

Suddenly the light-hearted discussion had become serious. Delphine and I had certainly fallen in love with Cairns and Leo's price of $32,000 for house, land, cane furniture and television set—he and his family wanted to leave it all behind—was absolutely reasonable.

We flew out next day, after going back in the morning to have a sober look. I had placed a $100 option to buy No.44 Dalziel Street, Stratford. If we decided against it (and that seemed likely) I would lose my $100. If we decided to buy, it would come off the price. Leo and I shook hands. The house was 34 years old. It had a study downstairs which would be ideal for me. And the view from what had already become Delphine's kitchen was breathtaking. But to decide so suddenly? It was ridiculous. And yet ... was it?

We sat up most of the night in our rented Sydney apartment and talked it over. 'Walnut', Delphine's little embryo, was developing. Could she have him (he was always thought of as a boy) in Cairns? Next morning I sent Leo a telegram: "Exercising option."

A week later we had vacated our flat, packed, and headed our 1971 Toyota Crown north. What had we done?

Leo met us in a floppy, wide-brimmed hat. He showed us the fruit trees, explained the tropical plants in the garden and how to clean the pool. "You'll like the people around here. They take the time to be nice," he growled.

The Cairns we immediately got to love was a paint-peeling old frontier town, with houses built on high stilts. Weatherboard and concrete-brick dwellings peeped from behind a confusion of bright-yellow allamanda; red and white frangipani and berserk bougainvillea. The sea sparkled, prawns were $3 a kilo and Morton Bay Bugs were being tossed back into the water as trash, because nobody thought they were worth eating.

In our first steamy Wet season we had 18 inches of rain in the space of 24 hours, the deluge clattering down on our iron roof like a train roaring through the London Underground. We hid in the bathroom through two cyclones, (said to be the safest part of the house because of its plumbing) watching helplessly out the window as huge old trees around the garden snapped in two. And the locals were indeed kind; they did give us the 'time'. Anybody arriving from further south than Innisfail, 80 kms down the road, was carefully given hours of the Far North Queensland 'Treatment'; a tried and true practice of judging newcomers by the simple expedient of forcing them to talk while the locals listened.

On our visit for the Sunday Times, we'd stayed at an elegant old beachside motel, and I noticed when we arrived at the restaurant, that there was only one other diner. As we finished our delicious crab, I said to the waiter that should the diner a few tables away, wish to join us for a drink later, he would be most welcome; we wanted to get to know the locals. It was agreed and the local, a developer, came and sat down with Delphine and I for a port.

He shook hands and then he said — nothing.

Embarrassed by the dead silence, I chatted trying to be friendly, in the end running out of things to say. The man later became nationally notorious for his controversial land speculation and I was informed by Monty that I was being given 'The Treatment'. "Let 'em talk and see what they're made of ..." This was the generous 'time' Leo was talking about.

When we settled in, it happened a lot. A Melbourne friend involved in the booming real estate industry had also endured it, but at the same time, he defended it. "These people," he said, "needed all their ingenuity to get where they have so far from anywhere. Cairns has a hard core of about 20 businessmen. They are some of the hardest, shrewdest characters you could ever meet. Isolation has made them that way. They leave so-called street-smart southern businessmen for dead. The Treatment, as you call it, lets them assess all the intruders."

In vogue at the time, was also the sport of 'shooting through'. Delphine and I had taken over a free weekly newspaper which we had bought after a dinner meeting with its tired owners. The paper's only income was from advertising, so early in our takeover we welcomed a newly-arrived Danish delicatessen who came in and took out expensive whole-page ads; every week. When his account was six weeks overdue I went to see him. "Oh, he's shot through," said his landlord, matter-of-factly. "Took a car he was trying out as a demonstrator as well. All the shop equipment was leased; the AGC financiers are still looking for him."

Annoyed, I went to the police station, then an ancient timber edifice on the sea-front. A detective sitting at an upright typewriter from which a mouse surprisingly emerged chuckled; not at the jumping mouse but at my predicament. It was a recognised FNQ custom, shooting through; much-admired, unless you were on the receiving end.

"There's this girl," said the helpful copper who wore wrap-around shades and yellow slacks, "who does the whole Coast every year and pays cash for everything when she arrives in town; dresses, grog, food. Then she does the rounds one day and says she's left her purse at home and would a cheque be all right? By now they all see her as a good customer and say of course it's alright. The cheques are met; and everything's great. Then one day she does the lot with her cheque-book — a restaurant, exclusive boutique, airline, delicatessen, jeweller — and disappears. Which one of them is going to spend the legal fees and air fares to bring her back?"

Cairns was still very much off the beaten track. There were no traffic lights, but there were parking meters, more often than not twisted in half by the impact of dust-covered 4WDs driven into town for the day by cattlemen and their wives to do the shopping. When lights were finally installed without warning there were bewildered drivers sitting in wrecks wondering what had happened. The town had one decent restaurant, a decade before its time; it was air-conditioned and had a fountain that trickled into a bed of flowers, picked every day from our garden by its two confirmed bachelor proprietors. It was called George's Bistro and it had style. It was regularly used by the town Madam to entertain her girls for lunch after a big night at the Bunda Street brothel, and as the fashionably-dressed wives of doctors, real estate agents, cane farmers and bank managers filed in to take their places by the window, the Madam would comment in a stage whisper "If my girls dressed like that they'd be damned hard up getting a fuck."

Even in the tropics, so far from 'civilisation', we drank surprisingly well. Every week I would choose the best French reds or finest Australian whites from the Burns Philp warehouse where the cellarman had an amazingly generous yardstick for the sale of wine. "White $1.50, red $1.75." The bliss came to an end when Head Office ordered a stock-take and the obliging fellow was replaced.

Our weekly newspaper wasn't an easy way to make money; the town businessmen tended to use it not only as an advertising medium, but as an overdraft. I took one belligerent smartie to court for a long overdue bill of $2.30 and won. It cost him $200 for his lawyer. It cost me $1.50 for a Warrant of Execution and a beer for the bailiff who told me how to do it.

When we purchased Focus News, its 'office' was the rear of a station-wagon where an IBM typewriter was stored. It used a printer, G K Bolton Pty Ltd., of McLeod Street, the only (and this is important) offset printer between Cairns and Mount Isa, where Sir Asher Joel had this new-fangled equipment.

I went to see 'GK' (as he was called), squatting on a rickety wooden chair in his small front office, a chair that seemed to have been made for a doll's house. I looked across at this large Englishman who had a frown that seemed to indicate the printing world was on its knees; Cairns was about to 'go under', and the Bolton empire headed for oblivion.

I later discovered that this was precisely the effect GK wanted. Had he sat behind a large executive desk, such a display of affluence might well have encouraged would-be clients to query some of his heady printing prices. But as Bob looked poor and worried, the client, on the other hand, was led to believe the price he offered was so low that GK and Mrs. Bolton, (always working twice as hard in the print-shop as anyone else,) might have been out on the streets next day, begging.

We came to an agreement to print my paper: cash in advance of delivery every Tuesday evening before the milk vendors came round to collect it and put it on doorsteps with the milk bottles. Bob had been 'bitten' by potential newspaper tycoons before. He said he would charge me $30 a page to print the paper, and his face showed such abject misery when he quoted, I almost thought I should offer him more.

GK, my new printer, had been a scrap dealer, had once

owned his own airline, was a brilliant photographer and no mean drag at sketching. He also loved music and was said to own two organs, one he had purchased and the other accepted from someone who failed to live up to his financial commitments.

Bob had an office controller, switchboard operator and general help called Flo. When chaos reigned, as so often it did in a shop that was printing a newspaper, books, brochures, wedding invitations and tracts, the calm voice of Flo was a joy to hear. Except when she was on the phone saying, 'Mr. Bolton would like to speak to you.' Then the heart sank. Either a page of my newspaper was late getting to him, or my ideas for a headline would not fit. Or the price was going up.

The price went up with charming regularity most Christmas Eves. Bob would proffer his hand to me, wish me a Happy Christmas and then look soulfully over his spectacle-frames and say, 'I'm afraid I have to raise your prices."

My mind would rush to Asher Joel in Mount Isa, the nearest offset printer, 1200 kms away, and the complexity of getting pages of typesetting on to aircraft and the huge cost of flying the finished product back to Cairns.

And I would shrug and give in. Bob would then smile benignly. It went on for years, each of us protesting greater poverty than the other, until there came a parting of the ways. A new offset printer was discovered 90 kms away, and I delightedly bade Bob goodbye.

It was a Christmas Eve and I invited him to our office for a drink. His cash-cow would no longer be there to be milked. He took the news rather bitterly. I told him how much I admired his technical genius and his enterprise, and I even had a grudging admiration for his shrewdness. But the party was over.

By now Cairns was being 'discovered' and there was talk of a new airport and, don't laugh, jumbo jets scheduled to land there. ("Pull the other one, mate.") Christopher Skase arrived in town in June 1983, and took me for coffee at the ritzy new Pacific International to ask if I would write a note to a television tribunal to say that he was a fit and proper person to own and operate a Townsville television station. I'd met him once at dinner in Melbourne when his talkative wife, Pixie, tried to sell me two $35 Italian leather handbags for Delphine. I turned down the bags but thought Christopher seemed OK and wrote the letter.

The following year we got our international airport and Cairns was 'on the map'. Travel writers came and explored our notorious Barbary Coast pubs, sitting goggle-eyed as young ladies in the bars offered: "Two bucks and I'll give yuz a flash", to retreat blushingly to interview the cantankerous old author, Xavier Herbert who was always annoyed to have to leave his ancient Hermes to talk to fools and turn off the noise-machine he used to drown out passing traffic.

They'd make the mistake of going on safari with the wily Percy Trezise, bushman, aviator, painter and world-renowned for his discovery of ancient Aboriginal art. Sucking hard on his cigarette-holder, Percy would tramp at such a furious pace, that broken men, nursing blistered feet and aching chests, would return weeping to the Pacific. That, too, had its problems. Mine Host was the rather unpredictable Paul Kamsler who owned the hotel. When I booked a serious American publisher of the Mormon persuasion into the Pacific, Paul, ever the joker, greeted us by asking if this was the gentleman I'd arranged the marijuana for? It sent the American pale-faced and jet-lagged to his room, wondering about the peculiarity of Australian humour and whether I was the sort of author he should have aboard.

That was Cairns. You learned to love it the way it was or pack your bags. We stayed on for 23 years until it started to be a poor-man's Surfers Paradise. We should have heeded the warning when we saw our first hippies, lolling in the winter sunshine on the Post Office steps beside the notice that said: "No loitering on the steps."

People got busted for smoking marijuana, and indeed it was the incidence of the drug in schools that had reluctantly persuaded Leo and Jane McKern to depart after 18 idyllic months. The Drug Squad had to resort to planting undercover police in Year 12 classes posing as fresh-faced 'students' (complaining to the Superintendent that it took them as long to do their homework as to write their reports). Satellite detection of marijuana arrived to save them and crops worth as much as $9m. at street prices were uncovered amongst the cane.

Delphine and I and new baby Adam, had a lifestyle that was as close to paradise anybody could find. I had seen Hawaii and Tahiti, but this was headier than both.

It is 5.30 am and the kookaburra adopted by the McKerns (or the other way about) has flown in for his breakfast and his loud chatter echoes around the slumbering hills that surround us. We put his special steak on a board and sleepily take it out to him by the pool. Up in the branches of the umbrella-tree he cocks a beady eye at the meat and then soars down to the board. His wife or daughter stays on the bough waiting; on cue, he takes the last piece of steak, flies up to her and pokes it into her beak. It is by now 5.45 am and apart from Kookie and the busy chatter of birds, including the Trumpet Bird, Urgent Ernie — who has a call like a frantic fire-alarm and Tuneless, a whistler so out of tune it makes you cringe — everything else remains fast asleep.

We sit by the pool and sip orange juice, looking down on a sweeping palette of dark and light-green cane fields, a silver river and the blue sea. I am reminded of the opening scenes from the movie South Pacific.

For breakfast this morning we have the choice of fresh

mangoes that have plopped down from a tree groaning with their weight; our own bananas hanging in a hand within reach of the kitchen, and fat, succulent papaws perfumed with the hint of frangipani which Delphine places at the ends of each slice.

Delphine pads about the house, tropical flowers in her light auburn hair, grappling with the problem of storing suits I have brought from London and which I will never use in Cairns. They must be packed in plastic covers, warn our friends, or they'll go green with mould in the Wet Season. The choice of dress each day is between the red swim shorts, the blue ones or the floral. We dress for dinner. I put on a shirt. Last night we were invited to a barbecue which was North Queensland Formal; thongs instead of bare feet.

Out on the lawn, fat, brown toads squat in a circle like a group of farmers discussing prices. When they dived into our pool to cool off I fished them out with the pool's leaf basket, but not any more. A veteran of Cairns-living advised me to hang a ladder of plastic roof gutter-protector into the pool so they could have their swim and climb out.

Cairns' first Madam would be dismayed today by the competition from 'escort' services. Her brothel has long-since gone. Old lady Cairns is no longer tatty and paint-peeled. She's walking 14 hotel stories tall, with (as I write) a struggling casino and a string of broken developers licking their wounds. Companies, resorts and shops for a while faced receivership, and old-timers wondered what happened to the laid-back years.

With fast food outlets and garish signs in Japanese, she's not the lady I fell in love with. She's now street-smart. They don't even bother to give the newcomers The Treatment.

Chapter 16

The Man Who Uncovered Schindler

As we became part of Cairns' society via our newspaper, we tended to meet interesting arrivals. And far from giving them The Treatment, we invited them '*à table*' to talk and enjoy Delphine's Cordon Bleu cooking. Food was her art and her ultimate enjoyment. A dinner preparation sometimes began two days before the actual event. Guests' tastes were established; who was to sit where, who would spark off who. And finally in her neat handwriting — place-cards. "Oh, you've gone to so much trouble!" was the comment that upset her most. It was never 'trouble', it was creating an event where people would meet and better know each other; maybe become future friends. I chose good wine and said why I believed it might complement the dish.

One guest was Robert Raymond, a man with a strange story to tell about the harrowing movie, 'Schindler's List', the saga of a German factory owner rescuing Jews from the Holocaust. We had Robert and his wife to dine just before the movie's world premiere and he held us in silent awe. He explained that if it hadn't been for his 'rather hurtful' criticism of the state of author Thomas

Keneally's worn briefcase, the epic film would never have been made.

Robert explained how Oskar Schindler, a German manufacturer saved the lives of countless Jews by insisting that they should be employed in his factories, which he operated next to the horror camps in which millions were being exterminated.

Raymond was a tall, sandy-haired Australian with a soft, persuasive voice. He had movies in his genes; his father was a writer and movie-maker and his grandfather once directed Marlene Dietrich in Ich Liebe Dich. His mother, four years old at the time, was in the film.

Raymond had been working in California as a literary agent, and on this particular day (he told us) he had been sitting in a Los Angeles hotel suite, plucking up courage to tell Australian author Thomas Keneally, that the battered briefcase he carried, was doing 'not a lot' for his stature in Hollywood, 'A town where first impressions are most important.'

Keneally, Australia's best-known author had gone to see him about the promotion in America of one of his books: The Confederates. His dilapidated Samsonite caught the jaundiced eyes of several Hollywood executives listening to Raymond's spiel.

On the night of our dinner, the launch of Schindler's List was still some weeks away, but even then there was world-wide publicity, hailing it as an epic. Robert had spent 13 years in America, he said. Now he had settled in Kuranda, outside Cairns.

"I had read most of Tom's books and had great admiration for his writing," Robert said. "Each book was about something different, and he gave them all such a believable background. The Confederates, his most recent novel, was a love-story set in the American Civil War and it was fascinating to me that an Australian had taken it on. I'd been back in Sydney a couple of times and while

I was there I contacted Tom and we met at Bilgola Beach. I asked him if he'd let me help him in the States. He had a London agent, and though she was doing all she could for him in London, I felt I might be able to help him a bit more in America. I said that if he came to LA, I could set up a publicity tour for him and his book, which was being brought out in paperback with a small advance to the author and not much publicity."

Raymond knew at the time, that 15,000 influential publishers, booksellers, agents and movie-makers were expected at an Atlanta Book Fair, and with so many authors represented, it would take a lot of pizzazz to attract interest to just one. He was determined that 'his boy' would be that author. So he went to a costume hirer and rented two authentic Confederate uniforms, with the appropriate insignia and badges, complete with side-arms for both.

"Mine looked great, but Tom's didn't fit. Tom has never been terribly interested in his appearance, he tends to wear suits that don't fit all that well and socks that don't go with the shoes. And his uniform needed some adjustment. He has big feet and the boots we hired were too small. We had to take a razor-blade to them so he could get his feet into them. His trousers hung rather awkwardly over the boots."

Quirkily, Raymond had made sure his uniform was that of an officer, Tom's a foot soldier.

"We went down 26 floors in the elevator and people looked at us as though we were pretty weird. They were gathered in their Amani suits and shiny shoes and nobody talked to us. I could see the head of publicity for Tom's publisher enjoying cocktails with hundreds of others and he didn't even recognise us. When the time came to announce Tom and his book they freaked out! We were noticed all right. We were a sensation! 'Confederates' went on and sold half a million copies."

Keneally then flew across to Los Angeles where Raymond now lived. "I was taking Tom around movie agents, because I believed that The Confederates was in the same league as The Red Badge of Courage and was screaming out to be made into a film. I'd booked him into the Beverly Wilshire Hotel and invited him on this Saturday evening, to come out to have dinner at our home. Tom was carrying around with him an old Samsonite briefcase. It was shabby, had faded labels on it and one of the catches didn't seem to close properly. It contained all his important papers. I said, 'Tom, I've got to tell you, I really think you should do something about that briefcase. It looks tatty, makes you appear to be down to your last dime.' Tom just laughed."

That hot Saturday afternoon, Tom Keneally could be seen wandering down South Rodeo Drive, Los Angeles, idly glancing in shop windows, thinking about presents for his wife and daughters back in Australia. His daughters had given him the offending briefcase years before. He came to a halt under an awning in front of a suitcase and bag shop called rather grandly, 'Beverly Hills Handbag Studio', and while he was sheltering for a moment from the sun, an elderly gentleman came out of the shop and said (the gentleman was to confirm to me later), "Why don't you come in from the hot sun, already? I won't try and sell you anything."

"As a matter of fact," said Keneally. "I am looking for a briefcase."

Leopold Pfefferberg, who called himself Paul Page in business said, "Have I something that is just right for you!"

"I noticed, (he said to me 14 years later) that the briefcase Thomas carried was very dilapidated. It had been made in Australia. I showed him one, made in Poland, in beautiful pigskin leather. Very light and very strong. It was $150, but I made him a very good deal and gave him 30% off. I sold it for about $110."

Keneally, pleased with the purchase, handed over an American Express card, issued in Australia, to pay for it. "In those days we had to wait 45 minutes for the girl on the phone to give the okay," said Pfefferberg. "If there is some problem or not a problem. And while we were waiting I asked Thomas what he did. He said he was a writer. I then said I would tell him a story — the story of Oskar Schindler, the papers about which I had kept with me for all those years after I left the German concentration camp. I was one of the Schindler Juden, and that man Schindler saved my life."

While the shopkeeper and Keneally awaited the American Express call, Pfefferberg took the Australian into the rear of the shop where he produced a stack of yellowing papers; files he had kept for 40 years; files he had spoken to journalists about, but nobody had been interested. "Until this miracle happened, (he told me later) this extraordinary human being, this jovial but humble man, came into my life."

Robert Raymond went on: "I was living off Mulholland Drive at the time, and I went that evening to the hotel to pick Tom up to have dinner with us. I noticed he had this shiny new briefcase. He got into the car and said, 'Listen. I've got to tell you about this extraordinary man I met. He has all these papers in Hebrew and German, an incredible story about a German who saved hundreds of Jews from concentration camps.'

"Tom recounted the whole story and I was fascinated. Next day a lawyer phoned him at the hotel and said he represented both Pfefferberg and Oskar Schindler and could they meet? They did, and the legal situation was a little hairy. I persuaded Tom to go away and write an outline of a book. Movies, I explained, are best when they come off the success of a book. He then had long talks with Pfefferberg and wrote a 27-page outline of the story. I saw it. I thought it was fabulous.

"Tom had originally wanted to write a film script first, but he decided to write the book, 'Schindler's Ark', with a promise that he would then have first crack at the screenplay. I said I would get him a deal five times better than his last book deal. I don't think he believed me."

Keneally returned to Australia, sat at his computer and delivered an enlarged treatment of the story to Raymond, who then set up a bidding war between publishers, securing a large advance from one — Simon and Schuster — whose Senior Editor, Nan Talese, wife of film star Gay Talese, said simply, 'We love it!'

"Nan is one of the most powerful people in American publishing, so what she said was important at that time."

Robert Raymond was getting 10% of future book profits in his role as manager/agent. He said, "I didn't wait for the phone to ring. I went out and hunted and fished."

The hunting and the fishing was to go on for several years before Raymond negotiated an option with MGM for the film rights to Schindler's Ark, which Keneally had now almost finished. MGM had, while Oskar Schindler was still alive, purchased film rights to his life story. Seven years before he died, Schindler had been brought to Hollywood by MGM and Poldek Pfefferberg and he signed. Raymond says: "I had to go to MGM and option the film rights from them prior to Tom's book coming out. The book rights from the various camp survivors, including Pfefferberg, were naturally ours. But to get other film rights we offered $1,000 a year, against a fat fee and a percentage of the eventual film's profits, MGM agreed."

MGM in 1995 made more money from Schindler's List — which they didn't make — than they made out of all the movies they actually made.

Oskar Schindler, the German to whom so many Jews owed their lives, died in 1974. Keneally never met him; nor did he meet his widow Emily, who lived in an Argentinean hovel. But Keneally talked to scores of death-camp survivors and when he had completed the book, Raymond offered it, in manuscript form, to various studios, only to be rebutted by one major studio after another.

"I woke up in the middle of the night and told myself this was ridiculous. One or two studios turned it down because they said a movie had been made about a vaguely similar story years before. There is not a lot of vision in Hollywood. I thought, 'I am going to the wrong people. Why not send it off to directors? They have more imagination. I should be going to the creative community, not the business community.' So I sent the book — it had not yet been published — to 12 directors, including Roman Polanski and Steven Spielberg. Every one of these directors, either personally or through their agents, called me and said they were interested. Polanski, who had lived through the same experience and escaped from a ghetto, as a child in Poland, wanted to write it."

It was then announced that Schindler's Ark had won the prestigious Booker Prize. "Earlier, when it was revealed from the UK that it was on the Booker Prize short list," says Raymond. "It made me feel that it was really going to be as important as we were hoping and the faith I had always put on it."

Raymond had by now had serious negotiations with Warner Bros.

"On a Saturday afternoon at home, I was just getting out of my swimming pool and my wife called me to the phone. It was Sid Scheinberg, then Vice-Chairman of MCA-Universal, considered at the time to be the most powerful man in Hollywood. He asked me if I would have lunch with him the following week. He said he represented a director, whose name he could not mention, who, he said, was 'the most important director in the world' who was very interested in the material. I knew it was Spielberg of course, but for some reason he did not want to mention it."

Raymond arrived at Scheinberg's black tower office on the top floor; met Scheinberg who took him to the rooftop dining-room. "We went through all the courses, right down to the dessert, and we talked for an hour-and-a-half about everything but the book. Its advance copies sent to newspapers ahead of publication meant it was being reviewed world-wide, but was still not in the bookshops. Sid Scheinberg had still not mentioned the name of the director apart from saying, 'You will know who it is.'

"I told him there was a negotiated deal in place with Warner Bros., but it had not been finalised. He had a little pad beside him at the table and wrote down all the things I considered about a film that I felt were important. I explained that the essential point was that we were setting up the Oskar Schindler Foundation, with some of the book's proceeds, that would help Jewish survivors from the death camps. I said when the film was eventually made and released we wanted a charity opening in Los Angeles and New York to raise more money.

"Sid Scheinberg then put down his glass of soft-drink, which we were both drinking and said, 'Robert, what would it take for you to sell us the project, with my director?' We had by now achieved a good understanding between us; I felt he was a very genuine man. But I was not prepared for an answer. I knew if I said something at that moment I would be bound to it. He knew Warner Bros. had made several itemised commitments and he said to me, 'How about I double them all? Would that do it?' It was just like falling off a building and you can see the ground coming up fairly quickly. I said, 'Yes!' We both stood up from the table and solemnly shook hands. I then had to put the deal to the people I represented in the project. Tom Keneally, Poldek Pfefferberg and the lawyer who represented the survivors.

"MCA-Universal decided the movie would be called Schindler's List and Steven Spielberg would direct it.

There was a lot of worry about that decision," said Raymond. "I felt strongly before I met him and more firmly after I met him, that Steven Spielberg was the director for the job. He was passionate about the book. But because he was best known for making 'ET', there were people who did not think he was the right man. It was felt that with his style of film-making might not do justice to such a poignant story. But I was never one of the doubters.

"Universal paid Tom to write the first draft of the screenplay. It must be realised that not many people who write books can write film scripts. He wrote 240 pages and it didn't work."

A new writer was given the task and the world-wide success of Schindler's List is now history.

In the final moments of the movie, dozens of Schindler Juden quietly line up to pay their respects to Schindler's grave in Israel, each placing a stone on it. Paul Pfefferberg was among them. He said to me from Los Angeles by phone after he had seen the film for the seventh time, "Nothing is added, nothing is taken away. It happened as the movie said it did. I cried every time I saw it.

"I had given Thomas my own testimony, Schindler's testimony and testimony from many Schindler Jews. I had kept these papers in my shop since 1945. Remember, this is the true story of someone like me losing his family and of the extermination of six million innocent bystanders, 1½ million children included. You have no other way when you see it, you cry. I am 81 now, and I was 33 when the war finished. I had been a professor in a Polish high school, a Jewish gymnasium and an officer in the Polish army. I had an eye and an ear open and I knew what was going on. And yet I still cannot believe this could happen.

"It was a miracle I met Thomas. You know, when I sold him his new briefcase it was 14 years ago. Do you think he might now need another one?"

Chapter 17

Mr Murdoch In My Moke

I flew down to Melbourne to discuss the promotion of my most recent book, and as we had coffee together, my editor, John Ross, thrust a rejected manuscript across to me asking if I'd like to write the life of Sir Keith Murdoch, Rupert's late father. The thick manuscript he handed across had been commissioned by Rupert, but he had turned it down.

"What's here," he said, leafing through some 500 pages, "is a record of Sir Keith Murdoch's business dealings and his newspaper acquisitions. But it's without colour and we can't publish it. If you're interested, I'll arrange for you to meet Rupert, see if he approves of you doing his father's biography."

It was a big ask. I would be dealing with the world's most powerful media personality, whom I had never met; a much more precarious undertaking than any other book I had done. With his huge battery of journalists and authors, it would be unlikely he would agree to me writing his Father's story.

I flew home to Cairns and began reading what was a detailed record of Sir Keith Murdoch's power; his business battles and the minutiae of dealings which almost sent him to the wall. But it was, as the publisher said, a skeleton without much flesh. Could a 'warts-and-all' biographer, which I happened to be, persuade the exacting Rupert to allow such a book to be written about his Father?

Rupert Murdoch was due to arrive into Queensland from the United States to spend a few days with his family on Lizard Island, off the coast from Cairns. I had arranged to fly out on the small aircraft he'd chartered, to pick him up and connect with a flight to Darwin to inspect one of his newspapers. We were to talk at Cairns Airport while he waited for his plane.

The Zwars owned an elderly but elegant, Toyota Crown sedan, used as a family car; and an untidy little Moke runabout driven badly by the staff of the free newspaper we owned; at weekends it was used for carrying sacks of chicken manure for our garden.

On the Big Day, Delphine needed the Toyota, so I parked Moke at an airport that was then only sheds and hangars. I climbed aboard a Bush Pilots Airways Cessna for Lizard Island, sitting up front with the pilot. We touched down on the tiny resort runway and a wind-blown Rupert Murdoch was waiting, briefcase in hand, suitcase ready to be loaded. He wore a suit and tie and a light tan from several days on a game-boat. He had an uncanny resemblance to Sir Keith; challenging, shrewd eyes, a set firm mouth. He climbed aboard, sat across the aisle from me and we took off. "Hi!" he said. "Good to meet you. Thanks for coming." A polite man but I got the impression he was nervous. He smiled a lot, but I noticed that many of his smiles were shy grimaces; a man who talked and thought fast, adding drawn-out extensions to words, giving his listener a chance to catch up. An end-of-sentence purr. "It was a very big problemmmmm." A man not at ease, but seemingly trying to bridge an uncomfortable gap between powerful media baron and the last cadet reporter his Father had hired for the Melbourne Herald before he died.

We shouted at each other over the noise of the twin engines for an hour, sharing the pilot's Thermos of black coffee, and then bumped down on the Cairns tarmac. I had faxed him my CV and a list of books I had written, and he said he now knew 'a fair bit' about me. We had an hour for discussion before his Darwin plane took off and he parked his suitcase with an Ansett desk clerk. Then he said, in his light, American drawl, "Look, I haven't seen a newspaper for days. Is there a newsagent nearby?" There wasn't one at the small Cairns airport, but there was one five minutes up the road. I said I'd drive him there—then suddenly realised it meant travelling in the grubby little Moke.

Too late to worry. The billionaire, used to chauffeured limousines, climbed over the side, strapping himself into a dirty, doorless little runabout, with its flapping side-curtains, clouds of chicky poo swirling around us. Then climbing out at the newsagent's, to buy an armful of papers and magazines, the assistant doing a double-take when she saw the Murdoch face on the cover of The Bulletin she had just sold him. As we chugged back to the airport he said, matter-of-factly, "I've checked you out. Think you'll do a good job. I'd like you to write Father's life." I forced myself to keep the wandering Moke straight ahead on the road.

When he was again due back in Cairns a month later, he had put aside time for a personal interview about his own memories of his father. I planned a lengthy talk in my study. A bottle of good Riesling rested in the fridge; the Toyota Crown had been polished, its tank filled with petrol, sheepskin seat-covers vacuumed spotless. I set off to pick him up in style this time from the Ansett terminal. I parked the Toyota in front of the arrivals gate of the airline he then half-owned, and met him. Warm smile, small-talk about the trip as I opened the door for him. I hurried around to the driver's seat as he strapped himself in. I turned the key. There was a sickening 'rrrrrrr.rrr' sound. And the motor died. *Dead battery.* A car leaving the airport was being driven by a neighbour who had seen her husband off to Sydney. I ran to wave her down. She opened the front passenger door for Rupert. Her small daughter stood beside him in the front seat, hitting him over the head with her woollen doll all the way up the mountainside to our home.

Could he use my phone, he asked? I offered to go outside, but with hair still ruffled, he waved at me to sit down. He made calls to several executives in Sydney and when he'd finished, talked to me about the father he remembered, explaining Sir Keith's determination to provide for his family; his shyness; his business gambles and his enemies in the Sydney newspaper world. Rupert also began talking about himself and some of the newspaper stories he'd been involved in, several of them *'exposés'* he'd worked on in the background and even 'broken', (one of them the notorious Khemlani Loans Affair). Rupert Murdoch, reporter; and from the telling, it seemed that this time might have been when he was at his happiest.

"My Father," he said, staring out the window to a riot of tropical allemanda and bougainvillea. "Was at times terribly badly advised; financially. He only had about five percent of The Herald shares, whereas if he had put his money into what he knew about instead of pastoral properties he had invested in, and rather than trying to be a Collins Street farmer, he would have died a very rich man."

Rupert's mother had earlier touched on her own worries about Sir Keith's borrowing. "In those days, bank overdrafts were much more frightening than they seem to be today," said Dame Elisabeth. "The way people

operate on overdrafts terrifies me, and I think it would
have terrified Keith. I could not sleep in my bed knowing I owed anybody money." She wasn't to know that
her own son was to one day soon face his own terror of
the banks when he, too, found himself at the edge of a
financial abyss.

But now the talk with Rupert was over, the bottle of
Riesling finished. There remained only one way to get
him back to the airport from our hilltop hideaway ... the
Moke. He nimbly climbed into its tatty passenger-seat
once more. "I'm beginning to think the Moke is compulsory," he laughed.

I had on tape the memories of the men and women
who had worked for Sir Keith, revealing the scary power
The Herald & Weekly Times chairman exerted over their
lives. Sir Keith probably knew few of our names, but to
cadet reporters, starting off on the first rungs of a career in
journalism, he was an awesome, greying figure, glimpsed
only in the lift or on his way down the reporters' room for
one of his 'getting to know you' visits. "Ah," he would
say, coming to a stop by your desk. "What are you on
[writing about] at the moment? What books are you reading?" Young reporters enthusiastically answered "Hem-
ingway." or "Scott Fitzgerald." And the last question as
he got up from the desk. "What are you driving these
days?" as though a cadet earning £5 a week changed his
car, even if he had one, as regularly as Sir Keith might
change his Rolls. "Still the old VW, Sir Keith."

Some of the memories from the interviews I had with
The Herald staff, past and present, created delicate deci-
sions of inclusion in the book. Along with the anecdotes
of Sir Keith's forays into the newsroom, came still-sur-
prised recollections of his behaviour that bordered on
the eccentric. He often seemed pre-occupied. Hearing
about the business deals he was doing at the time, when
he paid big money for newspaper shares he could ill-

afford, it was understandable that newsmen and women might have had the impression that while he was talking to them he was, to put it politely, thinking of something else. I recalled one morning, when I was head-down, typing, he strode through the reporters' room with startled newsmen quickly grabbing phones or suddenly bashing at upright typewriters. He noticed the dumpy figure of The Herald's Social Editor Miss Lois Lathlean, coming towards him.

"Ahh," said Sir Keith, coming to a halt. "Miss Lathlean! How's your mother?"

"Well ... Sir Keith," the diminutive Lois began, staring up through horn-rimmed spectacles at the tall figure towering over her. "Mother passed ..."

"Good. Good. Haven't seen her for ages. Tell her to get in touch with Miss Demilo (his secretary) and we'll have afternoon tea."

"But Sir Keith, Mother d ..."

"Good morning to you! I look forward to seeing her." And he went on his way.

I talked to Rupert's nanny about her memories of the family. She told me that when Rupert was about four he was 'extremely naughty' and she'd had to put him over her knee.

One of Sir Keith's former senior executives revealed to me that Sir Keith had serious political ambitions. The grand figure at the helm of arguably Australia's greatest newspaper already wielded heavy political influence; state premiers and prime ministers made their way to The Herald building to see him. But it wasn't quite enough.

One morning, said a former colleague, he'd heard Sir Keith talking to the editor of The Herald's sister paper, The Sun News-Pictorial, mentioning that 'some people were saying' it was time he might think seriously about entering Federal politics. "Well, Keith," said the Editor, (one of the few close enough to the press giant to call him by his first name) "I don't think so, yet. You are of course terribly well-known in the newspaper and business world, but not so well known among the ordinary people who would be asked to vote for you."

"Ahh," said Murdoch, having thought about it for a two seconds, "you could be right. I know! We won't go to the Melbourne Club for lunch today; we'll go down to the Athenaeum." A shift one notch down the social lunching ladder would fix everything.

I sent my finished manuscript to the Melbourne publisher and waited. Brian Stonier, Managing Director of Macmillan, had taken it on himself to be sure a copy was air-freighted to Rupert in New York and he would pass on to me his reaction. It came back on fax: Mr. Murdoch is 'seriously worried' about some aspects of the book and could you make yourself available at his mother's home the following Sunday to go through it? I felt slightly ill.

I was bidden to the delightful Cruden Farm, 2,000 kms away, where Dame Elisabeth still lived. It lay vine-covered and white-chimneyed near Frankston, outside Melbourne, and was reached by a long, tree-lined avenue. Sir Keith's widow had been charming and helpful when I had gone to see her and even loaned me some of her late husband's letters. Now, with apprehension, I flew down, and set off in a hire car for the meeting, getting lost twice on the way. I had brought with me two tape-recorders, one to place in front of Dame Elisabeth and the other near Rupert to record what each said as they made their way through the 150,000 words.

Rupert at the time, had a strike on his hands at the New York Post which he now owned, and was in Melbourne to face an inquiry into television network ownership. In between these concerns he was to juggle the problems of 'In Search of Keith Murdoch'

Mother and son came to the front door and we went into the lounge-room with its comfortable, old-fashioned furnishings, for coffee. Small-talk over, I asked Rupert if he could begin by going through his worries about the book. He'd already said as we sat down, "You talked to Kimpo, my old Nanny, did you?" I confessed I had. "Well," he said, shaking his head. "It's just not true that she put me over her knee. But I guess I was rude to her ..."

"What did you say, to her Rupert?" his alarmed mother wanted to know.

"I called her an old bitch, Mother."

"Oh, you didn't!"

"I did, because she was. But she didn't spank me. Father actually took away my roller skates for four days as punishment. By the way," he went on. "That little story about going to the Athenaeum for lunch. Father would have meant that as a joke." I nodded and made a note. It was now getting cold and the fire was dying a little. "Rupert, would you go out and get another log?" said his mother. Her son obeyed, and rattled the fire into life again.

He put down the poker and said: "Shall we go into the dining-room and have some lunch? What'd you like to drink?"

I said I would enjoy a glass of wine, thanks. "But maybe we could we go over the problems you found with the book, first?"

He peered at me over his glasses, surprised. "We just have. Otherwise it's fine."

Chapter 18

Doctor In Disgrace

I drove into town to get the papers and saw the front-page headline as I tossed them into the car. MCBRIDE ACCUSED OF FAKING — Thalidomide doctor inquiry.

Dr. William McBride? The Thalidomide Hero? Surely not?

The news story said that the former medical celebrity was accused of being a forger. He had allegedly been swept out of his scientific depth by his obsessive search for potentially dangerous drugs, and had gone on and faked laboratory statistics to prove his findings.

This was the famous Dr. McBride who had been honoured for his warning that the sedative drug Thalidomide poisoned the foetus, causing babies to be born with rudimentary digits where arms should have been; or without arms or legs; babies with one eye and short flippers on their shoulders; babies with only toes protruding from their hips. Babies born deaf, or blind. Following McBride's alert, Thalidomide had been taken off the world market and the Australian doctor became internationally renowned, heaped with honours. He opened a birth-defects research centre in Sydney and then quickly set about investigating other drugs that might be harmful to a baby growing in a mother's womb. Millions of dollars were raised for his work at Foundation 41, and McBride was seen constantly in the public eye as he pursued what was a relatively new medical science: the study of anti-cholinergics — drugs that cross the placenta and harm the baby. His gynaecological practice in smart Macquarie Street boomed.

Now — a faker?

I wondered whether my former newspaper colleague Phillip Knightley, who had written the definitive book on the Thalidomide scandal, and who had gone to school with McBride, could know about this? I phoned him in London.

"I am absolutely astounded," said Phillip, who, because of the long Thalidomide saga, and the campaign by his newspaper, the London Sunday Times, knew him better than any other journalist. "I have talked to Bill and he denies it."

Phillip Knightley's work for the Sunday Times had resulted in him being twice honoured as Journalist of the Year. His coldly efficient investigations were renowned for their accuracy. He said, "I just can't believe it."

I came away from the phone and said to Delphine that I felt there might be a book in the McBride fiasco. "What are you waiting for then?" she said. "Go for it!" Thank God for a trusting partner!

I sat down and read The Australian story in more depth. McBride (said the paper) had become suspicious some time ago, of the foetus-threatening potential of a mass-marketed morning sickness drug, Debendox, and had taken on its maker, the giant drug company: Merrell Dow, putting under suspicion their drug used by pregnant women worldwide for the past 27 years. He was claiming at least one of the drug's ingredients was harmful. Court actions had begun as mothers with deformed children came forward blaming Debendox as the cause of their babies' malformations. Cases, in which McBride was called to America as an expert witness, resulted in millions of dollars' damages against the huge Merrell Dow company, and the eventual removal of Debendox from the market.

So what had happened now, to McBride and his integrity?

The inside pages of the paper told the story; McBride's research work and ethics had been called into question by The Science Show, a radio programme put out by the Australian Broadcasting Corporation in Sydney.

Dr. Norman Swan, a Scots-born paediatrician turned journalist, announced that he would be talking about a morning sickness drug sold by the multi-national drug company, Merrell Dow, and which had been removed from the market, 'not because any government removed it, but because the manufacturer couldn't afford to keep defending law suits'. He went on, "One of the few researchers in the world to claim that Debendox is a substance that can cause birth defects is Australian doctor, William Griffith McBride, gynaecologist, Director of Foundation 41."

The ABC programme then methodically set out to examine Dr. McBride's credibility as a scientist, introducing one of his Foundation 41 research team who had worked for him on a rabbit experiment, designed by McBride.

Lab assistant Philip Vardy was the 'whistleblower' and came on air and said that during a research experiment, on the orders of McBride, six rabbits had been injected with Hyoscine, an ingredient of common motion sickness preventative preparations available over the chemist's counter. A further six rabbits had the drug mixed with their drinking water. One of the oral-dosed rabbits had produced a malformed litter.

Vardy then proceeded to itemise the evidence he said he had, which he believed showed his boss guilty of scientific forgery. Dr. McBride, he said, had written in a medical paper that there had been eight rabbits dosed with Hyoscine when in fact there were six. The doctor had included two rabbits he (McBride) claimed were experimented on by a friend, Dr. Jan Langman, at the University of Virginia in the United States. Dr. Langman had subsequently died.

I began my own file on the McBride saga as the papers were now full of it. Almost from the moment the radio programme ended, a press and radio campaign had begun with Dr. Swan at the centre, calling for a full inquiry into the ABC's fraud allegations.

The timing was, for Merrell Dow, one of the biggest pharmaceutical companies in the world, fortuitous. At this time in the United States, court demands for huge damages from the manufacturers of Debendox, were being heard and among the expert medical witnesses claiming the drug was teratogenic, was again, Dr. McBride.

Merrell Dow's lawyers acted fast following the ABC broadcast. In at least two courts, they introduced tapes of the Science Show and 50 pages of transcript as evidence, thereby throwing a doubtful light on the Australian doctor's credibility as an expert.

Back in Australia, the clamour for an inquiry into Vardy's allegations had reached such a crescendo that the worried Board of Foundation 41 began moving for an investigation to determine the correctness or otherwise of The Rabbit Experiment.

An approach was made to The Right Honourable Sir Harry Gibbs, former Chief Justice of Australia, and he agreed to take on a private inquiry for the Foundation, sitting with two medical authorities, neither of whom were teratologists. Merrell Dow accepted the invitation to give evidence.

Sitting in camera, the Gibbs Enquiry heard individuals giving statements that did not have to be sworn. McBride himself was questioned for 2¼ hours. He was not permitted to have a lawyer present to cross-examine witnesses. He could have refused to appear on the grounds that he was being denied legal representation, but (he was to tell me later) he felt if he did this he would appear guilty in the eyes of his peers. "Believing quite honestly I had done nothing wrong," he said. "I decided to go in unrepresented."

To his dismay Dr. McBride was found guilty of faking his experimental results. Worse, he had been warned by his lawyers that he was in grave danger of a further inquiry and that he could be struck off the Medical Register. The Gibbs Enquiry found that he had published statements he knew were untrue or did not believe were true. And he had, they declared, 'deliberately falsified' the contents of a scientific article.

Why would a man with such a reputation do that? Why would he need to do it? He had been the 'image' of the birth-defects Foundation he had founded with his own money 17 years before, and which over the years had used millions of dollars of donated research funds.

At dinner, Delphine and I now had one of our serious 'pre-book' discussions. Sydney was an expensive distance from Cairns. We had no idea how long any interviews with McBride would take, or how often I would have to travel there, particularly to attend court hearings. But yes—'let's do it!'

I bought my Ansett ticket to fly to Sydney. The thin premise of going to see Dr. McBride with the idea of writing a book had no more weight than my hunch that things are not always as they seem on the surface; nothing more, at this stage, than an inexplicable feeling that the story behind the story might shed a different light on the affair than the verdict handed down by Sir Harry

Gibbs. And as is the case with most non-fiction books an author sets out to write as I did, without a publisher's commission, it was a gamble.

By now I had researched and had published 10 non-fiction books. Why not go to one of my publishers with a proposal? The decision by any publisher is rarely instant. It requires editorial meetings, the place for such a book on forward lists ... half a dozen reasons that could mean hold-up, somebody else coming up with the same idea or the subject (McBride) not wishing to collaborate.

I telephoned Dr. McBride and when I was put through to him his reaction was hardly enthusiastic; he warily promised no more than to give me an appointment.

Flying over Townsville, I opened the book written by Phillip Knightley and the Sunday Times Insight team, 'Suffer the Children', published in the aftermath of the Thalidomide scandal. It described how Dr. McBride had been approached in August, 1960, by a drug-company salesman offering Distaval (the Australian product name for Thalidomide). At the time, McBride had one of the largest obstetrics practices in Australia. He had been [said the authors] aware of the drug and had read advertisements hailing its potential in The Lancet and The British Medical Journal. The salesman sitting in his office, introducing his product, praised the drug's effectiveness as a sedative during labour, having already convinced the medical superintendent of The Women's Hospital, Sydney, known as Crown Street, to try it. He had left a bottle of 200 tablets for the dispensary.

A fortnight later, McBride, supervisor of resident doctors, saw a pregnant woman whose vomiting could not be stopped. If it was to continue it threatened to bring about a miscarriage. He remembered Distaval and decided to try it. After two doses the woman's vomiting ceased and in April, 1961 the woman gave birth to a normal child. Impressed, McBride began to prescribe Distaval for pregnant women who complained of morning sickness, nervousness or inability to sleep. It was effective and had no reported side-effects.

On May 4, 1961, McBride attended the birth of a baby called Wilson. He was concerned to see the child had abnormalities of the arms, the radius bone was absent in each forearm and its bowel had no opening. After an emergency operation it died. In his seven years attending births at Crown Street, McBride had never seen such a peculiar combination of malformations; even though two to three malformed children were born in the hospital each week.

Twenty days later, he attended the birth of another malformed child, Baby Wood. Its malformations were strikingly similar to those of Baby Wilson. It also died after an operation. Then on June 8 he delivered a third malformed child, Baby Tait, again with limb deformities and an atresia of the bowel.

Disturbed, McBride spent the next weekend going over all the research material he had on malformations. He ordered the hospital records of the three mothers and the drugs they had taken before giving birth. Each had taken only one drug — Distaval. 'I was certain in my own mind, though I couldn't yet prove it, that Distaval was responsible for the malformations. That was all it could be.' It was Queen's Birthday long weekend, and on the Tuesday McBride went to see the medical superintendent of Crown Street and told him of his belief.

Dr. John Newlinds phoned the hospital pharmacy and ordered the immediate withdrawal of Distaval from use at Crown Street. Newlinds said later, 'Everything I know about obstetrics and gynaecology I learned from Bill McBride.' McBride was certain [he told the Sunday Times writers] that after his conversation with Newlinds he telephoned the Sydney offices of Distaval's makers, Distillers Company Biochemicals (Australia) Limited and asked the company to stop promoting the drug 'until we find out what is happening'.

He was told Distaval had been used in Britain for two years and if it caused malformations these would have already been in evidence. However McBride's suspicions would be passed on to London. On the same day, McBride said, he wrote a paper for The Lancet setting out his theory about Distaval-caused malformations in Sydney and began tests with the drug on animals. This paper, he says, was rejected by The Lancet. And DCBAL went on enthusiastically marketing its drug in Australia. When two more mothers who had been taking Distaval gave birth in September to malformed babies, McBride was convinced of the cause and angered that the company would not heed his warnings. He talked again to DCBAL and anybody who would listen to his evidence. Five months after his first report of his worries about Distaval, the company took a detailed statement from him and sent it on to London.

McBride then sat down and wrote a brief letter to The Lancet which was published in the weekly on December 16, 1961. In technical medical jargon it spelled out the birth horrors McBride was seeing. It was to be the first public warning about the dangers of Thalidomide.

That was the background of the man I had an appointment to see. Its complexity was to remain in my mind through our association as inquisitor and subject, a relationship that was to prove exasperating, stormy at one stage, and lonely for both of us in the face of his ridicule.

On the day of our first meeting I waited in the cool, austere foyer of the Foundation 41 building in Crown Street, Sydney. It was a stifling summer day outside.

Dr. McBride's solicitor, whom I also approached, had been matter-of-fact on the phone. If I wanted to meet the good doctor I should make my own arrangements. He relayed an unmistakable message that he and Dr.

McBride had had enough of the media. I glanced around and noticed on the lobby wall a large colour photograph of Dr. McBride, peering into a stereo-microscope at slides of chick embryos. It dominated the room. Around the instrument were broken egg-shells. I saw that on the day the photograph was taken, McBride had been wearing a Band-aid on his left index finger. Beneath the picture was a message: "How does a single cell develop into a human being? What goes wrong when the result is less than perfect?" It seemed apt; judges of William McBride were now saying McBride was less than perfect. The doctor who had been honoured around the world, was to all intents, in public disgrace.

Shortly after one o'clock in the afternoon I was shown upstairs to Dr. McBride's office. William McBride was standing by his desk. There were typed documents, newspapers and files strewn about and even stacked on a chair. He hurriedly moved them so I could sit down. The small room seemed to be in upheaval. His greeting seemed at once shy and nervous; his voice had that high note that signalled awkwardness. He wore a blue suit, had dishevelled grey hair and a set jaw, and he used his hands as he talked. He was thoroughly polite, but ill-at-ease, probably preferring to be looking through the lens of his microscope than to be talking with yet another journalist. Bags under his eyes showed worry and lack of sleep.

In front of him lay a copy of that day's national magazine The Bulletin with an article headed: The Good of McBride. It had a picture of the author, Phillip Knightley. I mentioned that Phillip was an old friend. "Oh," said McBride, brightening. "You know Phillip? I will be talking to him tonight in London." [I felt he was telling me that for a reason: he would check me out with Knightley. I found later that he had.] He said he was awfully busy, but would meet me again next day at my motel. The interview had only taken minutes.

He arrived looking dishevelled and still weary, took off his coat and said he wanted to take me to Foundation 41 to show me the white rabbits involved in the experiments he had been accused of faking. We hadn't even broached the subject of a book, but maybe he had already made up his mind.

We got into his car and he explained that in his crusade to prevent further drug-induced deformities in babies, he had been feeding the experimental rabbits with Hyoscine, a drug contained in most seasick remedies.

"Some drugs have been on the market for years and never tested for possible birth defects," he said as we walked around the rabbit cages. "Hyoscine, which has been around since the Ancient Egyptians used it, is one of them." He had first begun to suspect it when a woman had taken tablets called Benacine (containing Hyoscine) to settle her morning sickness. She had bought them from a pharmacy at the Sydney Harbour ferry quay, which sold them over the counter and without prescription to passengers worried about sea-sickness. The woman had been pregnant for about a month at the time she purchased the remedy. Eight months later her daughter was born with deformed toes and fingers.

I noticed McBride still seemed oddly cheerful, despite what he had gone through. He explained that he had been working for years to understand what drugs could do to the nerve cells, but when he had done a search on world medical literature he could find no reference to the effects of Hyoscine as a teratogen (causing monster defects). Yet this man in the rumpled blue suit standing by the rabbit cages had been branded a forger; had been found guilty of deliberately falsifying the results of what became known as The Rabbit Experiment. He had, said the Gibbs Enquiry finding, falsified the amounts of water and Hyoscine fed to New Zealand white rabbits through drinking spouts at the end of upturned milk bottles poked through their cages.

"I'll show you how ridiculous that was," he said. He strode over to a tap, filled a glass with water, drank some of it and then threw the rest on the floor. "There," he said. "You don't know how much I drank and how much I spilled, do you? It was the same with the rabbits. Nobody (in the research team) had thought of taking into account the fact that every time a rabbit brushed past, and knocked the drinking spout in its cage, some of the drug and water spilled out; on to its coat or on to the floor of the cage.

"I admitted altering the documents of doses. And time after time I explained why I did it. I knew the data recorded as the water intake by the rabbits were 'guesstimates' and I just made provision for this by averaging out. I stand by everything written in the paper I wrote, describing the experiment, and the resultant rabbit deformities. There were problems in assessing exactly how much the rabbits had swallowed. I disagreed with other workers' assessments, so I made my own. That may not be perfect scientific procedure, but it's certainly not fraud, because I didn't change the figures to deceive anyone. I changed them because I thought they were wrong.

"Dr. Jan Langman did experiment on two rabbits for me in America. One of them gave birth to a malformed litter. His letters were in the papers that were removed from the Foundation as 'evidence' by Vardy."

In the Gibbs Enquiry and a later Tribunal that would take years to deliberate, evidence was given that two of McBride's researchers had measured the wet patches beneath the drink bottles in the cages to determine what amount of liquid had been lost. The argument over the scientific value of that estimate and McBride's claim that he therefore needed to average out dosage, was the crux of the allegations and his eventual ruin; a career downfall that McBride darkly alleges had its roots laid down long before the Hyoscine experiment.

Sir Harry Gibbs and his two colleagues had, in their finding, met head-on the concern McBride had in some way been brought down by the drug company, Merrell Dow. Their finding said: 'It is claimed by Dr. McBride that the pharmaceutical company, Merrell Dow, is endeavouring to destroy his credibility because he has given evidence, and may again give evidence, in actions brought against that company in which it is claimed that one of its products, Debendox, otherwise known as Bendictin, is teratogenic (causes birth deformities) and that Dr. Swan and Mr. Vardy are assisting Merrell Dow. Indeed, we felt at times that Dr. McBride was concentrating more on endeavouring to establish impropriety or bias on their part, than on answering the allegations against himself. Mr. Vardy was in fact approached by Merrell Dow in 1984 and has since appeared for that company as a witness.

'There can be no doubt that Merrell Dow had a motive to discredit Dr. McBride. Merrell Dow has indeed sought to have his testimony rejected in proceedings brought against them and has relied on the discrepancies in the (Rabbit Experiment) article for that purpose. However, neither Merrell Dow nor Dr. Swan has any first-hand knowledge of the matters the Inquiry has to decide, and as we have indicated, the facts on which we rely in making our findings do not depend on their evidence or on the evidence of Mr. Vardy.'

The Gibbs Committee had dispatched one of its officers to try and establish whether or not Dr. Langman had in fact experimented with two rabbits on Dr. McBride's behalf before his death and Merrell Dow had sent its own representatives to the University of Virginia on the same quest, exhaustively interviewing colleagues and his secretary. The Company handed over to the Inquiry affidavits saying there was no evidence of such an experiment.

Next day Dr. McBride said he was hearing mysterious 'crackles' on the line when he lifted his phone. He told an interviewer he believed his phone was being tapped. "The whole campaign against me has been too well orchestrated. The timing is extraordinary. It would be a tragedy if Foundation 41 closed because of this, but it would be a delight for the drug companies."

The Gibbs Inquiry was unequivocal: McBride had deliberately falsified the paper he published regarding his findings in The Rabbit Experiment; the experiment was not done in accordance with proper scientific method and was not honestly reported; Dr. McBride was lacking in scientific integrity. He was guilty of scientific fraud.

By the time I met him, Dr. McBride had resigned his research directorship of Foundation 41 and removed himself from the Board.

"What keeps you going?" I asked him when I turned my tape-recorder on for our first interview. He scratched his nose. "It's my desire," he said in his high-pitched voice. "To see all children born healthy, which is why I published my Rabbit Experiment paper as an early warning. I see this as much more important than Dr. Swan's and Vardy's professed desire to see the preservation of the sanctity of science."

Six days before the Gibbs Inquiry had handed down its finding, Dr. Norman Swan had been awarded the Gold Medal in the prestigious Walkley Awards for excellence in journalism, for his exposure of McBride. "He destroyed me," said Bill McBride. "He got a prize. I hope he's happy."

I phoned Dr. Swan and asked if he would let me talk to him? A few days later he came to my hotel, a small, highly-strung man with a strong Scots accent, wearing spectacles with bright-red frames. I asked him how he felt, now that McBride faced further disgrace by the possibility of being struck off the medical register. Did he feel a sense of achievement? Swan was obviously unhappy with the question, but he said, "What I set out to achieve was several-fold. A gross injustice, in my view, had been done to junior scientists. They have all had major disruptions. It's scarred them all. The administration of science at Foundation 41 was quite clearly inadequate, and this was taking a considerable amount of the available research money for the city of Sydney from other research institutions which were peer reviewed and well run. It is important for the public to realise that they ought to be a bit more wise as to where they spend their charitable monies for medical research. And the other reason is that in Australia we have yet to set up a body to actually do something about scientific fraud."

As Dr. Swan's radio programme went to air, two more cases against Merrell Dow were being tried in the US, and the drug company had asked him, he said, to give evidence of McBride's character. He did not accept the invitation. "It was not," he said, "my duty to appear in court for a drug company to further their ends in litigation." He said he was particularly sensitive to the innuendo that he was 'in the company's pay'. "I have been careful as a medical journalist to always keep an arm's-length relationship with the drug industry. You have to be seen to be independent. Sometimes I do things for the industry on a commercial basis; for instance I might make an educational video which is sponsored by a drug company. But I am always careful to be in control of what goes out on that video.

"I have been careful, long before McBride started telling the world that I was being paid by Merrell Dow, to do this. So all I needed, after a programme like that, was to be flying off to Texas, courtesy of Merrell Dow."

If Norman Swan was refusing to go to the US to give evidence in courts, Merrell Dow had an easier time persuading key-witness and 'whistleblower', Philip Vardy.

Vardy, a 38-year-old biologist, having departed Foundation 41 and then studying for his PhD, was confined to a wheelchair, having been crippled in a motor-cycle accident. Three weeks after The Science Show broadcast Vardy was asked by Merrell Dow's lawyers if he would repeat in a video-taped deposition, what he had said on air. He agreed and flew off to the US, First Class. He gave sworn evidence at Santa Monica to be used in eight cases in which the company was being sued.

I met him at Sydney's Macquarie University Biological Sciences Department, where he was studying. Vardy wheeled himself though his lab doors to meet me and said straightaway that McBride's life had been 'a fragile pack of cards which has now collapsed because of an action on my part.' An intense, balding man he angrily denied that he had stolen the research papers for The Rabbit Experiment, which were used in the Gibbs Inquiry as evidence. "I was advised to remove them for safe-keeping and that is what I have done. I do claim I am entitled to possession of them up to the point where an independent inquiry determined whether or not a fraud had occurred."

Now the Department of Health was also interested in pursuing the McBride matters. He went on, "I think Bill has become obsessed with birth defects. Whether it is a way of trying to ameliorate his guilt, I don't know. But I know if I, as a young, ambitious obstetrician, cockily prescribed an untested drug (Thalidomide) to my patients and found that ahead of my colleagues I was responsible for malformations, I am not sure what would happen. Bill McBride, I think, is a Macbeth haunted by a bad dream."

By mid-1988 William McBride knew he faced further serious problems. He had been alerted that the New South Wales Government Department of Health had begun to interview colleagues, patients and Foundation

41 employees. The Department's Complaints Unit was headed by a tenacious public servant, Ms. Merrilyn Walton, who pursued errant doctors and had them struck off. Now she had written to McBride:

"This unit has been conducting an investigation into allegations of scientific fraud in relation to the (Rabbit) experiment. We have also been investigating a 'Debendox' experiment ... the third area of investigation concerns your practise as an obstetrician." (Medical records at two leading hospitals for women were being analysed and statistics prepared in relation to the rate of caesarean section at each institute.) "Indications are that your caesarean rate is extremely high. Eight individual patient records have been sent to senior specialists for their opinion ... we shall consult with the Medical Board in relation to your care and treatment of each of these patients."

McBride had indeed used caesareans with a considerable number of deliveries and he had good reason to do so, he said. In the meantime he did not have to be told how grave these charges were; if they were proven he could be struck off and disallowed to practise as a doctor.

Ms. Walton told a newspaper that after he had received her letter, Dr. McBride had 'virulently and publicly attacked the Complaints Unit.' But she admitted, "For anyone who is under investigation it is unpleasant and awful."

Bill McBride was not calmed by her sympathy. "This woman, Ms. Merrilyn Walton, a woman who has no medical training and who has been a social worker, is behind this persecution," he said to me. "It is extraordinary that she can spend two years laying charges against someone for carrying out their medical practice in which no-one has died and no-one has looked like dying. One baby died prematurely. I think, if I lose, God help the medical practitioners of New South Wales.

"I worked with doctors involved with fertility, I naturally had patients recommended to me who had—after much effort and medical help—became pregnant. One patient was 38 and having her first baby. In those days a caesarean was considered a major operation. I didn't do a caesarean and the child died while the woman was in labour. I felt terrible about this and fortunately she managed to get pregnant again and had a caesarean the next year and had a baby."

As the newspapers published details of the investigation and the allegations Dr. McBride faced, he said his practice 'has almost disappeared. Some doctors who have always supported you for years still send you patients, others have not, and their patients have told me their doctors feel there must be something in these allegations. It is hard to take. The Gibbs Inquiry and the Tribunal I must face has had a terrible effect on my family, and on Pat. (his GP wife) All my true friends have stood by me. I have played a couple of games of tennis, but no golf. I spend most of my spare hours with lawyers.'

I went off to attend my first session of the New South Wales Medical Tribunal that was to eventually cost a massive $6 million to hear 18 complaints against Dr. McBride. It sat in Sydney's Old Supreme Court No.1, a room that had seen better days. Paint flaked off the walls with six-inch pieces hanging precariously over the heads of witnesses. High up in the ceiling a bird-spattered skylight allowed weak sunshine to filter through dead leaves and the droppings. The Bench—comprising the neat, often testy, white moustachioed figure of Judge Wall and three colleagues: Professor G D Tracy, of the Royal College of Surgeons, Dr. Ewan Sussman, a Fellow of the Royal College of Obstetricians and Gynaecologists and Ms. M. Brophy, representing the public—was protected by an ornate, dark-brown timber awning that had the same carved elegance as the pews in the body of the court occupied by spectators, Ms. Walton, and Dr. William McBride.

They were to sit there, off and on, for a total of three-and-a-half years. Two years devoted to the gynaecological charges and during which, Dr. McBride underwent a heart by-pass operation.

On the day of the final verdict the tall, white-haired doctor walked to the court with his lawyers through a phalanx of television and newspaper cameras and took his place on the hard bench he had sat on for years. Merrilyn Walton was a few feet away and they studiously avoided one another.

The Judge announced that first the Tribunal would deal with the nine obstetrics charges, (distilled from 44 'worst performance' cases from the records of 2,000 cases handled by McBride over 10 years).

At the end, all these charges were dismissed. There was one admonishment; that he had left a patient waiting in hospital when he had gone overseas without arranging 'proper care'. The Judge said this was a 'minor and isolated lapse and out of character with his normal practice.'

Then came the charges arising from his experiment with Hyoscine. "The evidence," said the Tribunal, "establishes that Dr. McBride arbitrarily mis-described the experimental method and data and included spurious data in the preparation and publication of the Article." It believed he did it to: "enhance its publishability". It called the inclusion of experiments on two rabbits McBride said were done by the late Dr. Jan Langman "fraudulent" and "reprehensible". The Tribunal said he was an unreliable and evasive witness and that it was "highly unlikely" that Dr. Langman carried out such an experiment.

McBride got to his feet after the verdict and left the court shattered. He had been told that 'sentence' would take place at a later date: there was the grim possibility of being struck off.

He later returned to the musty No.1 Courtroom to listen to pleadings about his character—bad and good. By the lunch-time adjournment lawyers were still arguing and McBride and I went to one of his clubs and ate a meal of fish, cherry crumble and ice-cream. He chose not to discuss the Tribunal and instead talked about the Depression and Gallipoli.

With us was Frank Devine, former Editor-in-Chief and now columnist of The Australian. He and I had sat in the uncomfortable Press seats together for day after day listening to the evidence. At lunch he turned to McBride and said, "How's the book going, Bill?" Long ago Dr. McBride had agreed to co-operate with me and give me exclusive interviews; I reserved the right to be able to portray him critically if need be.

I answered for McBride saying, "It's cost me, but I think it'll be worth it."

"No," said Devine. "I mean Bill's book."

Bill's book?

"Oh well," said Bill McBride a little shame-faced. "I haven't perhaps told you. I'm writing my own book. Telling my side of the story. I don't think it will interfere with what you're writing."

I couldn't believe it. Bill McBride knew of my huge investment in writing a book to factually tell every side of the medical saga. Surely he would realise that another book—by him—would make mine redundant? Incredibly he did not. [And he went ahead and published a 'vanity' book, as it is known in publishing, selling a tiny number of copies.] I was still reeling with the man's insensitivity and lack of judgement as we went back to the Court.

Judge Wall was shaking his wigged head over the arguments now being put to him. "I have never struck such a case in all my legal experience," he admitted. He said he was going to adjourn the Tribunal to assess the situation.

Still disturbed from his vanity book revelation I went back with Bill McBride to his apartment to have dinner with him and Pat. His small grand-daughter, being 'baby sat' for the evening came in and sang "Baa, baa black sheep" into my tape-recorder and the doctor gloomily sipped a whisky. I asked him how he had survived it all. "It has been a terrible strain," he admitted. "Last night I didn't sleep. And the night before that. The Judge wondered why I had asked Dr. Langman for his help. Well, people do this. For confirmation. And he was interested. He said he would do some work on it."

"If they strike you off, what will you do?"

He looked at the floor for about 10 seconds, and when he looked up again there were tears in his eyes. "Well, I would be very angry and very unhappy and be very depressed. I would resign from the Foundation. I would walk out completely."

On a chilly July morning everyone filed back again into the dreary courtroom. Only one figure was missing. William McBride had flown off, by invitation, to a conference on medical genetics in New Hampshire, then to conferences in Oxford and Edinburgh. "It is a great honour," he said before he left. It was a move, to me, as odd as publishing his own book.

In his absence the Judge and his associates delivered their verdict after sitting for 198 days — the world's longest disciplinary hearing. "The Tribunal," intoned Judge Wall, "has given anxious consideration ... on the question of Dr. McBride's character and with profound regret has come to the unanimous view ... that Dr. McBride is not of good character in the context of fitness to practise medicine. Dr. McBride's character mirrors the classic tragic character — the person of eminence in public life, whose good deeds and interest in human welfare command respect and admiration, but is brought down by a fatal flaw in character."

He was to be struck off the New South Wales Medical Register.

When I got through to him in London that evening he said he was shattered by the verdict, but he would not appeal. "I just can't believe it," said the 67-year-old doctor. "I can't believe it."

Disgraced, but still allowed by law to use his 'Dr.' title ("the only way that is taken away from you is death") McBride applied in 1996 for re-instatement, but the NSW Department of Health's Tribunal said no, he would not be allowed to practise again yet. "I was told I had not shown enough remorse for my actions. What are you supposed to do?" he asked me, in his high, querulous voice.

Though he was barred from practising again as a doctor, the white-haired McBride stubbornly carried on with his experiments with Thalidomide at the now deserted laboratory of Foundation 41.

Working with colleague, Dr. Peter Huang, a chemical pathologist with a background in carcinogenesis who he had persuaded to stay on, McBride now claimed that their research with the drug had uncovered a new, frightening aspect of the horror it caused 40 years ago: that it can be embraced by the genetic system and, he suspects, is causing second generation malformations.

Their research with rats and rabbits had shown, he claimed, that Thalidomide damages the DNA strands of embryo cells, probably causing genetic mutations in the reproductive cells. If that happens in humans, he reasoned, Thalidomide malformations can be passed on from a grandmother who took Thalidomide in the 1960s, to her grandchildren in the 1990s.

Foundation 41's Sydney building had to be sold when the McBride scandal slowed donations for research into birth defects to a trickle. With nowhere to carry out their experiments, McBride and Huang flew off to England where pharmaceutical companies had initially promised them facilities to continue their Thalidomide investigations. "But when we got there we found that people higher up thought it too much of a hot potato," said McBride. "No-one wanted to get involved." He and Peter Huang were told privately by a pharmaceutical company representative: 'There are a lot of people who want you to be wrong.'

"So we went off to America to a lab recognised by the Federal Drug Administration, injecting it into pregnant rats' tails, then tracking its progress through their bodies. Thalidomide was found in the DNA extracted from the embryos. We later did the same thing with rabbits. That is where we got our significant findings; we used radioactive Thalidomide."

How does Thalidomide pass from one generation to another? Dr. McBride says it binds with DNA and damages the cells' genes that develop into ovaries and testes, depending on if the drug had been consumed at the time the primitive cells were about to become male or female. In Australia, there are 35 surviving Thalidomide victims, but no cases of second-generation deformity. However there have been, he says, 11 babies in England, and two in Italy, born with deformities that mirror their parents'. Some have come from Thalidomide-deformed mothers, some fathered by Thalidomide damaged males. Doctors opposing his view say the similar deformities are genetic. McBride does not agree. "In all the cases we have examined there is no history in any of the families of malformation before the grandmother took Thalidomide."

Drs. McBride and Huang published their paper in the specialist journal Teratogenesis, Carcinogenesis and Mutagenesis, and McBride had a letter on their findings published in The British Medical Journal 'on the condition that it also carried another by someone with an opposing opinion.'

I wondered what drove a doctor at his age, still smarting from what he believes was huge injustice, to go on spending years and thousands of dollars of his own money on such a quest? "The only way to prove that Thalidomide altered DNA in humans would be to use them in human experiments like those done on rats, an ethical impossibility," he says. "So instead, Peter Huang and I would like to see an international database set up to monitor the offspring of Thalidomide victims who 40 years after the drug was used by their mothers, are having families of their own. Then we would really know."

In the meantime he said he had vowed to go on pursuing the Thalidomide question that he has lived with since 1961. "When you see that these little white tablets can produce such horrendous malformations, you want to know how."

Though Thalidomide was banned as a morning sickness drug, it has been quietly brought back into medicine on an experimental basis. "It's been used to treat leprosy, here and overseas, for some years," says McBride. "It relieves the pain in some types of leprosy and helps with skin ulcers. I am cautiously optimistic about what it can do for AIDS patients where it is being used to help them gain weight by treating their mouth ulcers; they find it easier to eat. It is being used for advanced cancer and for tuberculosis. Once it gets FDA approval it will be able to be prescribed by doctors in the US for their patients.

"I am also optimistic about its therapeutic possibilities. It is a fairly simple chemical compound but, as we have seen, can cause tragic malformations. It ruined so many lives, including my own. Let us hope it can do someone some good in the future.

"We still don't know a lot about malformations; it has been my life's work to see what causes them. I think Peter and I have solved the question of how Thalidomide, and quite a few other chemicals, bind with DNA. There are thousands of chemicals coming on to the market which are tested on things like salmonella bacteria, a frequent cause of food poisoning; but they have not been tested on their combination with the basic building blocks of life."

McBride, then 71, never allowed himself to give up hope that he would one day be re-instated and allowed to practise once more. He had gone off to work in Pago Pago, in American Samoa, in early 1998, where his deregistration did not prevent him from working in obstetrics. After five weeks there, promising to return, he flew back to Sydney. In November he went once more to face the New South Wales Medical Tribunal; this time ready to 'be contrite' and admit that he had deliberately falsified his Rabbit Experiment.

In a unanimous decision, the four members of the Tribunal found he had 'finally gained sufficient insight into his actions' to apologise for the fraud. He would be re-instated as a doctor and allowed to practise medicine again.

The Tribunal announced: "He (Dr. McBride) has now frankly admitted that it was his dishonesty which caused his deregistration and that question was put as baldly as that to him and he has responded as baldly to it."

His re-instatement came with three conditions, including one that prevents him from undertaking medical research again. He would now be subject to approval of the Medical Board before he performed surgery and would be supervised by the Board for as long as it was deemed necessary. Outside the court a relieved Dr. McBride said, "It is a great stigma to be struck off, particularly after practising for 35 years with some distinction and honour. The original judgement was a life sentence. It has been five years of hell. I did a stupid thing; but I thought I did it for a good cause. I didn't want to see any more malformed children."

My book on Dr. William McBride, which in time and expenses cost Delphine and I about $20,000, was never published. Publishers, quite rightly, considered one book on the saga was enough.

* * *

In March, 2003, William McBride collapsed in a coma after suffering a severe brain haemorrhage and was put on life support. He emerged from unconsciousness and began talking to his family. Six months later he was well again and back in court; preparing to sue those he was claiming had defamed him.

Chapter 19

'That Snead Ain't Worth A Shit Either!'

"Golf," says Peter Thomson, Australia's most lauded golfer. "is an all-demanding endeavour that has no beginning and no end. It can devour a man with its insatiable appetite, or slowly torture and destroy him as surely as a disease."

How true! For myself, I caught the disease when I was about 10, the day I took my Mother's old hickory-shafted clubs out to the local course and began bashing at golf balls. I have been doing the same thing ever since. (Without a lot of improvement.)

And how could I have ever imagined that I was to find myself spending a year with Thomson on golf courses around the world? And, incredibly for a hacker, become a member of the renowned Wentworth Club outside London. Never stop hacking or hoping; something good could happen: all hackers believe The Secret may well reveal itself during the next round. Then the Pro Tour.

The Wentworth Golf Club is a revered course. Newspapers refer to it as 'the exclusive' Wentworth Club. Princesses, deposed dictators and the very, very rich live behind high walls and hedges on its 700-acre estate. And it was always out of the question for me to think of ever playing there, let alone having the gall to actually join the club; my golf was confined to the crowded public golf course at Richmond Park, gathering at dawn with other hackers. We wore jeans and trainers and nobody gave a thought to whether such dress might be acceptable. At Wentworth it would be a different story...

On the Daily Mail, I had begun a friendship with Peter Black, the television critic; who surprised me by saying he was a member at Wentworth; surprised, because Peter had only one arm. One of Fleet Street's most polished writers, he could be seen pecking out his column with his left hand on a clacking old manual typewriter. Peter had been born — years before the cruel effects on babies of Thalidomide — with the same legacy; a tiny, fingered hand at the top of his shoulder.

However golf, like typing, was no problem for the 50-ish, beetle-browed Black, who was a man who could be as awkward and as cutting in conversation as he was in his critiques. He was known not to suffer fools gladly and was treated warily by the Mail staff. His boss, the Features Editor, was so scared of him he would have one of his underlings phone Peter with suggestions, rather than risk a querulous one-on-one discussion.

I met Peter in the passage-way one morning and he asked me if I would like a game at Wentworth. He was a member and there were three courses to choose from: the East, the West (the long and tough Burma Road where the Piccadilly World Match Play was played each year) and a nine-hole course. On Saturday we would play the daunting Burma Road, 'if you feel up to it, Old Boy.'

I was immediately concerned about the standard of my game and how my hacking would be viewed by the wealthy English members. At Richmond Park, nobody cared.

I arrived early and parked outside the castle-like club-house, which boasted several bars, a grand ballroom and the centrepiece — a high-ceilinged baronial dining-room. Near the car park stood a far less grand building for the Artisans Club. Plumbers and carpenters played early in the morning before the Members time-sheet took over. There was not a lot of mixing.

Peter Black had earlier warned me that the clubhouse complex was ruled by the formidable Mrs. Williams, a manager who struck fear in the hearts of the staff, and every member from humble tradesman to multi-million-aire. "Be bloody careful if you run into her. She'll have you for breakfast, old chap."

Should I have doubted Mrs. Williams' right to enforce the Wentworth rules, I only had to read the framed item from the London Evening Standard in the passage-way outside the locker room, which I did with a few minutes to spare before our 8 o'clock hit-off. The cutting was from the paper's gossip column and it reported that Edward VIII, The Duke of Windsor, had been having a golf lesson at the nearby Sunningdale Golf Club one Sunday morning. The Duke had then invited the professional teaching him, to come to Wentworth, where he was a member, and join him for lunch.

They had just settled down, and were enjoying a sherry, said the article, when Mrs. Williams sailed in. "Your Highness," she said. "May I have a word?"

"Of course," said the Duke, smiling.

"Golfing staff," said Ena Williams, looking at the uncomfortable Sunningdale pro, "are not allowed in the Wentworth dining-room, I'm afraid you will have to ask your guest to leave."

And they did. The Duke took his pro across to his own castle, Fort Belvedere, where they had a quiet, less traumatic lunch. Phew!

And so it was, with Peter Black's nomination and a seconder, followed by a formal and rather stiff interview with the Committee, I became a Wentworth Member, parking my humble VW beetle next to Rolls Royces and Jaguars in the car park and being attended by Sutton, the well-off locker room attendant, who smoked only Cuban cigars.

Peter lived a few minutes from Wentworth, while my flat in Chelsea was half an hour's drive away. We had arranged to meet on the first tee at 8 o'clock. I waited nervously, then I saw Peter drive up; 10 minutes late. And I mentioned it.

The dark eyes under the cat-like eyebrows were raised. There was a moment's uncomfortable silence as he locked his car. Then he turned and said, "Sorry Old Boy." And it was the beginning of a friendship that was to last 30 years. Nobody had dared criticise the critic before and he welcomed it. Particularly from a 'bloody Australian.'

On the next Sunday I had put my name down in the Starter's Book and found myself playing with a trio of American oilmen; they were about the same standard as myself, which was a relief. After the game, we adjourned to the Golfers' Bar where dress rules were relaxed; no jacket and tie required.

One of the Americans was Bill Alexander, a hail-fellow-well-met Texan who sold mud to the oil industry (to cool the drills), and who chewed and spat plug tobacco. Like me, Bill was a new member, and as we settled into our chairs Bill noticed the formidable Mrs. Williams behind the bar talking to a barmaid. To everyone's horror, he hailed her: "Hey, old gal, get us a rum and coke will ya?"

There was a stunned silence in the small bar. Long time members stopped breathing, awaiting the coming explosion. There was none. "Of course, Mr. Alexander," said Mrs. Williams. And got him his rum and coke. It was the bully syndrome again.

Next morning, back in the office, I wandered across from the Daily Mail's news desk to the sports department to chat with golf writer, Michael McDonnell.

"Did you see that story in the Express about the young advertising executive who has given up his job to join the US golf tour as a caddy?" I asked Mike.

Mike said he had. The article said it was the man's belief that being a caddy would improve his game (his handicap was already a championship 2) and rubbing shoulders so closely with the pros, he felt, could lead to him eventually turning professional.

"What a life!" I said to Michael, whose one game with me had demonstrated my enthusiasm for the sport, if my lack of ability. "Wouldn't it be great to get so close to the pros? To live, eat and breathe golf and get paid for it. What a book that chap could write!"

"Well," said the paper's Mr. Golf, who was rather close to them himself, "why don't you do the same thing? You're still a bachelor, aren't you? You're nutty about golf and seem to know a bit about it. Ask your mate, Peter Thomson, what he thinks."

Englishmen have the odd belief that every Australian knows every other Australian, particularly if they're together on the other side of the world; and that they are 'mates'. They forget the size of the country. I had never met Peter Thomson in the flesh. I was aware of Thomson's fame, that he was five times winner of the British Open. Also, that he was a bit of a loner; like Peter Black he didn't give much time to fools. I admitted that no, Thomson and I were not 'mates'. But Michael was now running with his idea. "He's playing at Moor Park this week. Why don't you come out with me and I'll introduce you. See what he thinks."

Hang on! It was just a discussion! But Mike was now determined to check out the possibilities.

Peter Thomson, a good-looking, well-proportioned man with strong shoulders and brown, curly hair, was slogging balls on the practice fairway when we arrived. Embarrassed, I put the concept to him. He leant on his driver and rubbed his nose in thought. "I'll think about it overnight and let you know in the morning," he said. And went back to work. I got the impression that he was his own man, and a deadly serious one.

We met in the locker-room next morning as he was getting ready to go out and play the final round. "Look," he said, reaching into his locker for his spikes. "I've had a think about what you said; and I've had you checked out. Problem is you're off a 20 handicap, not a good golfer. As a caddy you need to be on top of what you're doing. As you know," he went on, pausing to do up the white shoes. "I write a column for The Age back in Melbourne, so I can write a bit. I've often thought of doing a book on the world tour; but you can't play golf and write at the same time, except for the small bit I do now. What about we go and do one together?"

Just like that. He'd checked me out overnight! Knew my handicap. I was impressed. And he wanted to work with me on a book! How long would we be on the tour? "Oh, about a year. Start on the Far East tour, then go to India, Kenya; the US and finish up at the British Open at Carnoustie. What d'you think?"

I thought for five seconds and a month later returned to Melbourne to join up with him. He invited me to his holiday home at Portsea, where he was spending Christmas and New Year with his wife Mary, and their three children, before setting off on the 50,000-mile tour. He had arranged a game of golf with friends and asked me if I'd like to play with them? Conscious of my sickening shank and long handicap I declined. I said I'd caddy for him if he wanted.

I noticed on the way around that everything Thomson did was purposeful. He strode purposefully, stood purposefully at the ball, swinging at it simply, powerfully and neatly. Nothing out of place. Then strode forward again. I'd read that Henry Longhurst, doyen of British golf writers, had once suggested, after Peter had won his five British Opens, that he write an instruction book. Thomson told Henry he'd give it some thought. Next morning he met Henry again on the course. "Oh I've written that book you were talking about yesterday, Henry," he said. And handed Longhurst a single page which, in a few paragraphs, explained how he took his stance and grip and swung at the ball. There wasn't much more he could say. For Thomson golf was as natural and uncomplicated as breathing. Surely you didn't need to think about it?

At Portsea I was frustrated by the difficulty I had finding the correct club when he asked for it. The soles of the irons were so worn it was almost impossible to see the difference between a 3 and a 4. The wedge had long since lost any marking at all. When we got home, he told me to 'chuck' the clubs under the house. I asked him, "Why do you use such an old set of clubs when Dunlop, (the company he played for), will surely give you anything you want?"

"No, they may be old, but they're the ones I use all the time," he said. They'd won several Opens. "You see, you groove your swing to the club, you get used to it. A new set can throw things out of kilter."

He wrote, "My clubs are in fact nine years old. I supervised the making of them in Sydney in 1959, and they became the prototype of the sets made by the Dunlop company with my name on them. I can't match them by having new ones made because it isn't possible to make one club exactly match an old one. There is always a variable in metals and wood. If someone steals my irons I will never be able to match them exactly." (And I'd "chucked" them under his house!)

Thomson made one thing clear to me about our collaboration; he didn't want to be 'ghosted'; he didn't want the book to be a 'first person' as told to, book with me doing the actual writing under his name. I'd done that with two earlier books and it was a split-personality exercise. To make that type of book sound authentic you have to become your subject; think the way they think; write the way they speak. I agreed with him. We decided to have what he was saying—his expert opinion of play and the efforts of other golfers—appear in italics. My descriptions of what happened on and off the course would appear in ordinary type so the reader knew who he or she was reading.

And it worked.

We travelled together, shared motel rooms at times, but tended to go our different ways socially. After 20-odd years on the world tour he had made lifelong friends and admirers who wanted to entertain him and they deserved to have him to themselves.

We flew from Melbourne to Singapore, Peter clutching the Life of the explorer Eyre, under his arm; me a small tape-recorder. He was to later write. "Three times a year I say goodbye and my small son weeps and says he doesn't want to go to school. He doesn't know why and it tears my heart so that I wonder why I am doing it to him, and whether it is worth the anguish."

And he went on with what happens on the tour. "You learn about life and human frailty, and wickedness and cunning and craft and all the other short cuts social man has contrived. If you're lucky, you'll learn about honour and trust and other high levels of behaviour. Most of all you'll learn about yourself."

This was an unusual professional golfer indeed. Among scores of different males from many countries whose topics of conversation seemed to be limited to golf and sex, Peter Thomson was a deep thinker and philosopher who even carried around with him heavy reel-to-reel tapes of performances of the (I felt) rather depressing composer Mahler. And yet the same man would come off the course, shower, lie on the motel bed with a tumbler of whisky and have the American television on full blast, waving a finger, shooting at 'baddies' thundering past in an ancient Western.

We had no sooner stepped off the Qantas jet at Singapore than we were whisked, baggage, golf clubs and Mahler into an air-conditioned limousine and out to an exotic restaurant for dinner. "You'd better get the hang of chopsticks," Thomson told me. "Otherwise you'll starve." I was hungry and when the first large shared dishes arrived, I had several helpings, believing that was it. It wasn't, they were just the first of some 20 courses.

Day One: Singapore Island Country Club's Bukit stretch was bone dry. A million gallons of water were being hosed into it every night from giant tankers brought in by the golf-mad Prime Minister, Mr. Lee Kuan Yew, handicap 12 and referred to coyly in the newspaper reports of the previous day's Pro-Am as 'A.N. Other'. This morning, members in turbans, Bombay Bloomers, safari jackets and shorts, were gathered at the practice tee by 8 AM watching the golfers loosen up, comments coming across in Chinese, Malay, Hindi and English. Cyril Horne was there, squatting on a shooting-stick and smoking cigars through a holder. The old British pro at Bukit was telling me out of the corner of his mouth about the PM's swing: "Backswing a little too rigid and exacting in the first 45 degrees. It contracts his muscles and is inclined to put him out of position at the top." Cyril had been a fixture in the East for the past nine years teaching sultans, Asian kings and directors of the big mining companies. He had become a rich man. He had given Sherpa Tensing, the man who conquered Mt. Everest with Sir Edmund Hillary, his first golf lesson. ('Good concentration'). Cyril's party trick was to sit on his shooting stick and smack a ball 220 yards down the fairway with a 5-iron, demonstrating there was no need for force from hips and body.

Out on the course, an enthusiastic crowd following Thomson watched dismayed as he shanked a ball. Facing an easy shot to the green on the 436-yard seventh, he had sized it up characteristically, left shoulder high up, right shoulder down, swung the club and ... "Ohhhhh!" A collective gasp came from his audience as the ball shot 45 degrees into a clump of trees to his right. Surely a shank only happened to people like his literary collaborator, not to a world champion? He said to me afterwards, "It happened because I was asleep. A shank sometimes occurs when a ball is higher than your feet and nearer to you, than you really want it. If you're a bit asleep and don't make the proper adjustment before you swing, you can be half an inch out laterally. Instead of hitting the ball in the middle of the club face, you're hitting it too near your feet, and consequently, the shaft. It was lack of attention."

The shank that day was the beginning of the end. He needed ten birdies to catch the leader, 'YY' Hseih from Taiwan, and there were only nine holes left to play.

* * *

Our flight-path from Singapore through what the British called the Far East, took us on to Kuala Lumpur, Malaysia, where Thomson was scheduled to play in the Pro-Am 'opener' with the Deputy Prime Minister, Tun Abdul Razak. Arriving on the tee the Deputy PM greeted the Australian with, 'I've just come back from Singapore where I took a ball off the P.M.' Making up the four was the diminutive Lu Liang Huan of Taiwan and His Highness, the Sultan of Selangor, a big man in wrap-around sunglasses, watched over by two bodyguards. He is not a good golfer. The Sultan stands with his hands far ahead of the ball at address, body drawn back for a furious lunge at the ball which surprises Thomson by going quite a distance. Tun Razak displays abject nervousness as he goes to the tee, and has a reaching, rigid address position, his body shaking as he prepares to swing. Somehow, again, the ball sails into the distance. The four move off, with caddies, umbrella bearers, fore-caddies and bodyguards.

There was a BBQ that night under the stars at the home of the Selangor club secretary on the edge of the 10th.fairway, and I was seated next to Sir Henry Lee, founder of Malaysia's ruling party and one of the chief negotiators of his country's independence. Tackling a chop, he told me of the 'precarious situation' in 1956 when he had flown to London to talk to the British government about the future of his country. The fate of Malaysia hung on what happened at another, grander dinner party. "In London, you see," said the small, greying 67-year-old. "They wanted us to have independence. But I didn't want it yet, we were broke. What could we do without money?" he asked me, sipping at his brandy-and-ginger. "On one particular night in Chelsea I went to a dinner with the official negotiating team and I was sitting next to a senior cabinet man. I told him, during the fish course, 'I'm off in the morning.' 'Where?' he said. 'Back home to KL.'

"'Why, for goodness sake?' he asked. 'The talks aren't over yet.'

"I said, 'No. But there's no need to discuss it any further. We haven't been offered any money. We can't afford independence without money. There would be political chaos, perhaps bloodshed.'

"The government man then excused himself," said Sir Henry, grinning. "He went to the phone and returned during the meat course. He said, 'I am sure there must have been some misunderstanding. You have an appointment at nine tomorrow morning with the Prime Minister, Mr. Macmillan, at No.10.'"

Around us that evening there were animal noises coming from the bush and the clear, starry sky seemed a long way from London. Sir Henry chuckled, "I talked with Macmillan next day and he offered us an immediate 37 million pounds. And that was how Malaysia became independent of colonial rule."

Next morning British golfer Peter Allis flew in from Hawaii, with a brief stop at Saigon airport, amid the turmoil of the Vietnam war, which was, by air, 1 hour 20 minutes away. "I saw burned out aircraft, military planes surrounded by sandbags, and jeeps buzzing about bearing machine-gun toting police, with bloody great green cigars hanging out of their mouths. It all seemed so incongruous. There were young Australian and New Zealand soldiers arriving to fight a war and here I was, a transit passenger, wandering quite freely about the airport. The week before, a couple of rockets had landed on the roof, leaving a bloody great hole in it.

"You saw on one side, burned out aircraft, and on the other, bored American guards hanging about ogling the wiggling bottoms of stewardesses as they walked up the stairs. It looked like they were just playing at war."

* * *

We fly in to Bangkok where the Bangkok Open is to take place on 18 holes sandwiched between the International Airport and the Thai Air Force runways, making it the world's noisiest golf-course. A hooked drive on the first tee can career down a connecting runway, past the green, 350 yards away and require a nine-iron to get back and out of the path of arriving jets. "It was not so long ago," a local told me. "that Sunday golfers had to dive for cover as a fighter coming in to land sprayed them with bullets. The pilot had inadvertently pressed the wrong button."

"It is," says Thomson, waiting for a caddy to fish his ball from a klong (canal), "a ragtime course."

At the pre-tournament cocktail party I spot a vivacious call-girl who has flown in from Hong Kong. In tiny mini-skirt and high heels she giggles that golfers 'are fun'; they also have plenty of time on their hands for 'little distractions'. She is standing a few feet away from a Scotland Yard-trained deputy chief of police. I drift over to him and ask, "Which system is the best? The American system where police are armed, or the British where they go unarmed?" He merely opens his safari suit jacket, revealing a revolver lying in a holster over one breast and a suspicious bulge beneath his shirt on the other. "Does that answer your question? My enemies have a $10,000 price on my head. It is wise to be ready."

Fanling golf course is up near the Chinese border, where Thomson is to play the Hong Kong Open; if his damaged wrist allows him. He has doctor friends all over the East, but apart from temporary relief after an injection of cortisone, none has been able to get rid of the unexplained soreness that causes him to use a driver to putt with.

In some desperation we are on our way to see Mr. Leon Seng, an old-fashioned bonesetter and osteopath, practising in the 'Suzie Wong' bar district. "Your doctors would call me a quack," says the iron-grey, crew-cut Mr. Seng — who fixed a British Ambassador's slipped disc and has a grateful letter to prove it — as he twisted the painful wrist and brought tears to Thomson's eyes. Then he stands up, hands behind bristling head, effortlessly pulling his head down between his knees. "You must do that a lot. Spine is problem, not wrist."

The advice doesn't work. Thomson performs Mr. Seng's exercises night and morning, but on the second day, the agony of pain forces him to give up. His arm goes into plaster.

We move, with a jangle of 80-odd sets of golf clubs, and golfers from the US, Britain, the Philippines and Japan and set off to Taiwan for the China Open. Kimono-style dressing-gown/pyjamas are laid out on our hotel beds and nearby, stone baths full of hot spring water are prepared to ease the travel weariness. The bubbling water smells of rotten eggs, leaving you refreshed but weak. A mama-san knocks on the door from her post in the hallway enquiring 'if golfer need girl for the night?' She has several takers, and the girls arrive on the back of motor-bikes driven by their minders.

And the tour hops on: from Taiwan to Tokyo, from Tokyo a long haul to New Delhi where we land, eyeballs feeling as though they have sand in them and go through Customs where every golf club has to be inspected, identified by registration number, noted in a book and signed for to be identified again on leaving. On from India to Kenya, to the Karen Country Club where there is a local rule: 'ANY BALL FALLING WITHIN TWO CLUB LENGTHS OF A SLEEPING LION MAY BE LIFTED AND DROPPED WITHOUT PENALTY.' "It's easier," a local member explains. "than having to shoo the lion away." I don't believe he was joking. The lions are said to frequently penetrate the seven-feet high fence enclosing their reserve and like to sleep in the rough jungle, bordering the fairways.

We fly into Indianapolis, USA, a world away from Africa, where Mr. Sam Snead is striding down the third fairway. 'Slammin' Sam' Snead is at this time one of golf's great characters. Egg-bald, he keeps his hat on at breakfast in the motel coffee-shop where we have adjoining rooms. "Goddam!" says a heavy-gutted admirer in a red T-shirt. "Will you look at that old man hit the ball?"

At the end of the day I find myself in a press tent with Mr. Snead and a veteran wire-service reporter who's taking him through his score-card. Sam, pork-pie straw hat on, with a brown Hawaiian motif bandana, is running through the 18 holes; without the aid of a card which is now in the secretary's possession. "Let's see, there. Driver, three-iron, chip two putts. Driver, wedge, one putt," recalls the millionaire pro. Then he spots my tape-recorder. "Whatyadoin with that thing?" I explain about the book. A scratch of the nose. "You any sortofa golfer?"

"No, Mr. Snead."

"See, I've got the worst golfer in the world at the club I represent. Hell, this fella must've had the world record if he ever kept count of how many strokes he took. There was no tellin' what he would shoot if he counted. Give him lessons and he couldn't even hit the ground!

"Anyways, he was watchin' television one night and he sees me give these lessons there, and he calls up the assistant pro.

"'Hey Jack, get the practice balls and meet me at the practice tee. I just saw that fella Snead givin' a lesson there and I got it. I finally got it.

"'Don't you try and tell me nothin', you cain't tell me nothin' about golf. Jest be there with the balls.'

"Anyways," Snead continues, a grin on his brown, leathery old face. "He gets to the tee and says to Jack, 'Jest tee one of those sonofabitches up.' He teed it up, and Jeez! He didn't even hit it!

"'Now wait a minute,' he says. 'I must've done something wrong. Tee up another.'

"And Goddam, he takes another whip at the ball and jest tops it off the tee.

"'Hell!' he says. 'That Goddam Snead ain't worth a shit either.'"

* * *

It's the night before the US Open, and there's a cocktail party at the Oak Hill Country Club, where I meet the gladhanders. 'Hi, Fred,' shouts a golf-ball distributor. 'Anything I can do for you, old buddy?'

Joe Di Fini is there, a huge brown Sicilian, eagle-eyeing the trousers as they walk past, for Joe manufactures 100,000 pairs of slacks every year and it gladdens his heart to see a pair of his trousers stride by. Joe and his sales manager, Jack Lust, Belgian-Jewish and with a patter that could sell sand to an Arab, are taking in the scene, highballs in hand. Jack, small and neat in wine-red jacket and grey Di Fini slacks, explains that Roberto De Vicenzo is one of the firm's professional advisers. "And I'm going to tell you something," says Jack, "that is one hell of a fine gentleman.

"And I'm gonna tell you something else," says Jack, looking around to make sure he's not telling the world. "You know what colour is IN next season for golf slacks? RHUBARB. Sure. It's gonna be rhubarb. We decided on it."

"We?"

"Well you don't think that the clothing industry hasn't got its head screwed on right do you? There are 'gatherings' of garment-trade executives, millers and wholesalers. The millers wanna know what the fashion colour is gonna be next year so they can run off and dye millions of yards of cloth and be ready. So we in the garment trade have this meeting, throw around a few ideas and come up with the Colour of the Year. Somebody passes the word to the fashion writers and the next thing you know somebody comes up with the great 'suggestion' that maybe rhubarb will be the 'in' colour next year!"

And Jack has one more piece of inside knowledge to impart to the hack. "You know why women's fashions are so crazy? It's because they are designed by effeminate men who hate women. Sure! Now you go away and think about that." Joe Di Fini and Jack Lust are nothing if not generous. They ask me what size slacks I wear and I tell them. Next morning there are three pairs in my locker, green, yellow and blue. No rhubarb.

In the afternoon, the blue slacks are no longer there. A tubby little Mexican called Lee Trevino, who has the locker next to mine, confuses the numbers and is wearing my slacks, tucked into his socks, good-naturedly hacking about in the boondocks for a TV crew looking for light relief.

He wins the US Open. In blue slacks that have been fixed so the cuffs (as they were given to me) are no longer left unfinished; they have been stitched to fit the stocky little legs of the 1968 winner who is overnight a millionaire.

The amiable Argentinean, Roberto De Vicenzo, told me that after he had won the British Open at Hoylake, he was back in the hotel exhausted, stretched out in an armchair, feet on his bag of golf clubs, caressing a well-earned beer.

There was a tap on the door and in came a Spanish waiter to refill Roberto's drinks cupboard. He immediately noticed the golf bag and the fact that Roberto was watching a Western on TV. "Oh Sir!" said Manuel. "You play golf? Not watch that on television. Have golf lessons on other channel. I switch for you!"

And he did.

Chapter 20

'Find A Pom A Week ...'

Delphine and I were up at dawn, padding barefoot around the house, enjoying breakfast by the pool; talking about the day ahead. She getting ready to work with a photographer on a House & Garden guest cook assignment; me on my way downstairs to the study, and back into the mind of Rudolf Hess ... my secret collaboration now into its fifth year.

We had the gift of a happy marriage and our son, Adam, had just left university and was also a newspaperman; (his choice, not mine). Because I'd had a family dynasty career hanging over my own head, I was determined our red-head should choose his own livelihood. When Adam asked what I thought he should do when he grew up, I'd answer, "Be happy!" But he had been involved in the phone dramas, heard the dinner-table stories and met newspaperman colleagues from all over the world; and he also got the taste for printer's ink, though acting, writing plays and films were later to emerge as equal contenders.

On Friday night, at the Zwar dinner table, we would open the traditional bottle of good red. And Delphine and I would get a little nostalgic for London. Whenever we had London friends to stay, they would tell us how much they envied our lifestyle and were astonished at our desire to 'one day' go back to Britain. The lure was there all the time; mental stimulation tasted and now absent. So on this night, like the others, out came the old subject once more: should we go back? "And if we did, what about money?" asked my wife.

Our sparkling blue pool, the whispering palms and blazing hibiscus outside our dining-room were 10,000 miles away from Cadogan Gardens, SW1, and our red-wallpapered apartment. A world away from chirpy Cockney humour; from journalism that nobody would deny was the world's best. But would anybody in Fleet Street still remember me? Probably not, I agreed (as always). And I got up from the table to answer the phone.

"Desmond? Louis Kirby here. Had a hell of a job finding you! Look old chap, the Daily Mail is putting out an international edition for Australia — it'll be called the UK Mail. And I'm editing it. Wonder if you'd like a weekly column? Sort of dispatch from your part of the world.

"How's the weather over there, by the way?"

Louis was one of my oldest friends on the Daily Mail and had become a Fleet Street editor.

"Would £150 a column be OK? You know, tight budget and all that ..."

I went back to the table and poured another glass. "To London!" toasted Delphine. It seemed like the first step and I noisily blew my nose. Next morning I started a list of Poms In Australia; I was to find one to write about each week.

* * *

We drove down to the Gold Coast on holiday and I saw the headline on The Gold Coast Bulletin's entertainment page: 'YOUNG MAX STILL SINGING.' It was advertising British singer/hoofer/comedian Max Bygraves — an institution like Buckingham Palace and the Goon Show. And I needed a 'Pom' for my column: Dispatch From Downunder.

Max ... 'young'? I'd met him back in London in 1960 when he was giving evidence in court for a lad he was trying to save from jail. And he was no chicken then.

'At 72,' the PR blurb assured his fans, 'Bygraves is still going strong.' Leaving the reader with the unfortunate image of an elderly singer-comic, tottering bravely on stage, voice trembling. A has-been, entertaining oldies. 'People with memories,' was how the publicity hand-out put it. But he was a Pom and I needed one this week for Dispatch. I drove down to the garish Leagues Club.

I got there to find the lifts in the gaudy entertainment-and-poker machine palace had broken down and the retirees and pensioners who had been bussed in, achingly climbing the stairs to the sixth floor. They paused gratefully for breath on the landings; welcoming the free cups of tea and coffee brought to them by girls bearing great pots. Walking frames and sticks left at the side of the auditorium, the capacity audience of gentlemen in slacks and sports shirts, then settled down with their ladies, who appeared to have just left the hairdresser, even at that hour in the morning.

And at last he came on.

A leap rather than a totter. Tall, trim, hair shining gold in the spotlight, the face looked exactly the same as I'd seen it in London 30 years before. He had on a white double-breasted suit (courtesy Austin Reed, as he showed me in the dressing-room later), and a bright green tie. He could have passed for 50. And that might have been stretching it.

Roars of welcome, claps and shrill whistles.

'Oh what a privilege and pleasure it is to be here!' he says, smiling the wide, naughty-boy grin. 'It's a pleasure to be anywhere!'

They roar, doubled up with laughter.

'I remember last year I was crossin' Leicester Square,' he begins. 'And some fella called out, "Oi! Max! You let us darn ..." I didn't know what the fella was talkin' about. What d'ya mean, I let you down?

'He said: "When Benny Hill and Frankie Howerd died we had you in a trifecta." He stands there, wicked look in the blue eyes. Waiting. And then goes on. 'Did you know that Eric Jupp' (the veteran accompanist across stage) and I were in the RAF together? I know what you're thinkin'. You're thinkin', what could two nine-year-old boys have been doin' in the RAF?'

The five-piece band strikes up "Jealous", and as though they've been rehearsing it with him, several hundred voices join in. He moves into a quick-step, the long legs as supple as a teenager's, the toes of his shoes tapping right on note.

'There was this fella,' he stops to tell them. 'Just about to close the Job Centre, you know, the CES. And he hears this voice, "You got a job for me?" And he looks around and all he can see is this duck. And it's the duck asking for a job! So the fella phones the Palladium and they actually need a talking duck! The fella tells the duck he will be paid a £1000 a week for a 14-week season. But the duck doesn't want it. "No good to me," he tells the fella. "I'm a bricklayer."

"Farrraway places, I've been dreaming about ..."

'There was this Australian,' (and he over-does the accent) 'waitin' at London Airport and he sees this beautiful girl sittin' there, and she's got a case with NSW on it. So he goes over and asks her if she comes from Noo South Wales. No, she says. The letters stand for Nymphomaniac Society of the World. She says she's been doin' this survey and she says the best lovers in the world are the North American Indians and just behind them, the Jewish race.

'By the way, she says to the fella. What's your name?
'Hiawatha Goldberg.'

He sings again: "You need hands ..."

Then he asks them: 'How old d'you reckon I am?'
Shouts of 72 from those who've read it. 'I am 84 years
old.' Roars of denial.

He's been on stage now for one hour 45 minutes and
appears reluctant to leave.

In the foyer after it's over, changed to open-neck blue
shirt and slacks, he signs $10 cassettes of his sing-along
songs for a queue of some 300. Then on his way to the
pokey back-stage dressing-room, he is shielded from
more followers by a minder. At last he settles in front
of mirrors, the shiny hair quite obviously his own, face
almost unlined.

I ask, 'When were the best times for you, Max?'

His blue eyes stare warily into the mirror at my reflection as he thinks. 'There's a lot to be said for the years
gone past. In the old days when we were in the theatres,
there were eight acts on the bill and there was always
somebody that you noo. That you could play golf with;
go off to a museum with. And have fun. There was always
lots of fun.'

He now had an 84-acre property at nearby Murwil-
lumbah, New South Wales; he'd bought it from an English couple who had set it up as a resort, but it had gone
into receivership. 'I swim in the pool, I play golf. I'm there
four or five months a year and then I go back to Bournemouth.' Was that the secret of his apparent agelessness?

He chuckles. 'Bert,' (his tall, balding minder) 'and I
were talkin' about this yesterday. Sayin' it's alright to be
doing this stuff and be under stress. But there has to be
some time in your life when you need tranquillity. You've
gotta have it sometimes. And I think I've had a lot of it
over the years. I've managed to live in places where I'm
not in a rush. I've got an apartment in London as well,

and it becomes a treadmill there, I can tell you.

'I write a lot of my own stuff. My friend, Eric Sykes, writes a lot. He's got some lovely approaches. My script-writer, Spike Mullins, died last year.

'You know,' he smiles as he turns around. 'There's nothing more rewarding these days, than to draw up a little routine, and go on stage and find that it's right. Though to get the laughs, you've got to wait. Gotta sit on it. You don't go out there and do 15 to 20 minutes and find it's easy every time; there are the silences. And when you're driving home afterwards, you think: "There was a moment there, and I missed it." That,' he said, 'is how you hone it. Try and get your act together ...'

* * *

Back home again I am on the phone to another Pom ... to Rio, and the Cockney grumble of Great Train Robber Ronnie Biggs bounces down the line. Britain's most noto-rious 'unofficial emigrant' says of course he is ready to talk about his new career in public relations; 'and that's no bullshit!'

Speaking from his exile where he entertains tourists ('a barbecue, all you can drink, a dip in the pool and the Ronnie Biggs Experience for $50') 64-year-old Ronnie is almost sobbing with nostalgia as he recalls the four ille-gal years he spent in Australia on building sites.

When the tears were wiped away he gets down to business. He'd just become South American agent, PR-man and shareholder (he told me over an echoing line) in an Australian invention, a revolutionary car engine that was going to change the world. And truly, 'it runs on petrol and water'.

Ronnie warned me, anyone who didn't get into it at $2.40 a share was a mug. So exciting was this inven-tion (by a New Zealand figure called Rick Mayne, now Queensland multi-millionaire) that some highly-titled Britons indeed, including the Duke of Marlborough, had hurried along to a London stockbroker's office a few months ago to get in on the action.

There is a complicated time difference between Brazil and London and I had mistakenly greeted Ronnie with a 'good morning.'

"Well, it's good evening if you want to speak to Ronald Biggs," said the old robber.

"You own shares in Split Cycle Technology?"

"Yes, I do, Sir. I don't know how many yet, 'cos I haven't received them. I am being given them so I'll talk about them."

He recognised my accent. "I would love to go back to Australia, I really would." Slipping into 'Oz' when every British detective was after him all those years ago seemed 'a piece of cake'.

"When my wife and family arrived in Darwin we drove down to Cairns. We went across to Green Island and saw the Great Barrier Reef. We looked at it from a glass-bottomed boat. I didn't fancy diving in, 'cos as a Pommie, I was frightened of those Noah's Arks.

"What I miss about Australia are the barbecues, the beaches, the Australian humour. I walked into a Melbourne urinal and there's this notice: 'Don't throw your dog-ends in here, people find them hard to light afterwards.'

"Australians work hard and play hard. I worked on building sites and the Melbourne airport hanging partitions and ceilings. The foreman would come around and if a fella didn't have his nail-bag on he'd reckon he was sick and send him home. He was hard on us; but at the end of the day he'd take us round the pub, order drinks for everyone and that same fella, who was cracking the whip all day, would pay the bill. That wouldn't happen in England.

"If I could be accepted back in Australia I'd go back, I really would. I appreciate the people and their philosophy. They rubbish the Pommies, but that is part of their humour. Australians have the best dirty jokes in the world."

Ronnie said he regularly talked to tourists from the UK who always asked him: Did he want to go back to England?

"When people ask me about England, I've got to say I really have no desire to see England again. Only maybe for a holid'y. In two years, when my son is 19, I face the fact that the Brazilian Government will ask me to move on to some country that has no extradition treaty with Brazil. That really narrows it down in this side of the world, to Venezuela or Costa Rica. And what if their presidents don't want me?

"They'll say: 'What're we gonna do with Ronnie?' I'll become The Most Unwanted Man!"

"In the meantime," he said, brightening, he was getting ready for the visit of 27 Australians taking part in the Biggs Experience tour arranged by travel agents. "It's one of my scams. Otherwise I'm not allowed to work. Fifty bucks and all you can drink. But I reckon I'm taking a risk with Aussies."

Mr. Rick Mayne, inventor, Lamborghini owner and listed in Australia's Richest to be worth $50m., had defended his decision to employ the old robber. He said that now he had Ronnie Biggs aboard if people didn't like it, well, "That is stiff bikkies. I come from a pretty hairy background myself. I have been pilloried in every Australian newspaper for being an ex-crook." (White collar fraud) "I did my time. I've come out. I've made good. I certainly don't stand on anybody else who's done their time. I realise the seriousness of Ronnie's offences, but I have no qualms about him being involved."

* * *

In a later Dispatch column I interviewed Cockney migrant 68-year-old Peggy Boakes, now living outside Adelaide.

Peggy's voice reminded me of a track on a record I'd treasured for years: Sounds of Our Time. It quoted a London taxi-driver who was making his way through devastated streets the morning after one of the Luftwaffe's heaviest raids on the East End. He said, "I saw this woman, sweepin' her front doorstep. And behind her, her house was almost disappeared. I thought, now I'm gonna hear if 'itler's father and mother were married ... but she saw me and shouted, 'You ain't seen my bleedin' milkman, 'ave you?'"

That was also Peggy Boakes' spirit. She admitted she and her husband didn't have much money; he still ran a small mechanical business. "But we're happy, luv." Then she said, "I'm phoning because you wrote the other week about Max Bygraves. I've been in love with Max for 40 years. Do you know when he's coming back to Australia? It'd be great to see him again before I die." I said I'd phone Max. And his answer was: "Melbourne in February."

So Peggy left Ron, 65, at home in Moonta, South Australia, (pop.2,500) at his small mechanical workshop and flew to Melbourne to stay with her son, getting two of the last seats for Max's sell-out concert. "I saved up my pennies. I have been a fan of Max's since I saw him in a second-rate movie playing the part of a sailor. I said to my friend: 'One day that man is going to be famous.'

"We could only get two seats three rows from the back. But he was lovely; so handsome in his cream suit, he looked 40, rather than over 70. When he came on he said, 'A friend of mine is in the audience today, she's 95 and she's brought along her grandmother.' I wept with laughter; my son, who is 29 and doesn't know much about Max, wanted to hide!" Had she gone backstage afterwards to meet him? "No." Peggy said she was too shy. "Oh you can't do things like that!"

Next morning, back home in Adelaide, she phoned me.

"This is gospel," she began. "I had just sat down at my computer to write to thank you for ringing Max for me in Bournemouth, otherwise I'd have never seen him and to tell you what a marvellous show it was; I wept through a lot of the songs. I had to turn my back on my son otherwise he would have been embarrassed.

"Then as I was about to type, the phone rang. It was my husband, Ron, from his workshop. And he said, 'Are you sitting down?' I said yes, I was. And he said: 'Well, have I got a surprise for you! Because you were so lucky finding out through Mr. Zwar when Max was coming back, and getting the last seats, I bought us tickets in the War Veterans Art Union.

'"We have won a million dollars!'"

* * *

I heard that Anthony Shaffer, the renowned British playwright and author of the world's most famous whodunit, 'Sleuth', was said to be living near us in the dark blue wilds of Miallo, in Far North Queensland; a somewhat spooky rural outland, seething with suspicion and with inhabitants showing plain hostility to strangers. Would I go and find out what he was doing, said Louis?

Rainforest-clad mountains, surrounded 'Karnak', the property Shaffer and actress-wife, Diane Cilento, called home. They had astonished the locals and not a few friends, by building a $1.2m. theatre—the Karnak Playhouse—miles from anywhere, with 500 seats, a dramatic stage crowned with a shiny brass sun; audio-visual box, a restaurant, bar, advertising department, administrator's office, faxes and switchboards. Karnak lies 20 minutes from the sleepy little northern outpost of Mossman, two hours from Cairns, set in the middle of cane-farms and tired old fibro cottages, and where the popular rumour was, that the couple were eccentric.

Tony Shaffer, when I arrived to meet him, was sprawled, white-haired on a sofa in his study, an airy room lined with books, a solid English desk, and a huge sculpted wooden manta ray. He sat me down on another sofa opposite, and walked around me a few times, then screwing up his eyes behind mauve-framed spectacles, drew in smoke, and pondered the question: "They want to know what on earth you are doing here?"

The man who wrote the renowned stage-play and movie 'Sleuth', 'Whodunit?', 'The Wicker Man', and adapted Agatha Christie books for the movies, then recalled for me the chat he and Ms. Cilento had after dinner four years earlier. "I said to Dee we just can't live in Rip Van Winkle Land all year around. There's no theatre to go to. (A suck on the cigarette). Not just because it is one's profession, but because it is also one's passion and pleasure. D'you know what I mean?"

La Cilento, the lady whose face goes on provoking love-affairs with cameras, had agreed. "Why don't we build one?" she said. Shaffer is trying not to be put off his train of thought by the harsh ring of the Fax behind him and the rat-tat of hammers and the whining electric saws across the valley outside, where they are building 'the monster we have created'.

On his knees rests a yellow-bound script, which four actors would bring to life in a fortnight, and from which he said he would read to me, his new play, 'Murderer'.

He recites the lead actor's opening speech that will launch it in London, and now having its world premiere at the Playhouse.

'To become a murderer ... that, in the last few years, has crystallised into my single, constant, unappeasable passion.

'Not a casual killer in a bar-room brawl. Or a senseless slayer in a squalid domestic squabble, but a great classic murderer ... who knows that once a man has killed deliberately, his inhibitions are destroyed.'

At midday, with the sun streaming in, there is, nevertheless, a chill atmosphere. Mists are swirling about the jungle-clad hills outside. I still feel the weird sense of hostility that seeps in from the lonely roads. On one-way bridges on the way to 'Karnak', where a driver pulls to one side to let a farm utility pass, instead of getting a wave or a nod of thanks one is greeted with a cold, suspicious stare.

It suits Shaffer down to the ground. He flies in and out of Cairns International Airport, 40 miles down the road, to London or San Francisco, as frequently as he might have caught a No.9 bus into the West End to his law practice years ago. What happened to that career? He draws heavily on his cigarette, going back over the somewhat painful memory.

"I had, you see, been engaged at the time in an undefended divorce action. There is, presumably, no easier case for a solicitor. Unfortunately there was this mix-up in court. There was this woman in the box, the one I thought was my client, and I was asking her questions we'd gone over about her husband's behaviour and astonishingly she was shaking her head. No, she said, he didn't do that. But what about the other thing? No, he had never done that either. I was getting a bit frazzled about all this when the judge suggested a short recess and invited me and the other solicitor into chambers. He said, 'I am afraid you have cocked things up!' I hadn't been questioning my client at all! It was another woman of the same name and I lost the case. Probably the first lawyer to lose an undefended divorce case in the history of British jurisprudence."

Tony took himself out of the Law Courts and across the road to where a cinema was playing 'hour-shows' of shorts and cartoons. While he was sitting in the one and fourpennies, licking his wounds, he idly noticed the Pearl & Dean screen advertisements. "They were terribly boring and I thought: I can do better than that." So next day he made a call to Britain's biggest screen advertising agency and asked for a job. "I told them I was a lawyer and that didn't excite them."

He was given a lowly position and found himself writing commercials for Durex contraceptives. Nevertheless his climb up the advertising ladder was spectacular. "I eventually found myself with a chauffeur-driven company car and earning an enormous amount of money. But I was not, you know, happy."

Tony's twin brother, Peter, was already an established playwright, living in New York. His 'Equus' and 'Royal Hunt of the Sun' had been hailed wherever they had been staged. Tony decided he might be able to write plays as well; he'd had one on his mind for 20 years. So he gave up his advertising directorship, handed back the car and rented a small flat in Putney to work in, sitting down at a typewriter for six months tapping out 'Sleuth'. When it was completed he bundled up the manuscript and airmailed it off to Peter, asking him to have a look and see what he thought.

Peter Shaffer read it and sent his brother a telegram, 'Welcome to the Club, Old Boy.' 'Sleuth' was staged all over the world and made into a movie with Laurence Olivier and Michael Caine. It left Tony Shaffer with the problem of writing a play that was better. "Otherwise they will be waiting to cut one down. The tall poppy thing, you know." (Annoyed suck on the cigarette).

He said that some weeks before I went to see him, he had been back in London for research and had attended the court trials of the Yorkshire Ripper, Peter Sutcliffe, accused of killing 13 women. "I wanted to see what a man who had done such terrible things was really like. He seemed a perfectly mild little fellow. Scruffy, really. Undersized. I couldn't see how he could have done that sort of stuff. While I watched him ... our eyes met."

Now the pages of yellow legal pads on the table

before us held the lines of 'Murderer', the play about such an inadequate serial killer who had an eagerness to be caught. He read from the pad: 'If I cannot be famous, at least my crime will make me infamous for all time. People will wonder enviously if they, themselves, can cross that great divide between timorous man and proud killer.'

When he'd finished he told me why a lot of locals plainly did not want the Shaffer-Cilento Karnak Playhouse. It meant strangers driving up from Cairns and across from Port Douglas. And strangers have to be watched. "The opposition was violent," says Shaffer. "I don't mean I was personally assaulted. But I do mean I have had poison-pen letters addressed to me. Of a vile kind. And there was an attempt to 'stitch me up' with a police charge. (An allegation of 'flashing' on a beach).

"There was some concealed agenda. And I didn't know what it was."

It was only after he and Diane had returned from a trip to New York that the scales fell from the bespectacled Shaffer eyes. A neighbour who had contracted to slash the encroaching jungle on the sprawling 'Karnak' property, took him to task. 'Naughty! Naughty! You shouldn't be doing that sort of thing.'

"What sort of thing?" asked a puzzled Shaffer. So 'one' was taken for a drive to one of the boundaries. "There was, of course, a marijuana plantation. Fenced off with bandicoot wire. Someone had been growing dope, not just on our land, but all around this valley." Police helicopters flew out bags of the stuff, arrests were made and charges laid, which still remained unheard. And reality at last sank in. "Of course they don't want hundreds of people coming in here. People means police."

Concerned that hundreds of theatre-goers cars would cause serious congestion on the narrow, one-way bridges and wreck their roads, the Douglas Shire at first said no to the Karnak project. Ex-lawyer Shaffer went to council meetings and dug in his well-shod heels. Were the narrow roads and bridges the only objection? They were. "All right. We'll use the Ballyhooley." The Ballyhooley, a little steam train that once hauled sugar-cane in and out of the nearby farms, now carries tourists in bright-painted, open carriages. "They'll be met by buses before the troublesome bridges and brought on to the theatre, just as they do at Glyndebourne in England."

But who will come?

"In this area there is absolutely no entertainment for tourists. Not even a cinema. We bring plane-loads of people from all over the world and at night give them nothing to do. And people living in Mossman, Port Douglas and even Cairns, 40 miles away, are starved for good theatre. At Port Douglas the Sheraton Mirage has someone playing the piano and a girl singing."

He found himself turning away these days, from the Hollywood he enjoyed when he scripted Agatha Christie's 'Death on the Nile', then 'Evil Under The Sun'. But he wasn't fazed by the future. "The Hollywood film industry is in a state of virtual terminal disgrace. I don't see it as a fit job for gents. I don't see it possible to write to accommodate the kid-world where there is an average IQ of 70 and a vocabulary of less. And that's just what they are trying to do. They achieve their purposes with violence and sex; ice-picks used on people who are in the middle of orgasm. Hollywood has lost its mind. A whole lot of middle-aged men, trying to second-guess and palliate whole generations of uneducated cretins. I think they should be ashamed.

"Here, we will show people what is enjoyed in the West End and on Broadway. Here," he pauses, seemingly still bewildered by the reality, "on Upper Whyanbeel road, Miallo."

Chapter 21

Vet In The Clouds

We were invited to a barbecue under the stars in Cairns and I found myself sitting next to Don Lavers, a vet. He was chatting about a horse he'd just treated on Cape York Peninsula, about 800 kms away.

"How long did it take you to drive there?" I asked him. It was, at the time, the Wet Season, and for months settlements and townships were isolated as downpours burst the banks of creeks and streams.

"I don't drive," smiled the craggy-faced Don. "I fly. Got my own plane." His vet practice was in fact twice the size of England!

He held the table fascinated as he recounted emergency dashes to injured or dying animals and memories of the unusual outback characters who owned them. In the back of my mind I was saying, "What a book this fellow has in him." But we'd just met and this wasn't the time.

We saw each other a lot after that. But it wasn't until Delphine and I, and Don and Dell had another dinner together prepared by my Cordon Bleu lady, that we talked about it seriously. "I'd like to write a book with you one day," I said. "Fine," said Don. "Why don't we start next week?"

He was a rugged character with a boyish thatch of fair hair and a slow, querulous, amused voice that stretched out the humour and the pathos of his stories. He came to my study at Stratford, a couple of mornings a week to chat on the tape-recorder. As he quietly remembered the dramas of dying animals he'd arrived too late to help, we sometimes had our handkerchiefs out, the recorder switched off. We'd take our time before we tried to talk again.

Don seemed nonchalant about his life—he could be treating wheezing Peke dogs in his surgery in Cairns in the morning and in the afternoon find himself at the controls of his small plane high above cattle ranches the size of some European countries.

It was on the first session, when we sat down for coffee, and he opened the batting with the story of his tutor, Professor Hamish Dunstan, a man with a pinched, craggy face that permanently expressed disappointment.

"'All I can say,' said the professor as yet another student fumbled a catheter insertion into a horse, 'is God help the p-o-o-r animals.' Professor Dunstan hated the Queensland heat, loathed the Australian accent; and thoroughly disliked women. No matter how hard an aspiring girl vet tried, the professor would whisk his stained white coat in annoyance and wonder why on earth a woman should ever wish to become a vet? One of his students was an astonishingly beautiful blonde with an upturned nose and hair that cascaded down to her waist. She was quiet, self-effacing and determined to be a vet. Prof. Dunstan had a First World War veteran, called Sgt. Blain, assisting him at his practical lectures and on the day in question he had asked Blain to extract a horse's penis to its full length.

"'In most horses,' Professor Dunstan droned, 'unless

they are very n-e-rrrvous, the penis will come out quite a distance if you hold it firmly and correctly. You will then take your catheter, which will have been lubricated beforehand and insert it into the orifice.' He called for each of the students to step forward and grasp the penis, to demonstrate the procedure."

Don recalled that it was then the turn of the fair Mary Thomas. And every eye rested on the poor girl. She had stepped forward and reached for the organ, which was becoming, after much handling, a little slack and weary. Nevertheless she seized it confidently with her left hand, just as she had been shown, and, awaiting the Professor's order to proceed, turned to him expectantly. "It was at this point that Professor Dunstan deliberately looked away from the girl and began lecturing us on the irritability of horses. He droned on for five minutes before he turned, in mock surprise, to rest his gaze on Mary. 'It would appear, Miss Thomas,' he said, 'that you enjoy holding that thing?' The normally quiet Mary looked him straight in the eye and still holding the horse, said, 'Not really, Professor. But if it gives you some peculiar satisfaction I'll hold on to it. I am here to learn. Not to object.'"

Don's flight-path when he left his Cairns surgery to 'go bush' would often take him over beautiful Princess Charlotte Bay on Cape York Peninsula; over saltwater creeks abounding in fish, oysters and crabs. Around them, was the most exotic bird-life in Australia; wildfowl-ducks, geese, plain turkey, magpie-geese and thousands of majestic, long-legged cranes. Every cattle station has its own airstrip, some of them well-cared for and smooth like an airport tarmac; others potholed and rough, with the ever-present danger of huge Brahman bulls wandering across in front of a tiny aircraft as it came down to land. A growth on a horse at Rutland Station had to be operated on under an umbrella-tree; the next 'hop' to

Coen involved pregnancy tests for cows and then, by chance, another meeting with the famous 'Oink' the pig.

"The old Exchange Hotel at Coen was built of timber and corrugated iron a long time ago," said Don. "The verandah and floor were rotting and sagging and taking a drink at the bar was like standing in a blast furnace. Coen has about a dozen homes occupied by whites, and 50 by Aboriginals. It has an airport located on the other side of the river 14 miles away, and in the rainy season, when the whole country is flooded, you need a boat to reach it. For five soaking months an aircraft is the only means of getting out to the rest of the world.

"When I landed, I went to The Exchange for a beer with Billy James, a farmer. And there I saw my old friend, Oink. He was sprawled asleep on his chair on the verandah; the fattest, laziest, smelliest pig in the whole of the north. He had begun his days as a lean 'Captain Cooker', the breed directly descended from domestic pigs released by Capt. James Cook from his reef-bound Endeavour in 1770. Since then, Oink's hungry-looking razor-back relatives have become a pest on the Peninsula and are hunted by white and Aboriginal. They are not as pleasant to eat as a domestic pig and many have TB. But when things are tough in the back country, men tend to overlook a lot. I told a station-owner friend one day that the bacon hanging in his cool room had maggots on it. 'Them bastards at it again, are they?' he said. 'And they eat a lot, too.'

"Oink had been brought to The Exchange by an itinerant who had swapped him for beer, and the pig had stayed on as a pet ever since. Housed at first in a pig-sty, but latterly spending most of his time on the verandah or in the hotel's old-fashioned bar, and fed by the publican on choice left-overs from the dining-room and given the stale beer that overflowed into the drip-tray. Oink's eating and guzzling had made him enormous, and his stale beer intake was added to by as many as a dozen fresh glasses given to him daily, by locals and travellers delighted to tell their friends: 'I was having a beer with a pig the other day ...'

"When Oink had consumed all available beer he would ponderously make his way out to the verandah where he would flop into an ancient, low-slung squatter's chair, a construction of wood and canvas that had long extensions on the arms with holes in the ends for glasses. When you sink into a squatter's chair on a hot day with the beer in one of the holes you never want to climb out. Every morning Oink sprawled into and over the chair and would remain there until the publican, cleaning out the bar from the night before, would shout: 'Where's that bloody Oink?'

"Instantly the great mound of bristling flesh would heave itself up and Oink would propel his 200-lbs. bulk through the bar-room door to his dish filled from the drip-tray. Snorting noisily with pleasure he'd guzzle the beer and then lumber back to the verandah, contented to drop off to sleep again in the creaking, stained chair. Until a stockman with a throat as dry as a burnt chip and needing somebody to drink with would shout for the umpteenth time that day, Where's that bloody Oink?'

"One day a salesman arrived in town, had one or two more beers than he could handle and staggered off to a chair on the verandah — Oink's chair. Oink had finished his own slurping and looked around to see if there was more, but there wasn't. He turned and plodded towards the door and got to within two or three feet of the relaxing salesman. He stopped in his tracks and shook his head, as though to clear his brain. Then he lurched forward again and without ceremony launched his massive body onto the chair and the salesman, sitting half-asleep in it. There was a cry of surprise from the salesman and a simultaneous cheer from the bar. 'Give him back his chair, mate! Don't be cruel to the poor little bloke.'"

There was an Alsatian dog that Don almost had to destroy, it was known as 'Smokey' and he was uncontrollable and ferocious. It was rare for Mrs. Dorothy Brown, the patient and kindly woman who ran the Stratford Animal Refuge in Cairns, to admit defeat. But Smokey was so badly behaved he had no future. 'We may have to be put him down,' she told the vet. He had been owned by a couple who were both deaf and dumb and their efforts to communicate to the canine ear, were unintelligible. Don promised to come up with some sort of solution, but when he made his next visit to the Refuge he still had none. He was ready to put the dog to sleep. As he walked in the gate to a chorus of barks and yaps from strays and boarders, Mrs. Brown smiled a welcome. "Do you remember Smokey?" she asked. "Well he's as bad as ever, but he's gone to a lovely home!"

Who on earth would take him on? "A very kind lady, who is determined to save him. She is a psychiatric nurse and she is planning to treat him as a disturbed human being. She has been in touch and says that Smokey has already changed."

"When I phoned Mrs. Joan Dryburgh," Don remembered at one of our morning sessions, "she said she knew he was about to be destroyed but was now part of the family. I was welcome to go out and see him.

"The afternoon I arrived at their property I heard furious barking and saw a German Shepherd rushing towards my car. I decided to stay where I was. I noticed a lot of earth-moving equipment and a series of sheds as a slim, bespectacled woman in shorts, appeared and grabbed the dog's collar, dragging him to a chain 100 yards away. She returned and invited me into the house for a cup of tea. Mrs. Dryburgh said she and her husband had previously owned a cattle-dog that had been killed. They had chosen Smokey, which she now called 'Ringer', to be their new guard dog. 'He's been so well-behaved,' she said. 'But you wouldn't think so today, would you?'

"She had," he went on, "chosen Ringer because he was the first dog to bark when she walked into the Refuge and she had liked the look in his eyes. 'I looked at several other dogs, but kept coming back to this terribly disturbed fellow. Because of my profession I felt that if anybody was going to get rid of his savagery I might be the one. I was told he had been deliberately made ferocious; the previous owners had allowed someone to try and train him to be a guard dog. This person had wrapped padding round his arm, as the police dog trainers do, urging him to attack.'"

Mrs. Dryburgh had not been allowed to take the dog from the Refuge immediately. He was too much of a problem. Instead she had visited him in her off-duty hours and had stood outside his kennel talking to him as he raced madly backwards and forwards barking. It was some days before she ventured into the exercise yard. 'He raced right up to me, skidded to a stop and began sniffing at me. But he did not attack,' she said to Don. When she eventually got him home he ran into a cattle-crate where he remained for two weeks, snarling and skulking, before he seemed ready to be let out. When she was able to get a lead on to his collar, she took him for a 45-minute run; then on the following day, another. Soon she was taking him for four runs a day.

"Then came an important stage in their relationship: she decided it was time to be able to pat Ringer. She realised that his reaction would be unpredictable. 'He was still nervous and distinctly savage. I crouched down on my knees, hoping he wouldn't spring at my face, and said, 'Come on, Ringer. Come over and let me pat you. I clapped my hands together and repeated, come on! He trotted over and let me pat him on the head. But he was trembling with fear.' She then said to me, 'Would you like to make friends with him?'

"We walked across the yard where Ringer waited, chained to a post, his coat shining. As we approached, Mrs. Dryburgh said to me quietly, 'Don't make any rapid movement. Stay quite, quite still. I'll get him on his lead.'

"As Ringer saw this stranger coming towards him he started his hysterical barking again, straining the chain, trying to get at me. The dog seemed quite crazy and I wondered if all she had said about his transformation had been true. Ringer was clearly going to show this stranger who was the master.

"As she got right up to him Mrs. Dryburgh slowly extended her hand. Immediately, the dog ceased barking and began wagging his tail. He didn't look fierce any more. Rather, he gave the appearance of a shame-faced, naughty puppy. She slipped his collar on and then unclipped the chain. She pointed across at me. 'This is Mr. Lavers, Ringer. He's a friend of ours.' Ringer stared at me, cocking his head to one side in curiosity. She repeated, 'Ringer is a good boy. And Mr. Lavers is our friend.' She was now walking the dog around me in a crescent, gradually drawing nearer. I was standing as motionless as it is possible to be.

"Ringer remained suspicious and apprehensive; ready, I knew, to react instantly if there was a move from me. She said, 'You tell him he's a good dog now.' They were now about 12 feet away and I said, 'Oh you are a good dog, Ringer. That Ringer is a good dog indeed.' When he approached to within two feet I was overwhelmed by the obvious potential violence he had in him, and the damage he could do to a human being. I felt a simultaneous contraction of my bowels and hoped that the dog remained unaware of my fear. (Dogs sense fear and this sense can make them attack.)

"Mrs. Dryburgh now said, 'I want you to put your hand out to see how he will respond.'

"I had always known never to put my hand out to a savage dog. Once a dog seizes it and gets a grip, the hand can be badly torn before it is wrenched free. 'Do you really think that's wise?' I asked. 'I would prefer not to.' But she was determined. 'It's all right now. He's quite happy to be close to you and look, he's sniffing at you. You can put your hand out now.' The dog had its nose within a foot of my knee and was now snuffling at me. I debated for two or three seconds whether I should extend my hand and then made up my mind. Slowly, I extended it.

"The effect on the dog was dramatic.

"He jumped, sprang away, cringed and began hysterically barking again. Then he came at me. The leap he made was, fortunately, not a determined one. If it had been, I'm sure the slightly-built Mrs. Dryburgh would not have been able to hold him. He bared his teeth and saliva spattered from his mouth. But he stopped just inches from my hand. I slowly withdrew it to my side, and my voice was tremulous as I said, 'You're a good dog, Ringer', hoping the high, nervous squeak that came out would somehow convince him of my sincerity.

"He withdrew, suspiciously, and a few moments later came up to me again and put his nose against my leg. He sniffed for a few seconds, then cocked his leg and urinated. I quickly moved my shoe out of the way and let my hand encompass his snout as it pressed, sniffing, against my trouser-leg. My fingers rested on the top of his head and I patted him.

"You're really a good boy Ringer, I said, overwhelmed with relief.

"He looked up and wagged his tail."

Chapter 22

The Bio-adventurers

I 'd arranged to interview Australian scientist Sir Macfarlane Burnet, in Melbourne. Sir Macfarlane was a renowned Nobel Laureate whose inquisitiveness had taken him to the forefront of scientific knowledge; a man hailed by his peers as a genius.

What had began that day as a routine newspaper profile, was to lead to a book and a 20,000-mile sortie around medical laboratories. The Magic Carpet syndrome again and my enthusiasm running wild. But I had no idea this was to happen when we met.

The day of the interview was dry and gusty; pollens were being swept over Melbourne and into the supposedly invulnerable Walter and Eliza Hall Institute for Medical Research. The swirling pollen was making me gasp with asthma, and when I discovered he was sneezing as much as I was I said, "I would have thought, Sir Macfarlane, that with your skills in medicine, you would have cured yourself of hay fever?" He emerged from behind his wet handkerchief and said there was no cure. But if there ever was, I would be the first to know about it.

Burnet had long ago retired from the helm of the great

Institute where he had been required to be not only a scientist, but an ambassador for science. The internationally respected Institute was supported by public funding and the task of the man at the top was not only to direct research, but at the same time explain, excite and inspire individuals and companies to give money to search for a cure for a host of genetic diseases. To do this efficiently this scientist had to be a tabloid-style interpreter, able to equate a donation of $1million to the possibility of curing the company director donor of his prostate cancer in the years ahead; or his wife, who might contract breast cancer.

This was no easy task. Many scientists, I had discovered, are notoriously bad communicators. They can chat to their peers about genetic strands and hooking up pieces of DNA. But to relate this to the board of a pets' food conglomerate, or the team of dedicated women money-raisers invited into the Institute once a year to see what is going on, requires superb public relations skill. 'Mac' Burnet had it. His voice might have been dry and his delivery unemotional, but he succeeded in simplifying the most complicated of scientific experiments, showing their relevance to human health.

Over a cup of tea, Sir Mac explained to me genetic engineering — the tampering with DNA — the very building blocks that make up our bodies; the manipulation that recently spliced human genes into pigs. "I am," he said. "A bit sceptical of the bright enthusiasm of the young. I am not terribly interested in DNA recombination work. I might be proven wrong in five years, but I don't think anything is going to come of it, apart from an understanding of the various aspects of the machinery of DNA. I think they'll find that Nature has had three billion years of dealing with interferences of one DNA by another. Every bacterium has had bacterial viruses living with it and dealing with it; and with all this going on there has been the necessity of DNA functioning properly. The more I know about genetics, the more I am impressed by the extraordinary power that has developed in Nature, maintaining her integrity of DNA." He then spoke, rather contemptuously, of an American scientific team claiming 'breakthroughs' and 'exciting results' from genetic manipulation.

"I think they're beginning to wonder if they've been making too much fuss over something which is becoming very unimportant." The American team was working on three genes of a virus called SV40, hoping their gene-splicing technique would eventually lead to an understanding of the elusive mechanism of cancer.

Burnet said this was also frightening him.

"I have been worried," said the man who had won the Nobel Prize for his immunological science. "That if this genetic engineering did work, the amount of error that would have to be tidied up, might just possibly turn out to be dangerous. If you put something completely unusual into a genetic system ... it might just go funny, blow the genetic system to pieces, because that's what viruses do."

This genetic tampering was, he said, precisely what the American researchers were now doing. In the sprawl of departments that makes up the renowned National Institutes of Health at Bethesda, Maryland in the US, a senior virologist, Dr. Andrew Lewis, had been working on a monkey virus, SV40; identified as positively causing tumours in animals, but not yet proven to cause cancer in man. Dr. Lewis had discovered that he could produce a hybrid that was part SV40 and part an adenovirus that is the cause of the common cold. News of this mix had gone beyond his lab and he began getting calls asking for samples of the hybrid so other gene-splicing scientists could play with them. Disturbed, he sat down and drew up a memo of understanding that would ensure, fellow researchers would take special precautions with his hybrid if he let them have it. They would also have to sign a declaration that they would not pass it on to another researcher who had not agreed to abide by his rules.

He was astonished by the reaction. Distinguished biologists, including a Nobel prize-winner, refused to sign and said he should "hand out" his viruses "in the usual manner with no strings attached." One of them, Paul Berg, was already experimenting at Stanford University with SV40 and was trying to unlock its genetic code to discover which of the virus's three genes caused tumours, and how they did so. He was handling SV40 in a highly purified, and infectious form. The SV40 in tumour cultures he was working on, readily transformed individual human cells and the cloning 'vehicle' Berg was working with, naturally lived in E.coli, and E.coli naturally lived in peoples' guts.

When Lewis's concerns were made public and Berg was contacted by outraged colleagues he said, "At first it got my back up." Then he, too, had doubts about carrying on with his work. He decided to postpone his experiment. "This moment was," a top American scientist told me later, "the end of the scientist's traditional right to play God." The cancellation did not come a moment too soon. In a lab., two floors below Berg's, Stanley Cohen, a balding, bearded scientist of renown, was to unearth a remarkable plasmid (the small piece of DNA carried by certain bacteria as extra chromosomes) that had the ability to 'take on' a new gene and slip easily into the human gut's E.coli. It was being requested by other scientists who (Berg said) had 'horror' experiments planned. "But I had been in the same position myself two years before until somebody called me up and asked if I had thought of the consequences."

In Melbourne, nibbling at his afternoon tea biscuit, Sir Macfarlane Burnet went on, "I am all for stepping out into the unknown except where you have very, very serious reasons for being chary of doing so. Handling viruses that are potentially pathogenic (capable of causing disease), at the level of molecular biology is dangerous. Viruses are the only things which are small enough for us to be able to understand completely. And I'm scared stiff that somebody will understand the polio virus completely and do experiments that will let something bad out."

My God!

What sort of people were these adventurous scientists?

Did the general public have any idea what was going on?

Sir Mac had talked about an introduction to Sir Gustav Nossal, his successor as Medical Director of the Walter and Eliza Hall Institute who might make introductions for me and pave the way to get me into laboratories if I wanted to write an in-depth article about research. But I had boldly now decided to write a book on medical science and had asked him if he believed it could be a 'goer'. He outlined the obvious snags: the lay writer, blundering along the pungent corridors of medical research, is greeted with suspicion, and rarely with trustful cooperation. Too many boffins had been burned by ignorant journalists shouting that the men in white coats had found a cure for cancer.

Sir Gustav Nossal was the glamour figure of Australian medical science. Austrian-born and as handsome as the most glamorous of his country's legendary ski instructors, he was the epitome of Continental fine manners; his conversation exuded excitement and hope for the future. His eyes danced with enthusiasm for his job, his scientists and his Institute.

I wrote to him and then went to see him about the book possibilities. He was enthusiastic! We came to an arrangement. I confessed I knew nothing about medicine or about medical science (I would be hard-pressed to define a cell) but I wanted to write a book about it that might attempt to explain it. He said he would read my final manuscript for errors and if he felt the book worthwhile, he would write its Foreword. He would allow me to roam his Institute's corridors but only on specific appointments arranged by one of his senior researchers. I could use the library as a base and while I was there ... learn what a cell was. "Now, the best of luck!"

For weeks I had the run of the Institute. I attended lectures which I grasped as easily as if they were delivered in Mandarin. I was allowed to peer into microscopes, and clicking on my tape-recorder, pose questions about pancreatic islet cells, Interferon, leukaemia and skin grafts. I was immediately caught up in the almost tangible excitement and eagerness, but, at the same time, baffled by some men and women who had no idea how to translate for me what they were doing; only rarely finding a gem of a worker who could clearly and simply make the whole thing understandable. One day, in exasperation at being unable to understand a bench-man's science, I told him that he and his kind were equally to blame when journalists, with the best will in the world, but with limited deadlines, so often 'got it wrong'.

Scientists are gossips. Within half an hour of my outburst I was approached by a female researcher who said she'd heard what I'd said. "We all have a problem with this," she said. "I've talked to Gus and he wonders if you'd address the whole Institute?" (Bloody hell!)

Next day, with an auditorium, a rostrum, pointer and a Melbourne Herald pinned to a lectern to explain newspapers, I spent an hour introducing 60 wary scientists to journalism. "The big problem you and the reporter have to get over," I said. "Is the fact that the writer has limited space. If he is preparing an article on the latest research into leukaemia, he has space allocated in the paper for maybe 1,500 words; and it has to be ready that day. You have the habit of making a statement and then qualifying it; you cannot say tomorrow is Tuesday without qualifying it and saying that one assumes we will see the next day. There is no space for that. In an ideal world the reporter would go away and write his article and come back with it to be checked. But time and rivalry for news gets in the way of that. If he doesn't get it right, because he doesn't understand it, it is both his fault and yours for not being able to say what you want in laymen's terms."

There were friendly and some aggressive questions from people in stained white coats, and not a little negativeness from those who would probably never welcome the lay public into their private worlds. "OK," said one young scientist, "What can be done about it? We need the publicity to generate funds; but we retreat into our shells every time somebody gets the story wrong. D'you blame us?"

I noticed Sir Gustav Nossal, in his immaculate, unstained white coat, looking hard at me as I answered. I had not had the occasion to speak to him since our initial interview. I took a breath and charged in. "What I believe the Institute needs is a professional writer-interpreter. If, for instance, some advance has been made here in research into leukaemia, the newspapers could be told the brief facts and if they are interested, be invited to ask questions. Those questions could be taken to the relevant scientist, the answers interpreted and written up by the professional writer and then taken back to the scientist immediately for review; so what has been written down is accurate. The newspaperman can then be given the draft and introduced to the scientist. The Institute can then feel more confident about the coming article being accurate and every newspaperman would be overjoyed that the science he is interpreting to his readers, is both understandable and correct."

Gus Nossal had been leaning against a bench. He moved forward to say he believed such a person was exactly what the Walter and Eliza Hall Institute required. He asked me directly if I would be that man and spoke of an attractive salary.

I had a meeting with him in his office; it was only two weeks since he had given me 'the key' to the Institute. I thanked him for the offer, but said I had started a book and it might take another year. Sir Gustav said, "You must not confine yourself to science in Australia, Desmond. You are just getting to know what we are about. Go off to institutes around the world. I will give you the introductions."

***

It had been explained to me that because of the genetic uniqueness of the individual, a potential graft is going to differ in more than one hundred ways from the host's molecular structure. Only identical twins have a perfect genetic and chemical match. That was why transplants couldn't happen between 'foreign' donor and an ailing recipient.

Nevertheless, British biologist Dr. Peter Medawar, had demonstrated about 40 years before, that he could make mice accept skin grafts from other mice if the recipients were injected with cells from the donor before they were born. The hypotheses that the body learns before birth to tolerate all those cells that it encounters prenatally, was an idea the Australian Macfarlane Burnet had put forward and which Medawar had taken up and then experimentally demonstrated: the phenomenon of immunological tolerance.

It was only after this laboratory success that transplantation of organs was actually considered as a clinical treatment. Medawar said he believed that graft rejection was basically an immune phenomenon and occurred in most cases because of cell-mediated immunity; rejection did not seem to depend so much on antibody formation, but, rather, on a response by the cells themselves to the grafted tissue.

Today scientists say, in more modern vernacular, that graft rejection is due to the activation of the thymus-derived cells, the so-called "T-cells."

The invaders aboard donor material ready for transplantation were termed by Medawar (now Sir Peter) "transplantation antigens" and he believed that the binding of this transplantation antigen to specific receptors carried by these T-cells, caused the angry reaction resulting in the graft being rejected. The transplantation antigen was the villain and therefore the major barrier to tissue grafting.

If that was true, there would only be two things you could do to get over such an obstacle. You could match the donor and recipient so they were the same antigenic type (a mammoth task in a randomly selected population, as New Yorker Dr Robert Good was to find out when he searched the world for a matching bone marrow donor) or you could immunologically suppress the recipient, and that was hazardous.

Sir Peter Medawar and Australia's Sir Macfarlane Burnet had spent a long time investigating the ability of the body to distinguish between "self" and "not self" and their eventual findings after years of experiments earned them the Nobel Prize in 1960.

It was five years after Medawar had operated on his unborn mice before the first human kidney transplant was performed. Doctors subjected the recipient to massive doses of radiation directed at the lymphocytes and other cells of the immune system to put them temporarily out of action. This knocked out almost all the active, circulating lymphocytes and the macrophages, or "scavenger" cells. It was a sledgehammer approach, and it was quickly discarded as unacceptable and not particularly effective.

Surgeons then turned instead to immunosuppressive drugs which had been perfected to be used against the proliferation of malignant cancer cells. It was believed that they somehow interfered with the manufacture of the nucleic acids — DNA and RNA — in the cells. (A cell has to double the amount of DNA it carries in order to provide a set of chromosomes equipped with full genetic information when it splits and prolifically multiplies into daughter cells.) But immunosuppression is a tricky undertaking; at the same time the patient's ability to respond against the antigens of donor tissues is being suppressed, his vulnerability to viral infection is equally increased: as desperately-ill AIDS patients have since discovered. "Clinically," doctors who have used the system say, "we have to walk a very thin tightrope. We have to try and immunosuppress the patient sufficiently so he won't reject the graft, and at the same time allow him to retain a little immune activity so he can cope with infections that come along. Today the whole transplant problem revolves around immunosuppression."

But one lone voice said perhaps there might be another way to avoid such hazardously suppressive pre-treatment.

Working at his laboratory at the Australian National University in Canberra in the early sixties was a scientist called Dr Kevin Lafferty.

Chapter 23

The Painted Mouse

K evin Lafferty, a burly, bearded microbiologist then in his thirties, had been studying how antibody molecules combined with viruses and other biologically-active molecules like enzymes. And now the always restless scientist felt he had satisfied his curiosity in this direction. The next research plan he contemplated was thought by some of his colleagues to be academically risky.

I went to see Kevin Lafferty, and he told me his fascination with biology centred on its admixture of conservative determinism with elements of chance variation. It gives the biological system a uniqueness and freshness that is both alive and beautiful.

"What I wanted to know now," said Lafferty. "Was how lymphocytes actually gather the information about their environment? How do they learn not to attack their own organism? How do they know to respond immediately to foreign agents like bacteria or viruses or, for that matter, foreign tissue some adventurous surgeon has sewn into the organism?"

It was the same wondering that Medawar had done. But dare he say it? Lafferty was not absolutely convinced that Sir Peter Medawar's Nobel Prize-winning conclusion had been correct.

In the down-to-earth, no-nonsense manner typifying his Australian birthright, Lafferty felt that there might be flaws in the immunological theory that said transplantation reactions were due to the immune system 'recognizing foreign antigens' on the transplanted tissues. He had been experimenting with sheep and chicken cells, and had discovered a situation where sheep lymphocytes he had treated, confronted with chicken cells undoubtedly carrying antigens foreign to sheep, yet gave no response. "There either was something completely wrong with the theory, or some trivial explanation for our results."

Lafferty realized that if he was going to take this line of almost sacrilegious thinking further, he was in effect implying some "inadequacy" in the concepts of transplantation immunology that had won the most coveted award in science for Medawar and his co-worker, Sir Macfarlane Burnet, two of the recognized giants in world immunology. "Research of this kind was considered an indication of lack of faith in current immunological dogma, if not lack of intelligence; a view put to me politely by my colleagues within the university, which is dependent on government grants, and somewhat more bluntly by those outside this institution." Kevin Lafferty, his battered tennis racquet lying in a corner of his office, knew this game he was playing could have dire consequences for his career if he was wrong. And that was more likely than not. Might he be kissing future funding goodbye?

Lafferty just could not believe that antigen recognition, the sighting of the 'fingerprint' or 'pirate flag' was, in itself, sufficient to activate and summon the outrider lymphocytes into attack.

To try and prove it, he did one experiment after another, confronting diverse tissues from sheep, pigeons, and chickens with one another. He watched interactions between chicken lymphocytes and individual tissues from incompatible chickens; bone, liver, heart, and kidney. And he came up with a fascinating clue. "It soon became obvious that we only observed damaging reactions when the target tissue contained blood cells, or part of a blood-forming system. The damage produced in these tissues could be accounted for by the wild, uncontrolled proliferation of these blood cells. Heart muscle from incompatible embryos was not attacked if the blood cells were carefully washed out of the tissues before testing. But the muscle was destroyed if the blood cells were purposely introduced!" Lafferty did his experiments again and again and sat back and watched microscopic 'explosions' within the tissue that destroyed not only the target cells, but the surrounding muscle cells when blood was present. When he transplanted bone, the fierce rejection centred around the blood-forming cells of the marrow, the reaction so violent that the whole bone tissue was destroyed.

He knew clearly now that blood cells carried in a transplant of tissue, played a vital role in the process of graft rejection. And that transplantation antigens long considered the culprits, appeared unable by themselves, to activate a specific immune response in a host receiving a foreign transplant.

There was only one villain: the "S" or stimulator cell in the blood, which passed a secret message to the responsive cells in the host and caused activation.

"Get rid of all the blood cells from the transplant," declared Lafferty pugnaciously. "And the tissue you're going to transplant won't stimulate a violent reaction in the host." As simple as that.

Lafferty might well have been sure of his facts, but he also knew his discovery was doing to cause a scientific rumpus.

On a crisp Canberra spring morning Lafferty packed his bags and pages of laboratory results and flew off to

San Francisco to attend the Fourth International Conference of the Transplantation Society. His purpose was: "To meet fellows working in my own field and to pick up little bits of information that circulate freely within the scientific community, but which receive little or no attention in the published papers."

As the conference got under way, the slightly jet-lagged Lafferty listened with particular attention to a paper given by a tall, good-looking scientist from Minnesota. His name was Dr. William T. Summerlin. The topic of his discussion had Lafferty's full attention. Summerlin, a man about Lafferty's age, was saying that he had discovered that both human and mouse skin could be successfully transplanted if the tissue was kept growing in a laboratory culture medium for several weeks prior to transplantation.

In short, he was claiming he had eliminated the transplantation barrier.

Skin grafting on man, from one part of his body to another using his own skin, had been carried out in India as long ago as 600BC. But grafting between unrelated donor and recipient had never succeeded. Summerlin was now saying he had succeeded.

Looking at the lecture in hindsight, Lafferty recalled for me, "many were sceptical about the whole procedure. But I was much more enthusiastic, because Summerlin said he had done what I had been trying to do for so long. He had found a simple but effective way of removing the passenger cells, the major cause, as I saw it, of graft rejection."

Lafferty buttonholed other scientists to talk about it during the coffee break. One shrugged, "You may well get rid of the cells in this way; such blood cells do indeed die off in culture. But what about the antigen left on the surface of the tissue cells?"

That was no problem said Kevin Lafferty. "I was already convinced that antigen on the surface of most tissue cells was unable to activate the immune system anyway!"

Frustratingly, he had no opportunity to meet Summerlin in San Francisco, but he had been invited by the leader of Summerlin's group, Dr Robert Good, to lecture at Minnesota on what he was doing in Canberra. "It was at the time that Good and his workers had been using bone marrow transplants on SCID infants, (children born with severe combined immunodeficiency, destined for a painful, early death) so there was now considerable interest on the bearing our studies might have on the exciting findings Summerlin was reporting.

"We spent a couple of days in Good's laboratory thrashing out these issues. Bob had attracted around him an active group of young research workers who had a keen interest in both clinical and basic biological science. Then I spent the afternoon with Bill Summerlin and I became extremely enthusiastic about the possibilities of his culturing procedure. He showed me banks of stainless-steel incubators containing a range of different tissues he was preparing for transplantation; there was skin, cornea, and adrenal gland. I peered through a microscope at thin pieces of cultured skin and all looked well. It was an impressive, 'big-time' lab and had an atmosphere of confidence and excitement."

That day, the lab and its workers gave no hint to Lafferty of the disaster that was soon to engulf it, making waves that would even hit him in Australia and cause his own research to become a hot potato nobody wanted to handle.

Lafferty travelled home full of enthusiasm for the organ culture procedure and a little envious of the group's obvious success. "We had been wrestling with the problem of effectively removing passenger cells and had found no practical solution. I'd never even considered the possibility of culturing the tissue prior to transplantation."

Kevin Lafferty might well have been prepared to plod along for years after a hunch, but that did not mean he wasn't always ready to grasp new ideas. As a careful thinker, he was cynical about empty talk not backed up by repeatable results. So he was still not sure in his mind at that stage that what he had heard and seen in the United States — The Summerlin Effect — was entirely due to inactivation of passenger cells. What needed to be done now was to patiently await confirmation of the American group's initial report and so determine the working mechanism that gave the claimed results.

However, that could take months. So the impatient Australian decided to try and do it for himself. He began culturing. Culture technique was designed to grow pieces of whole organs, as small blocks of tissue, in a nutrient medium outside the body. It was initially developed to study factors involved in organ development and growth, and the behaviour of whole organ fragments in isolation from the rest of the body.

"I set about the task, although I had no previous experience with the transplantation of skin," he said to me later. "A trip to the library and a little practice showed that there was no particular problem associated with the technique. Skin-grafts between mice that were of the same inbred strain — isografts — healed in and survived. Skin exchanged between different inbred strains — allografts — initially healed in, but was rejected about three weeks later."

Lafferty's team now began to transplant mice skin that had been in culture for a couple of weeks. But the results were dismal. Cultured skin, regardless of whether it was transplanted to a compatible or to an incompatible recipient, became dry and hard within a few days and was eventually sloughed off. "Neither type of transplant showed any evidence of ever healing into the wound made on the mouse recipient's back. We must have transplanted some fifty to a hundred mice, all with the same result," he told me. "The graft took on the appearance of a dried up old boot and then began to fall apart. My colleagues were not surprised. They had never expected the experiment to work.

"Well," Lafferty said. "I did expect it to work. And after all, I hadn't shown Summerlin to be wrong just because after organ cultures, I couldn't transplant skin to a compatible animal. Maybe there was something wrong with my technique. The real problem seemed to be that blood vessels were not growing back into the transplanted tissue before it simply dried out and died. This wasn't rejection it was a failure of the tissue to take."

Perplexed, he sat down and wrote to William Summerlin: 'Are there any particular tricks to your grafting technique that I've missed?'

Summerlin replied. Yes, there were some difficulties associated with the technique and he was preparing 'a few technical notes' that he would mail to Lafferty when they were completed.

"Nothing ever arrived," said Lafferty. "I was irked by the old-boot appearance of the skin I was so carefully transplanting, so I decided to switch to another type of tissue.

"We needed something that could be transplanted to a site that had a good blood supply; that seemed to be the cause of our troubles. Again, if it were an internal site, maybe we wouldn't have to worry so much about the tissue drying out before the blood vessels grew back."

Why not, Lafferty asked himself, transplant under the kidney capsule?

The technicalities of this procedure were complex. They involved experimenting with mice, using the tough membrane which fits tightly around the kidney, functioning as a bag to hold the organ together. This 'bag' could also hold transplanted tissue in place. Lafferty had chosen thyroid from the gland that lies in the neck in front of the windpipe and which regulates the body's metabolism and its physical and chemical processes essential to life. He would transplant two types of thyroid — cultured and uncultured. (Culturing meant 'growing it' in an atmosphere of oxygen and carbon dioxide.)

First he transplanted uncultured thyroid between incompatible (i.e. genetically different) mice, inserting thyroid which was half the size of a match-head. The invading thyroid was rejected after 10 to 15 days. Then he transplanted two batches of cultured thyroid to two groups of incompatible recipients and after the usual percentage of mice dying after or during the operation, was left with four survivors in each group.

For 15 days the burly Lafferty waited and watched. During his wait the telephone in the lab rang. A fellow scientist was on the line: "Have you heard about Bill Summerlin? He's been accused of faking his transplant results."

Dr. William Summerlin, the bow-tied, researcher he had met in the US, had moved to New York's Sloan-Kettering Institute for Cancer Research, the foremost cancer investigation hospital in the country, to work with its chief, Dr. Robert Good. He had been working on transplanting skin between incompatible mice. The man on the phone said, "Bill has been accused of touching up the transplanted skin with a felt-tip pen. All hell has broken loose." A few days later, while the disturbed Lafferty was still waiting for his own transplant results, Time magazine confirmed the worst: Summerlin had admitted to faking. "I felt decidedly sick," Lafferty remembers. He went and re-read a paper Summerlin had written and had sent him. It made astonishing claims for the medical future.

'The phenomenon which this paper describes ... may well allow for utilization of grafts from any donor — living or cadaveric.

'The era of banking organs, at least skin, may be much closer than ever before.'

Dr. Summerlin talked of surgeons having available to them 'banks' of hearts, corneas, lungs, livers and kidneys which they could, using his techniques, readily insert into unrelated recipients. An incredible scientific achievement if it was true. But had Summerlin gone 'off the planet' and faked these conclusions as well? Lafferty wondered.

He had at that very moment an experiment underway which could show, as was most likely, Summerlin's theories to be nonsense. But on the other hand, what if they proved his claims? In an atmosphere that was stinking with what was being described as the worst scientific fraud in a century, would Lafferty even want to tell anyone he had succeeded?

The 15 days were up. It was time for his lab technicians to kill Lafferty's mice, remove their kidneys, and see if the transplants had survived. Lafferty went through the ritual with a sinking feeling in his stomach. He didn't need what had happened. He kept asking himself, "Why did Bill do it?"

First, the workers removed the kidneys carrying the uncultured transplants; they had been rejected.

Now it was time to take out the cultured thyroids. Lafferty and his assistant, Alison Bootes, hurried with them down a corridor to the counting room where a y-counter, which would read the radiation from iodine isotopes that had gone in with the thyroid, would tell them whether or not the thyroid was still functioning. The tube carrying the transplanted kidney with the cultured thyroid inside its sac rattled into the counting chamber.

"The counter sat quietly for a few seconds, then it took off at a crazy pace! It was fantastic," said Lafferty. "Ten thousand counts per minute!" (Compared with 500 counts per minute with the failed uncultured transplant.)

"The cultured thyroids were functional! And kidneys from other mice in the group told the same story.

"On the face of it," said Lafferty, in perhaps the scientific understatement of the year. "We had managed to sidestep the transplantation barrier."

The team, hardly able to contain their excitement, nevertheless agreed to tell nobody at this time. "In the light of what had happened to Bill Summerlin, we were now in tiger country." They did new experiments using different strains of mice and had two other scientists overseas, independently do the same experiment. They achieved the same remarkable success. A German researcher, using the Lafferty Culture Method at Wisconsin, in the U.S., transplanted cultured rat thyroid into mice. "I was now certain that organ culture could prolong the survival of thyroid tissue in an incompatible host." Declared a now confident Lafferty.

Now the huge next step had to be faced: could the culture system be used clinically to transplant from one human to another? As Summerlin had said it could. Organs like the pancreas, livers and kidneys, that were no longer functional could easily be replaced with organs saved from dead people.

By now, Dr. William Talley Summerlin, then 35, a rangy six feet one inch, had been banished in disgrace from New York's Sloan-Kettering Institute and advised by his boss, Dr. Robert Good, to seek psychiatric help. All enquiries as to his whereabouts failed, since the front-page publicity surrounding the saga he had vanished. Having been to Canberra and questioned Kevin Lafferty about what was certainly an historic scientific breakthrough, I determined to locate the American who despite all that had happened, might well be right after all.

Sloan-Kettering Institute, when I phoned, was decidedly unhelpful. They did not want to know about the man who had brought them such humiliation. Colleagues

with whom he had worked so closely asked me to leave
them alone. They had no idea where Bill Summerlin had
gone and neither did they care. One night, in a call to a
sleepy bench scientist who was intrigued to have a call
from Australia, I got a clue. "He was last heard of somewhere down in the arsehole end of Louisiana. A little
place called Houma. The man still puzzles me. He is a
great scientist and had everything going for him. Then
he threw it away; just like Rembrandt putting his foot
through one of his paintings. Now for Christ's sake let
me get some sleep!"

I found a clinic in the Houma directory that specialised in oncology and allergy, among other persuasions,
in a town of 30,000 people. I called it and asked for Dr.
Summerlin. He was there and he came to the phone.
"No," he said. "I am sorry. I have no desire to meet you
if you come over. What happened in New York is behind
me." He put down the phone. I then decided to write to
him. I had, I said, recently spent many hours interviewing the one man in the world who might prove his theories right and I had his unpublished paper describing his
transplantation success.

Summerlin changed his mind. "Yes," he said. "Please
come over. I'd like to see you ... and bring Lafferty's
paper!"

To get to Houma I had to fly down to New Orleans
and then take a Greyhound bus to a small oil-rig supply
town that seemed to have remained frozen in time. The
afternoon I arrived, the streets were eerily empty; shop
windows contained clothing styles that were trendy 20
years before. My motel was adjacent to a rubbish dump.
When Bill Summerlin walked into the lobby I saw a tall,
good-looking man wearing a spotted bow-tie and a welcoming smile. He had a high forehead and brown, pen-
etrating eyes that had an odd habit of momentarily dilat-
ing with his moods. He said he had to get to his clinic,

but would take me out to dinner that night. "After what I'm going to tell you, you will not sleep. It is a story that nobody else knows ... that nobody could imagine. It is about extremely powerful people and the serious dangers of their power."

That evening he picked me up and we drove in some silence to his country club. We sat down, ordered and he offered me a beer. I said I was allergic to beer; but if I believed I was to have a free consultation from a top allergist I was mistaken. His thoughts were at Sloan-Kettering. "Can you imagine what it was like?" he asked me, face twisted in pain, his food hardly touched. "For a year we were lost and out in the wilderness. Rebecca [his wife] cried herself to sleep every night for weeks. They told me at Sloan-Kettering that I should see a psychiatrist. I didn't need to then; but after the relentless persecution that followed, even I began to wonder about myself. I had a good talk with a psychiatrist friend of mine and he advised me to start running; 'just get out there in the countryside and run.' So I did. I started marathon running and last year I competed in the Boston Marathon. I run up to 15 miles a night."

I moved to switch on my tape-recorder so we could talk about the saga that had brought me 10,000 miles. But he put his hand up. "No. You're going to have to bear with me for awhile. I've now met you and I will talk to Rebecca tonight. The three of us will have breakfast in the morning at your motel." He called for the bill.

Next morning Bill Summerlin came alone to the motel. His face was tired and he had shadows under his eyes. We ate our pancakes and drank our coffee almost in silence. He then said, "I have been persuaded not to talk to you about the past. I'm sorry. But I'd like you to come and see my clinic anyway."

We drove to a modern brick complex that had 25 doctors working on oncology, x-ray therapy, radiology, ear-nose-and-throat, orthopaedics and several other disciplines. He led me down a carpeted corridor to his own office. There were framed medical and scientific scrolls on the walls, a facsimile of the Declaration of Independence, a family photograph and a news shot of the start of the Boston Marathon. He then took me to meet the clinic's business manager and two of his medical colleagues, leaving me with them while he attended to a patient. They told me Dr. Summerlin had never spoken about his Sloan-Kettering experience to them; and they had never questioned him. I said, "Maybe he wants to do it now, with me asking the questions. I'll go and have a cup of coffee and leave you alone to talk to him about it." It was a slim, but unlikely hope.

When I returned, Bill Summerlin was back. He said, "I would like to tell you everything, in front of these gentlemen."

Nervously at first and then gaining confidence as he went on, he told the gathering for the first time, the full story of what had happened in the saga now referred to as The Case of the Patchwork Mouse.

He explained that he had been working in a Texas burn centre and had become obsessed with the need to vastly improve skin grafting. "We could only use what cadaver skin that was available to cover a wound temporarily for two or three days, sometimes pig skin for the same period. I was appalled by the paucity of thought and effort in that area." He had become fascinated by skin culture and its possibilities and had been allocated a bed for his research at the Stanford Clinical Research Center. One patient occupying the bed was an adult Negro male who had sustained a 10-cm third-degree burn to his left flank. Summerlin set about culturing skin from a live Caucasian and transplanted it on to the Negro. "After four weeks I discovered the white skin was not being rejected! The man's body did not seem to recognise that the donated tissue was foreign. I shared it with a few people and they said, 'Gee whiz, that's just a fluke. I wouldn't say anything to anybody about that. They will question your sanity!' But it happened. The Negro patient's scar was covered and it healed and he did well."

Summerlin, excited, began experimenting with female-to-male grafts and discovered that 'fresh female skin would be rejected. Her skin that had been cultured, however, was not.'

How many people to your knowledge are living today, with 'donated' skin, grafted by you? I wanted to know. "About six, who were done at Stanford. Six or eight more at Veterans' Administration Hospital. Then about three or four who were done in New York. As far as I know though, nobody else has done it on humans at all."

Now the Mouse Incident?

Summerlin said he had been getting 'exciting results' at Sloan-Kettering in New York working with mice. He had set up a 'rare' meeting with his 'mentor', Dr. Robert Good, for 7AM one morning and had slept at his laboratory overnight.

Why did he describe meeting with Dr. Good as a 'rare' occasion?

"Our meetings were increasingly far apart; frequently months between encounters and discussions." He had awakened at 5.00AM and after he had showered and shaved, two of his secretarial staff arrived with crepes and champagne to celebrate the coming occasion, when Summerlin would demonstrate to Good the astounding evidence that he had crossed the transplantation barrier.

He then had 18-22 mice brought up in cages. On the way to Dr. Good's office, in the elevator, Summerlin decided to give Dr. Good a little test. "He knew, or should have known, that you can't put black mouse skin on white after culture and expect it to turn out completely black. The hairs grow grey at best. I had some hairs [on the graft] growing in very nicely, but they weren't very dark. So on one or two ... I just took out my pen like this ... (he reached into his white jacket pocket) and I darkened them. Just to see if he would pick it up. Dr. Good must have spent a maximum of about two or three minutes glancing over the mice and talking with me about the work and I was summarily dismissed from his office."

Down again in the elevator went Summerlin and his mice; then the carry-cages were taken over by the man looking after the mouse colony. As he removed some of the mice from the carry-cage black felt-tip ink came off their backs on to his fingers.

"I had done something very foolish," said William Summerlin. "Next morning I called Dr. Good to try and sit down with him and visit with him and tell him I felt like I needed a rest. Later, I said to him, 'Well, you know, you SOB, you didn't even notice the mice! You weren't even looking. You flunked the test.'

Dr. Good had coldly replied, "I call that scientific mis-representation and fraud." Within hours Summerlin had been suspended and − he claimed − all the experimental mice destroyed.

"One of the things that still rings in my ears is Good's last words, 'You and I could have gone to Stockholm together,' a reference to the potential of a Nobel Prize 'but now, I promise you, you will be dead in science and medicine forever. Dead! Dead! Dead!'

"He had picked up a heavy glass object from his desk. I literally fled the room. It was macabre."

So was that it? The stupid, unbelievable end to what might have been an historic scientific breakthrough? The hopes of millions now dying, dashed?

William Summerlin shrugged. "I guess so."

Chapter 24

Back To London

We made our decision during a Friday night dinner in Cairns to go back to London. We sat down to a fine red with our fillet of beef and Noel Coward on the stereo. I would phone London about midnight.

"Of course, old chap," said Louis Kirby as he arrived for his London morning and sat down at his UK Mail desk. "Come over and write your column from here … Dispatch from London."

The column would pay our living expenses while I got back into Fleet Street.

The night we arrived, we went straight to the nearby Star Tavern. It was the same elderly, well-worn back-street pub I'd always known. It boasted a downstairs bar for butlers, chauffeurs and the tradesmen, and an upstairs 'private' bar for the pick of British criminals.

Attractive 'working' girls made their way up the stairs to drink in what had become their exclusive club. The Star stood behind the German Embassy in Belgravia, but no ambassadors trod its rickety stairs.

To wander heavenwards by accident or to have the gall to walk in uninvited was a foolhardy and often dangerous mistake. The bar was presided over, from the customers' side, by mine host, Paddy Kennedy. A stocky Irishman with a square, florid face and something of a drink problem; a gruff bully whose roar 'scared the shit' out of strangers and delighted the social butterflies, actors and wealthy layabouts who climbed the stairs on a Sunday morning. Paddy rarely took his place behind the tiny bar from which hung ruby-red goblets kept for an Indian maharajah and lady-of-the-moment, Christine Keeler. That position was reserved for a quiet, unobtrusive gay barman, who uncomplainingly took insults and patiently listened to the slurred outpourings of thieves and frustrated homosexuals.

In the centre of the mean room the burly Paddy held court, mingling from group to group, insulting the young nobility, touching up bosomy actresses and keeping up the boisterous, nonsensical banter that made atmosphere at Paddy's such an attraction. Nobody went there to enjoy the decor or the service. Bump Paddy's arm or approach him and you had a crystal whisky glass shoved under your nose, "Make it a loooorge one," he would roar. It was a bad idea not to oblige. He also had a quirky sense of humour; when a titled lady across the mews planted spring daffodils in a window-box, Paddy saluted the season and put a row of plastic flowers in his. When a racing 'certainty' given to him by an identity in one of the smart residences around the corner failed dismally, he got on the phone and had a lorry-load of ripe horse manure dumped in the tipster's front garden.

I'd originally gone to the Star to write a three-part Sunday newspaper series on Paddy's life. The crime reporter friend of both of us who arranged this precarious exercise, said it was no good talking to him when he was 'in drink', as it were; we communicated on a hand-held tape-recorder as he walked his dog in Hyde Park at nine o'clock in the morning. Paddy relatively sober and clutching a bag holding the previous night's takings, ready to be banked.

It was Upstairs where I first met Christine Keeler, who, with her blonde friend Mandy Rice-Davies, had set London on its ear with their cavorting in what became known as The Profumo Affair. Because she had chosen to sleep with Mr. John Profumo, the Secretary of State for War, and a Soviet naval attaché, Eugene Ivanov. The lithe Christine had caused such a scandal that it almost brought down the British government. Christine and Mandy made huge amounts from selling their stories of their various liaisons. Their go-between, Stephen Ward, suicided and Profumo, having lied to the House of Commons about the affair, was left ruined by the Sunday newspaper disclosures. I had been suddenly summoned on my day off by the news desk because I lived a block away and arrived just as they carried Stephen Ward under a red blanket from an ambulance into St. Stephen's Hospital in Fulham; an officer said to me out of the side of his mouth, "E's gone, Guv. No 'ope."

Christine Keeler liked to drink incognito at The Star, unpestered by a Press acutely conscious of the menacing Paddy and his dubious clientele. I had a 'privileged' entree to talk to the notorious call-girl and it was a Sunday morning when Paddy introduced me. She was a dark-haired, pale girl — far more attractive than she appeared in The News of the World — quietly spoken, almost lady-like, certainly not out of place in the foyer of a Mayfair boutique. We sat on stools and sipped red wine at Paddy's bar and talked, of all things, about the sanctity of marriage, until it was time for the pub to close.

Closure at The Star was always a ritual. Paddy would glance up at the ancient clock in the wall, unsteadily check the time with his wrist-watch and then bellow (not the usual 'Time, Gentlemen, Please') but, "Get your fat arses out of my shop!"

With obedient alacrity we obliged, extortionists, petty villains, celebrated criminals (like George Dawson, 'The Cockney Orange-Juice King', who'd made Paddy's his first stop after release from prison), painted ladies and myself. I had with me, this evening, a handsome Australian dentist friend, Maurice. He had watched my conversation with Christine with undisguised jealousy; but despite his undeniable attraction to women, he drank by Paddy's rules: you did not approach a 'personality' unless you were invited. Tossed out, as one, the Star clientele made its way to Sloane Square where a club had a late-night licence and it was permissible, under the complicated City of London ordnances, to drink until the early hours. With us, came Christine, and out of nowhere, Mandy Rice-Davies, (otherwise known as 'Randy Mice-Davies') tottering along in high heels and wearing an expensive mink coat and little else. Maurie and I had reached the club in time to see Christine and Mandy departing the bar for a table in the corner. But hang on! Out of the corner of his hungry eye, Maurie noticed Christine coming towards us, appearing to be heading straight for him.

The oldest teenager in the world ran his fingers through his boyish thatch of greying hair and put on his little-boy-lost grin, the one he used at the dental chair to put patients at their ease and to charm girls from 18 to 80. Christine now thrust her way past the tables and immediately confronted the weak-at-the-knees Maurice. He smiled a huge welcome. "You didn't nick my fucking gin, did you?" she demanded, pointing at the empty bar counter.

* * *

Paddy wasn't all bad. As gruff and rude as he was, he was known for his generosity and quiet support for many a 'punter' having a hard time. He was informed one evening of the plight of a well-known movie actor, who happened to be dead. "The problem, Pad," confided a regular, "is that no bugger will bury him."

"Why?" demanded the bemused publican.

"Well, it appears that when his dad died, he 'knocked' [didn't pay the bill] for the funeral expenses. Now the funeral directors have declared him black until they've been paid for both, the job lot, as it were."

Paddy was flabbergasted. The dead actor had been a regular and his name was a household word. "We'll take around the hat," he announced. Donations were solicited (demanded might not perhaps be too strong a word) from Messrs. Jack Spot (a scar-faced criminal known to use knives with terrible skill), Ruby Sparkes 'Burglar to the Nobility', and the now-wealthy Profumo Affair girls who said they would attend. A West End club owner 'volunteered' to open his establishment on a Sunday as a fund-raiser and amid the popping of champagne corks the stocky Paddy took around the hat. To his concern one villain found the temptation too much as it reached him — and took £10 out. "The little tea-leaf was taken outside into Bond Street," Paddy recalled, "and Ruby Sparkes scored a goal with him through a jeweller's window."

It was a few days later. A hung-over Paddy was sitting in the sunshine outside his pub when a tall, lugubrious gentleman in a black homburg and ankle-length black overcoat approached him and announced he was from the funeral directors. "I didn't think you were from the fucking Crazy Gang," growled Paddy and handed over the money.

Patrons needing an early morning heart-starter at The Star would notice sitting at the end of the bar, as permanently as one of the rickety bar-stools he squatted on, an elderly gentleman in a homburg with untidy grey hair spilling beneath.

Paddy whispered to me that he was once a judge 'and a bloody top judge at that'. His Honour had, it seemed, fallen on hard times.

The Judge, whispered Pad, in a voice that could be

heard at the other end of the room, was in the habit of 'having one or two' during the luncheon adjournment. It appeared that on this particular day, he was trying a particularly complicated higher court fraud case, and had enjoyed rather more than the one or two. A little tired and emotional, he had emerged from the curtains behind the bench to take his seat while the body of the court stood in respect.

He then reached unsteadily to a drawer in front of him and withdrew the dreaded black cap, used only in past years when the gravest offence had incurred the delivery of the death penalty. Donning the dusty cap, Judge X had stared down at the unfortunate before him, facing charges of having fiddled the books and said, "There has been far too much of this dishonesty lately. You will hang by the neck until you are dead."

"At that moment," said Paddy, "a hand reached out from behind the curtain and grasped the Judge, helping him to leave the bench. He's been coming here most days ever since."

* * *

At the Daily Mail next morning it was announced on the daily news-room news list that Frank Sinatra was coming to town. It would be an exaggeration to say that reporters were fighting for the assignment to meet him. 'Cranky' Frankie had notoriously departed an Australian tour in the wake of unions bans that had left the entertainer unable to fly home to the USA when he wished. He had in the meantime made it clear what he thought of all journalists, women journalists in particular, dubbing them 'two-bit hookers'. He had been in a decidedly bad mood with everyone, vowing never to return to Australia. And now he was heading for London.

Sinatra was making a television series to aid disadvantaged children, a heart-warming effort we all agreed; but his minders had made it clear that the media were nevertheless to keep away. No interviews. No pictures. No approaches. We breathed a collective sigh of relief. No coverage.

I was called in. Frank Sinatra, said Deputy News Editor, Monty Court, would be at a home for blind children in Surrey that day. I was to go down and cover the visit.

"But what about the ban?" I protested. "He doesn't want to see anyone?"

Court, a roly-poly Cockney unknown to take no for an answer, said, "Just go down and see what happens, my Lad." It was a 'thin' news day.

An angry Sinatra accompanied by his notorious heavies was not an exchange I looked forward to. As I got out of my car at the home I saw Sinatra being 'shown' through the children's workshop by a blind boy, David, who was about eight. He had the entertainer by the hand and was leading him to the area where Braille was being punched into paper. Frank, I could see through a window, was being patient, kind and interested. There was no sign of bodyguards, just a bored chauffeur standing smoking beside the black Rolls Royce that had brought him down to Surrey. And certainly no sign of television or newspaper reporters.

When David finally let go Frank's hand, allowing him to be taken by officials to another part of the work-room, I quietly went up to the little boy, introduced myself, and asked what Mr. Sinatra had said to him. He told me Frank had said he had never seen Braille being processed before and was interested in the keyboard that produced it. Then he took my hand and said, "Could you show me Mr. Sinatra's car? He said he came here in a Rolls Royce!"

By now Frank was squatting in a sand-heap 50 yards away, talking to some kids; one of them idly fingering the bald patch on Sinatra's head as he kneeled. "Certainly, let's go," I said to David. The longer the distance between Frank and I the better. We made our way through the building to the front entrance and with his right hand in mine, the blind David ran his fingers over the sharp, warm, gleaming radiator of the Rolls, imagining its stateliness and power, the chauffeur standing a short distance away.

Then to my dismay I heard a voice: THE voice. "Hey," said the voice. "I left my cigarettes in the car, Charles. Could you get them for me?" Little David also heard the voice. Still clutching my hand, he called, "Mr. Sinatra! Mr. Sinatra!" and reached out with his free hand to grab Frank's. It was a difficult situation. David had the famous Frank Sinatra, who hated the Press tightly held by his left hand and the banned, unwelcome Press in his right. Frank's famous blue eyes—hard, clear blue eyes that were scaringly alert—now bore into mine. Who the f---- was I demanded the eyes that in seconds seemed to go cold with anger.

"Uhhh, Mr. Sinatra," I tried. "This is uhh, a bit unusual. I happened to be here writing about the children here and, ... er, you arrived. I was just showing David your car. I am, uhh, from the Daily Mail."

I hunched my shoulders ready for the onslaught. But he was terribly nice.

His tanned, rather battered face broke into a smile and he said, "Don't ask me any silly questions and you're OK." Hand-in-hand with David, he gave me a pleasant, long interview about what he'd been doing in Europe, what he felt about kids, what he felt about England. And in a moment it was over. A lady superintendent called for David and he let us both go, running inside.

My story next day was bannered as an exclusive and the cheery Monty Court given accolades by the Editor for his initiative. "I told you there'd be a bloody good story down there, didn't I?" Monty grinned.

Chapter 25

The Queen Dons Rubber Gloves

" The Queen yesterday had to have three stitches inserted in her left hand after she tried to separate two Corgis fighting each other in the Palace — " The Times.

I had just come on for the 11 am to 7 pm shift at the Mail and the News Editor called me into the glass booth, where he sat with his deputy; two assistants manned switch-boards, filtering out nutters like The Genuine Elect of God (about whom, more later).

"Zwar, grab a cab to the Palace. Find out what goes on with those horrible little dogs. How come they can bite Her Majesty?"

'Over to the Palace?' What does one do? Go up to one of the Coldstream Guards and ask to be let in? Knock on the iron gates?

A good reporter, a good Australian reporter, did not ask questions. In the, here-today, gone-tomorrow ruthlessness of Fleet Street, it was necessary to be noticed; to have an edge. Mine was never to ask questions when given orders, you answered: "Jump? How high, Sir?" "Phone Comrade Khrushchev? Of course." The reference library was there for the details, the phone numbers and how to go about it.

The first edition of the Evening News which came out, incongruously at 8 o'clock in the morning, had a picture of the Queen with four of her pet corgis on leashes (two of them joined by one leash) and alleging those two were the villains. It was an educated guess because who was going to ring up and argue? The Queen, it said in the caption, 'was recovering'.

I found Buckingham Palace in the A-D section of the phone book and dialled the number. Could one perhaps speak to the Press Secretary? One could, sniffed the operator and I was put through to Miss Anne Hawkins, Her Majesty's Assistant Press Secretary. Could one help, she enquired? I wondered if one could actually come around to the Palace and sort of, well you know, have a word about the ... er dogs? "There would be no question," Miss Hawkins said frostily, "of speaking to the person in charge of the corgis who is, of course, The Queen herself." But, she went on, one could come around and have a background chat and park one's car at the east entrance. She would alert the police on duty.

It seemed too good to be true! I drove my Volkswagen to the gates, was saluted by a policeman seven feet tall and waved through. Once at the appropriate door, I knocked. It was opened by a gentleman in tight jacket, pantaloons and buckled shoes. A flunky. In great ceremony he led me down a hallway lined with elephant tusks, shields, glass cases of silver trophies and I was taken to a small room at the end of the corridor. Miss Anne Hawkins' tiny office held a tiny desk, two chairs, a mini hand-basin, a single-bar radiator and the tall Miss Hawkins, in pink twin-set and wearing two rows of pearls.

Where would one care to begin? She demanded.

Well, I said, 'one' wondered about the temper of the corgis. They were persistently in the news for biting policemen, palace sentries and the odd station-master when they were alighting from trains. Had there ever been an attack on a Royal before?

"Oh, they are no less boisterous or mischievous than any others," dismissed Miss Hawkins.

"Well," I tried again, as Miss Hawkins glanced at a small clock on her desk, "who scolds them when they do wrong?"

"Oh, one cannot really go into that ..."

Who trains them? "Oh," a smile at last. "They have been taught to do tricks. They sit up and beg for food. And they roll over on their backs."

Yes, but who taught them to do that? A shake of her immaculately-coiffured head. That question, again, was out of bounds.

'One' was quite obviously not about to tell the world about the private lives of Her Majesty's cantankerous little Welshmen. "Perhaps if you would like to leave your questions I may be able to talk to The Queen?" she volunteered, but not too convincingly. It was obviously a polite way of ending our fruitless little chat.

Back along the passage with the aloof and wordless flunky I went; past the elephant tusks and African tribal masks. A fizzled assignment. Unless ...

I drove the VW back to my flat and typed out a list of questions and then drove back again, saluted this time by the policeman, and handed the flunky the sheet of paper.

Back to the Daily Mail office where I admitted I might well have failed to get a story. "Well at least you got in, old boy," said the surprised News Editor. "I have never been there."

Then two days later ... a phone call. Miss Hawkins had not only spoken to Her Majesty, but the Queen had, seemingly quite enthusiastically, answered my questions! One returned rather fast to the Palace.

My first question: How and where were the dogs fed? "The Queen, whenever she can", said Miss Hawkins. "has the dogs' food sent up in a dumb-waiter to the drawing-room at Buckingham Palace, or Windsor, or Sandringham, at about five o'clock. It is retrieved by a footman who hands it to Her Majesty, who has donned rubber gloves. On the floor, on a table-cloth, stand their individual bowls, each with the dog's name on it, into which Her Majesty mixes meat, vegetables, gravy and biscuits." (I marvelled at the scene of Her Majesty on her knees) " And when the corgis finish their meal, the Queen clears things up and returns the bowls to a tray.

"She very much likes to look after them herself, and of course they go where she goes," said Miss Hawkins. "If you see her in the Palace" (a little unlikely, I felt) "on her way upstairs to one of the state rooms, the chances are that there will be a corgi or two with her. They just wander about with her everywhere. If they happen to wander in when a photograph is being taken they are included."

Miss Hawkins gave me a pencilled royal corgi family tree, explaining that Her Majesty was firmly in charge of breeding. Even when Tiny, a corgi, gave birth to seven puppies fathered by Princess Margaret's dachshund, Pipkin, it was, she insisted, "a planned marriage".

Would one care to speak to the Queen's kennels? Mrs. Thelma Gray, of the Rozavel Kennels, at Pirbright, Surrey, had enjoyed a 'By Appointment' relationship with the palace for years, and the kennels-palace friendship probably still exists. Mrs. Gray's stud corgis had been mated with the Queen's bitches on many occasions. The kennels had enjoyed its royal association going back to 'Dookie', the dog taken there for mating by the late King George VI in 1933.

Mrs. Gray said to me: "Her Majesty has done me the honour of discussing her dog-breeding plans with me, and on occasions I have suggested outstanding dogs owned by other owners as being the best choice of sires."

And on the delicate question of whether bride goes

to groom, or vice versa, Mrs. Gray said, "The stud dog is always taken to visit Windsor." The particulars of the stud dogs chosen by the Queen had never been widely broadcast and were known only to a small circle of people, she firmly pointed out. "Therefore, such a stud dog's fee is in no way altered by his having fathered a litter of puppies to a Royal corgi bitch; nor is the demand for his services in any way stimulated."

The Queen, since she was 18, had generally mated her bitches with dogs outside the 'family'. Because corgis had become trendy, ill-considered breeding has developed a strain of nasty-tempered pets in residence at many English top peoples' homes. When she wanted Heather 'married', she chose Mrs. Gray's high-strain gentleman Lees Maldwyn Lancelot.

And who house-trains the puppies? Her Majesty. If one of them does terrible things to a Palace axminster, she rubs his nose in it. "The puppies are always house-trained by the Queen herself," said Mrs. Gray.

There was one more link in the doggy saga. Mrs. Alma McKee, who was for many years a cook at the palaces, recalled to me, "I often used to take up the menus to the Queen Mother, when she was Queen, as the dogs were having their meal.

"When the Queen Mother and Princess Margaret were together at Clarence House, their dogs' feeding time was a ritual. Mother and daughter took rather a formal tea together at a small table covered with a white tablecloth, in one corner of the drawing-room. Afterwards, they laid another tablecloth on the floor on which the dogs were given their meal. The royal corgis fully appreciate their privileged position and have the run of the house. By day, when I was there, they conducted a private war on the policemen who were always on duty to guard the house. The corgis hated their patrolling habits, or uniforms, and in the kitchen we were always sheltering enormous policemen who were being pursued by these small, but relentless dogs!"

A Corgi called Bee used to torment cook McKee. "In Scotland I had to walk up the same stairway as the Queen when I went to my private rooms, and Bee used to lie in wait. One day she refused to let me pass.

"After lunch, the Queen's corgis used to come down to the kitchen when they knew nobody was about, to see if they could snatch something to eat. I had a feeling all the time that these little dogs knew they belonged to a very special person. They had quite an aloof air. They did not want to talk to you unless you were very nice to them. They usually had ordinary meat, but they did enjoy venison. And they loved green vegetables. When the vet came to see them, one of them would get very excited and make little noises. She would run to the vet and roll over on her back so that she could listen to her heart. Then she would look up at her — ever so seriously — as if to say, "What do you think?'

"The dogs had their own little beds in the day nursery when Prince Charles and Princess Anne were babies. The blankets and cushions were pale brown and gold, to go with the dogs' colouring. One had a special blue cushion with red spots. At night, if Sugar did not think her basket was made up properly, she would get out and make it again herself."

Chapter 26

'Mister Daily Mail'

Every desk in the great newsroom was suddenly deserted, with sub-editors, reporters and photographers jammed around a Foreign Room teleprinter clacking furiously.

A sub-editor, dashing back to his desk said an astronaut, Yuri Gagarin, had been launched into space by the Russians. The news-desk phones had gone mad. Reporters in Daily Mail offices around the world were being ordered into action. "Interview scientists and leaders", the Foreign Editor was shouting over the phone to Moscow. "Get the background on Gagarin."

"Zwar!" I hurried into the 'home' newsroom responsible for all that happened in Britain. "We want a back-grounder London piece. Get up to the Soviet Embassy and find out what they're doing. Are they celebrating? What's going on? Get a talk with the Ambassador." I raced out and took a black cab to Kensington Palace Gardens, better known as 'Millionaires' Row', the centre of foreign embassies. I found the high-walled Soviet Embassy already surrounded by milling reporters and photographers.

"They're not playing," a disgruntled Daily Mirror man told me. "They say Come back in the bloody morning." I pushed past him and made my way to a great oaken door, pressing the buzzer. The door took a while to creak open and a fair-haired man in blue suit and brown sandals glared at me. He didn't even want to know who I was. "In ze morning ..." And the door slammed closed. The mob waited, staring up at the sky as if expecting the spaceship Soyez 11 to appear above. Then Eddie Laxton, a burly, foot-in-the-door specialist who looked more like a boxer than an Express reporter, suggested we 'doorstep' somewhere more comfortable; like the nearest pub. To my amazement, as one, the pack departed, heading for Kensington High Street.

I was unsure. I had just joined the Daily Mail and I knew I wasn't going to get the story in a pub. I went with them because it was obviously expected; but once they were gathered at the bar—I did what I now know to be unforgivable in the street-smart code of journalism—I broke ranks. I left them and headed for a bottle shop, an 'off-licence' as they were quaintly called. I saw on the shelf a bottle of Stenochka vodka, labelled 'Very Strong. 150 Proof.' I bought it and headed back up the leafy pathway to the Embassy, rehearsing my speech and glancing about to see if there were other reporters around. Mercifully there were not. I walked through the Embassy gates and again knocked on the formidable brown door and waited, clutching the bottle wrapped in brown paper. The brown sandalled servant opened the door and before he could say, "in ze ..." I launched into my prepared speech.

"I am from Australia. I come here on behalf of the Australian people who are delighted to congratulate the glorious achievement of the cosmonaut Comrade Gagarin. I wish to ask Soviet Ambassador Soldatov if he will take this as a gift and toast Major Gagarin with the people of Australia." Then I drew breath.

Brown sandals peered suspiciously, first at me and then at the brown paper wrapping, slowly removing it from the bottle in case it was a bomb. "You vill vait," he said. And taking the bottle, closed the doors. Heart thumping, I looked around to see if by now any of my rivals were around. I stood on the step for what seemed like 10 minutes and the doors swung open. It was the stony-faced flunky. "Come!" he beckoned. And I followed him into the Soviet Embassy, down a long corridor to a great room lit by a heavy chandelier. There stood the egg-bald Ambassador Soldatov I had often seen on television; beside him stood a waiter with my bottle on a tray and two small glasses that were already filled. Ambassador Soldatov then smiled, lifted his glass and motioned me to take mine. We drank. "To Comrade Gagarin!" he said. "Comrade Gagarin!" I said enthusiastically. He turned on his heel and left.

The Daily Mail now had its 'London end' to the story; I had an exclusive on the front page: "AMBASSADOR TOASTS ASTRONAUT".

But I had become a marked man. The threat filtered through from the Daily Express night duty driver to our night driver, the recognised backstairs communication between rival newspapers. I had erred by breaking ranks. The 'heavy mob' (reporters renowned for their persuasion on doorsteps) were upset. I was to be punished.

And they didn't wait long to deliver.

One wet, miserable winter's night I was told to get to a police station on the M1 Motorway where a bus-load of young convicts had overpowered their guards and the driver delivering them to Birmingham. The prisoners had all escaped.

The Heavy Mob arrived in their duffle-coats and sheep-skin jackets at the same time as I got there; and I heard mutterings of my recognition. The police were adamant: the guards had already left, and the bus-driver, whose coach stood in the mist-covered yard was not going to talk to anybody. We might as well all go home.

Reporters and photographers climbed back into their cars and waited, staring through the fug of tobacco smoke and frosted windscreens at the 'nick'. Every hour one of us went to the front counter and pleaded. We were told a statement would be issued by Scotland Yard Press Bureau next morning and really, we had better all go home to our beds because even the coach driver had been whisked away and his coach would remain where it was.

At 1AM, after I had called my news desk for the fourth time saying there would be no interview, they told me to go home. I had just emerged from the phone box when one of the 'mob' said, "We're all calling it a day. They're not going to play." And half a dozen cars drove off. I got into mine and headed back to London. Next morning I got all nine newspapers. To my dismay I saw, in six of them, quotes from the coach driver that he had been overpowered and had been in fear of his life. It had been a "dreadful experience."

I was carpeted and told in no uncertain terms that my good record had been smudged. The Daily Mail had been the only national newspaper without the quotes.

That night Alf, the night driver taking me out on a job said, "They got you, didn't they? The Mob didn't talk to that coach fella. They got together and made up a quote. They all used it. Except you."

* * *

London was bathed in summer when weeks later, Yuri Gagarin, a smiling, boyish soldier in uniform, now safely on land, had arrived in Britain as part of a grand tour and the world that was pleading to know, "What is it actually like in space?"

He was taken by the Soviets to Earl's Court, a huge auditorium packed with the hundreds of press and fascinated onlookers. Standing up on stage with officials from the Embassy and an interpreter, the cosmonaut was called on to answer questions from the body of the hall. In those days it was a frustratingly ponderous procedure to televise questions as one reporter after another, with his or her hand up, was chosen from the stage. A BBC television crew wheeled its camera through the throng to the particular reporter and the interpreter translated. Because the whole procedure was slow, there were no more than six questions asked — one of them, mine.

Watched by hundreds, and knowing I was to be telecast around the world, I got to my feet, suddenly scared, as the man-in-charge pointed at me. I waited for the camera to be wheeled from one side of Earl's Court to where I was standing and then began ...

"Major Gagarin, I am Desmond Zwar from the London Daily Mail. Could you please tell us how your experience has affected you? Now you are back on earth, are you disturbed by dreams of being in space; do you have nightmares, believing you are still there?" There was a ripple of interest and some laughter as the interpreter told Gagarin what I had said. I remained standing. Then, in cultured English the interpreter gave me Gagarin's answer, "Major Gagarin has never had any mental instability, either before or after his experience in space. He is quite well." A peculiar mis-representation of my question, or Gagarin's answer, and I have often wondered why. (My world fame on television was spoiled that night by the television network's difficulty interpreting my name because of my accent. The caption under my face on the news that went out on millions of television sets said I was, Dennis Waugh of the London Daily Mail. So from then on 'Zwore' (the way the family name was pronounced in Australia), became Zwar, as in car. It was easier for the English to understand.

Because it was cheap transport and I couldn't afford

a car, I had a Lambretta motor scooter which I rode to and from work, avoiding waiting for the all-night 'N' buses after a 2 AM shift. It was particularly useful getting through traffic jams. I was assigned to use it to follow Gagarin about London for the next few days.

I arrived ahead of the news pack at Karl Marx's grave at Highgate, where the astronaut ceremoniously laid a garland of flowers. Last on the list of his engagements that day was to be a party given by the Anglo-Soviet Friendship Society at the Hyde Park Hotel. And this was out-of-bounds to the Press. The Soviet Embassy media office had made it clear that this occasion was a strictly private party which the Prime Minister, Mr. Harold Macmillan would be attending. "Forget that one, old boy," said the News Editor. "Take the night off." (He didn't understand Australian reporters. A non-invitation to me meant the exact opposite: Get in there!)

I parked the Lambretta in a side-street off Piccadilly and walked up the steps to the old, dignified hotel. It was around 7.30 PM. Gentlemen in lounge suits, medals clanking on their lapels, made their way up the curved staircase to the first floor; ladies on their arms. A steward in dinner-jacket stood half-way up the stairs, taking invitations. I walked up and made as if to walk past him. "May I have your invitation, Sir?"

"Oh, it's alright. Daily Mail." (I had always noticed sardonic enjoyment on the faces of petty officials when they were empowered to say 'No!' to a reporter requesting information or access to their establishments.) This one almost salivated.

"There are no Press tonight, Sir. None at all." He stood in the centre of the staircase and barred my way. I turned and walked downstairs to the lobby again where an anxious Manager was standing watching the last invitees arrive. He remained just inside the front door. He glanced at me. "Waiting for the Prime Minister."

I went outside and waited myself.

From time to time, the worried-looking fellow came out through the doors, looking at his watch, glancing anxiously up and down Piccadilly. By now it was 8.15 and if Harold Macmillan was coming, he was certainly going to be very late. At 8.30 the Manager came out for one last look, turned on his heel and went inside. He had obviously given up.

At 8.35 PM an aged black Humber saloon drew hesitantly up to the front of the hotel. Its driver got out and held open the back door. Harold Macmillan, Britain's Prime Minister, alighted and stood, like a bewildered old walrus looking up at the hotel. There were no security people, no police, just the chauffeur, who got back into the car and drove off.

I stepped forward from the now deserted lobby. "Good evening, Sir. Would you be looking for the Anglo-Soviet Friendship Society?" "Yes. Yes," said the PM.

"Then please come with me." He obviously took me for some sort of official and followed me inside, moustache quivering, a tired look on his face.

The Prime Minister and I made our way up the staircase where the flunky was still rigidly standing guard. "Good evening," said Mr. Macmillan as we passed. "Good evening," I said to the flunky. He went red in the face, but said nothing as he bowed to the PM. I opened the door to the convention room and a hubbub of voices greeted us. First to step forward was Valerie Hobson, wife of the Prime Minister's War Minister, John Profumo. "Harold!" she smiled. "Can I get you a whisky?" And turning to me: "Whisky?" She had no idea who I was, but I felt an acceptance would have tested my luck too far. I thanked her, but said no, and melted into the crowd. Gagarin was at a piano and they were playing the 'Volga Boatmen's Song'.

* * *

An unlikely notoriety of the Cold War was Miss Nina Pomenolorov, an Olympic discus-thrower for Russia. A massive woman, built like a lorry-driver, Nina was largely unheard of until she was accused of theft.

Late one afternoon Scotland Yard Press Bureau put out a news flash that police were searching for her in London. She had been charged with the theft of five ladies' hats from C&A Department Store in Oxford Street and had been ordered to appear in court that day. The Yard said she had not shown up. She had vanished. The incident had occurred at the lowest point in East-West relations and diplomatically could not have come at a more sensitive time for Russia or Britain.

I was at C&A's in 10 minutes, but as I tried to interview department managers and shop assistants it quickly became obvious that the shutters were down. Orders had come from the British Government — one manager whispered 'MI5' — that nobody would be talking to the Press. I did my best to charm young shop assistants, but the attitude was unanimous: nobody knew anything. Noticing a table of woollen hats were on special sale I asked a girl if they were the collection of hats from which five had gone missing. She just nodded. I bought five and went back to the office. They were photographed and used above next morning's banner headline on the front page that said Nina had gone into hiding.

The News Desk said there was one place she could be kept hidden away out of the reach of the police or even the government: the Soviet Embassy. A foreign country's embassy is considered to be that country's territory, inviolate from intrusion and able to carry on any activity within the host country without interference. It was no secret that the Soviet Embassy had sophisticated listening and broadcasting devices and was run by a staff largely recruited from the KGB. One of its buildings bristled with sophisticated antennae.

The Yard divulged that the diplomatic law regarding embassy vehicles was now a problem. Embassy vehicles were considered Soviet territory and if Nina was indeed in the embassy, she could step into a Ziv limousine within the grounds, be driven to Tilbury. And the car, with Nina inside, could be lifted by crane on to a waiting Russian ship. And the police would be powerless to do anything about it: other than watch.

By the third day of Nina's disappearance, Millionaire's Row looked like a tent village. Police had put up makeshift tin roofs attached to walls opposite the Russians to keep the rain and sleet away and were working in shifts, fed by mobile canteens. The siege situation had become grave. Munching a Scotland Yard sandwich I asked a detective-sergeant how long he thought the cat-and-mouse game would go on. "We are merely here to make sure she doesn't go without us seeing her. We can't go in and arrest her, even though we firmly believe she is inside," he said miserably, rain cascading down his face.

Always eager for the scoop, I made my way up the driveway of the high-walled embassy and knocked on the heavy door for the third time that week. This time it was opened by the same fair-haired man I had met before. And this time he did not close the door in my face. He invited me inside! 'You vill please follow me?' (God! I was going to meet Nina!)

I followed him down the same passageway I'd gone down to see the Ambassador, but this time we turned right. The fellow opened a big door and I noticed it was lined with green felt, like billiard-table cloth. This led to a second door, similarly lined, six feet further on. It was like being in a Swiss hotel that had double insulating doors for warmth in the severe cold. He opened that and led me through to a large room. The walls and the ceiling, were covered in green baize as well. The room was sound-proof.

The Russian motioned for me to sit beside him on a couch and by now I was more than apprehensive. There was no sign of Nina the discus-thrower and I was obviously to be the centre of this discussion. I became seriously worried.

He turned to me, his expressionless flat face close to mine, I saw leathery pock-marked cheeks lined with small scars. "Mister Daily Mail," he began. "For many dace now we haf been pestered by the Press of the world, in particular your Fleet Street. But in particular moreso, we haf been annoyed by you. We watch what you write in your newspaper. Why don't you leave us alone. Mmmm?" I tried to explain that Ms. Pomenolorov's whereabouts had caused a serious international incident and that every newspaper was interested. Pock-marked ignored that. "You will plis keep away from this embassy. Otherwissse: trouble." I agreed that was a good idea. He got up from the couch and I followed him to the front door which was banged behind me.

Outside in the private road the uniformed police with their two-way radios were hard at it and an inspector came forward. "Did you get to see her?"

I assured him I had not, and to use his own jargon, added, "Just making routine enquiries."

Nina eventually came out of hiding and made her overdue appearance in court and the international incident died away. I never went back to the Russian embassy.

* * *

Back at the office I was temporarily given news desk duty, which was a change and despite the frenetic pace, a little cosier than playing hide-and-seek with Nina. The world's nutters, when they are not annoying police station night-duty sergeants, turn their attention to newspaper news desks. Assistant night news editors sit at their switchboards until the wee hours, fielding calls from the angry, the disturbed, and the put-upon. They know someone will listen to them because it might just be a story; and if the operator is a bit short with the caller he might go to a rival newspaper. I have, on occasion, had to accompany an almost naked mental hospital escapee who had arrived at the inquiry desk, as he set off to find and murder his wife; hoping the police we had alerted were waiting at the address as promised. Yawning at three o'clock in the morning, waiting for my desk duty to end, I received a call from a famous and very sexy London actress. She asked if I could come over 'right away' to her Belgravia flat for a drink. When I called back at five o'clock to say I had finished work she had, unfortunately, changed her mind.

Without fail, around midnight, we would get a call from 'The Genuine Elect of God', warning us, as he had the night before and on many other nights, that the end of the world was nigh. If you had time to humour him you would point out that he'd said the same thing earlier in the week and we were all still here. He would then get angry and say he was 'going to call the Express' and we'd all be sorry.

Chapter 27

'Can You Hear Me Sweetheart?'

After some years back in Australia, we made another nostalgic trip to London and I walked down what was left of Fleet Street in the late 90s, past where the Daily Telegraph had been, and was no more. It had gone to the "dogs" — the Isle of Dogs. The ghastly black glass Express building was now empty, with the ghost of Lord Beaverbrook probably still rasping out orders. Where was the News Desk man who had come down the stairs 40 years before to tell me, "Nothing at the moment, Old Boy"?

I turned right into Whitefriars Street, which I had done so often on my way to the Daily Mail, at first with apprehension and latterly with notes of features ideas. I arrived at Northcliffe House this time and saw it was locked and boarded up. No longer did the pavement rumble beneath your feet as the great presses roared into action. No longer did the brilliant Vincent Mulchrone amble across to the pub for a glass of champagne, or Gordon McKenzie bustle up the steps late, but with brilliant features ideas scrawled in the margin of The Times.

My appointment that day was at the 'new' Northcliffe House — where Barkers of Kensington High Street had been — to talk with the Editor of The Mail on Sunday. He had told me on the phone that he 'rather liked' the idea of a column, similar to my UK Mail 'Dispatch from London'. This one would be topped by a cartoon Aussie with a corked hat and would 'take the piss' out of the Brits. What an excellent scheme he said. On the strength of the phone conversation Delphine and I had already begun a search for an apartment; a column in a national Sunday was obviously worth a lot of money.

At the new Northcliffe House I checked in with uniformed Security and was directed upstairs in the glass elevator. The Editor and I shook hands and I sat down ready to sign the contract. But he was hesitant. All, apparently, was not well.

"I'll come straight to the point, Old Boy. You Aussies have recently shown that many of you favour a republic; getting rid of the Queen and all that. I couldn't run a column by an Aussie now, could I? My readers would hate you."

We flew back to Australia the next day.

Another Magic Carpet turning-point: from the concept of a luxury flat in Chelsea to the mayhem of Heathrow, sitting in a cramped Economy seat on Qantas for the next 23 hours.

We still had a life in Cairns. Adam, our son, was now a newspaper feature-writer; had written his own play and was appearing on television commercials. Delphine's expertise in food and interior design were in demand by the glossies. I had started book No.17. This one.

In 1992, the black cloud. Delphine had been diagnosed with breast cancer, had a mastectomy, and then thank God, had been free of the disease for the next five years. A complete remission said the medical rule of averages. I was forbidden to disclose to anyone what had happened. Her doctor had said to her, "They'll have you with one foot in the grave."

My girl had regular check-ups in Melbourne at the hushed, air-conditioned rooms of her oncologist and we would leave him, smiling and not needing another appointment for three months, safe in our warm love. We celebrated with lunch at our favourite restaurant.

Then on the next visit 'routine' x-rays were ordered. This time a dark cloud drifted in once more. And yes, there were 'hot spots' seen on some of the bones. That meant bone-strengthening therapy and chemotherapy, but 'not to worry'. How do you say that to a husband sitting with a sickening anticipation that all was not the same with the woman I had lived beside and loved so deeply for the past 33 years and be believed? For Delphine it was a brave reaching into her inner being for courage and hope; her diary now listing medical appointments for radiotherapy and chemotherapy, but no 'thoughts'.

This lady of mine, at 60, was still a girl. Fair, delicate features and body, dark, dark eyes; always cheerful and re-assuring to anyone who had a problem; caring. Child-like. As a language of affection she and I used Adam's growing-up words. It was a code that said we loved Adam and each other. I would ask her if she had had a good 'seeps', and if — as so often happened — her generosity of help to someone was ignored she would just shrug it off: "Peops are funny."

As pain in her ribs persisted and the many x-rays discovered the extent of the secondaries, our knowledge of cancer and the newest drugs increased. Neither of us admitted even to ourselves that she could die. When it was discovered that there was a large cancer on her femur that threatened to disintegrate the bone, she had a long operation and a steel rod inserted. With the stoicism that was part of her nature, she smilingly did her physio and learned to walk again. There were alarms — like the possibility of the secondaries going to her liver. When the x-rays showed it was clear, the new oncologist, Kerrie, and Delphine hugged in the hospital passage-way and I had to turn away and look through tears out the window.

And then came something neither of us had thought about, or knew how to handle. One morning I went into her bedroom with morning tea to find her sitting on the side of the bed, patting it.

"What are you doing, darling?"

"Nothing," she answered and went on patting the mattress.

I called Dr. Kerrie and she ordered a brain scan for the afternoon. It was negative and she came around to the hospital suite she had admitted Del to, to tell us. More tears and hugs. But then, "I want to do a lumbar tap. I just want to be sure. It might be the medication causing it, but there is nothing in the literature."

This was done and we sat for seven hours waiting for the pathology result.

It was bad. There were cancer cells in the spinal fluid and almost certainly the sheath of the brain.

It took only another week and my little girl had — in personality — disappeared inside herself. She had just gone somewhere else; away from our world. I sat with her at the end of the bed and she had her head turned from me. There was no conversation from the frail person lying so restlessly, now and then trying to climb out of bed like a naughty child.

"Darling!" I'd ask. Nothing.

Then, "Can you hear me, Sweetheart?"

"I am still here."

Another try. Again nothing.

Did she feel she was going to die? I had no idea and to this day don't think so. I just hoped not. Our prayers and our faith had given us hope for so long and God could do it again. Couldn't you God?

At the end of the third week she could not get out of bed to the toilet. She was on a drip and then morphia. I was assured she had no pain. I would drive home each evening, 60 kms through the countryside denying it all. It couldn't happen to my girl. She would come through it. I walked across a golf course each morning before setting off to see her, shouting aloud 'The Lord's Prayer.'

On the last afternoon there was such silence between her breaths that the nurse and I thought she was no longer with us. Then a huge breath would follow and Delphine — and hope — were still alive.

Adam had come up and she was quiet and contented as he combed her auburn hair which had begun to grow back strongly after the chemotherapy.

That night the hospital called. She had passed away. Peacefully.

I drove to the hospital and kissed her cold forehead. As she had wished, Delphine was cremated and at the service Adam gave this eulogy:

'Yesterday, Dad's cousin Michael and his partner Suzie, wrote in an email: 'Delphine was one of the most beautiful people that God created.'

Her friend Pamela said: "She was my dearest friend. She's in heaven now wearing a very fashionable halo."

And Mavis — our neighbour in Cairns for 17 years said she was a "true lady".

It is true Mum did enjoy a touch of glamour. It is a prerequisite for someone who wrote so exquisitely for House and Garden, Home Beautiful, Gourmet Traveller and Vogue. Her writings made her a legend among women and, more particularly, gay men.

But the fact that she was so stylish and had impeccable taste and was a fabulous cook and writer, did not make her elitist. Mum helped out every bird with a broken wing; the ill, the sensitive, the grieving and the artistically talented but emotionally fraught. She had an uncanny knack at seeking them out and listening to them and caring for them and writing them cards and inviting them around for one of her famous dinners, overlooking the pool in Cairns or the sea in Broadbeach. And if she and Dad had been invited to someone's house for dinner, she would send a thank you letter in her beautiful handwriting the next day. No one practised manners and etiquette more thoroughly and with greater style than my Mum.

Then, there was the other side that few people saw. It was her sense of humour which was wide-eyed and self-deprecating. She called herself "Sadie" — as in "the cleaning lady". And she would tell me on the phone about the latest restaurant she'd been to with Dad and she'd say, "Sadie got an airing last night." Of course she was being ironic. Sadie got an airing most nights. She lived a full and busy life — gym sometimes twice a day, plus work, plus social commitments. Less ironic was when she'd be chatting to what Dad called, one of her "patients", and she'd wrap up the conversation by saying, "I've got to go. Des and Adam are waiting at the dinner table with their mouths open." Indeed, we were a pair of chickens in constant need of being fed. Who could blame us? Earlier this year, just before she went in for a serious operation, she said, "Not to worry. I'm not going anywhere. I need to be around to look after you and Dad."

If Dad — a staunch advocate of heterosexuality — had to put up with Mum's gay friends monopolising her time and drinking his whisky, then Mum's job was to tame several of Dad's journalism friends. These were tough, hard fighting, hard drinking men who would think nothing of downing three bottles of red before filing 2000 words of sparkling copy on deadline before brawling over who had the better intro. But they all behaved impeccably around Mum. No doubt, as Mavis says, they knew they were in the company of a "true lady".

Mum and Dad's marriage was a great love affair. They fitted perfectly into their masculine and feminine roles. When going to a party, Mum would always take a while to get ready and, to hurry her up, Dad would start the engine of the car. Clever trick, but she remained defiant,

"I will get ready in my own time." So Dad would turn the car engine off and wipe his brow — then, he'd turn it on again. Still, she wouldn't be hurried. Ditto for leaving a party. Dad got to know the life stories' of many a doorman and cab driver while waiting for her to emerge. The only thing she liked better than socialising was food — and often they'd go hand in hand. But her love for Dad transcended everything and their disputes about time management and who wasn't listening to who were always coated in love. She talked glowingly about him — particularly, when he wasn't there. Mum was never one for throwing high emotion into someone's face — it went against her principles of taste. She showed you she loved you by linking arms with you or holding your hand or in practical ways such as conversation, emotional support and food. Over the past two years, during Mum's illness, Mum and Dad grew even closer. Dad devoted himself full-time to her and in her diary, which we opened two days ago, she often wrote, "Thank God for Des". The other day when I thanked Dad for his great commitment, he said it "wasn't commitment son, it was love".

Mum settled me into boarding school, then, to University college, then to my first flat with my third girlfriend, a situation I knew she wasn't ecstatic about. But she was always there to help me settle-in and then rescue me when it all turned bad. She knew the names and personality profiles of all my friends and girlfriends — even those she'd never met. She was shrewd too. She would get "vibes" about people who she called "bad eggs" and she was always right.

If you have known Delphine — you knew what it was like to be cared for, worried about and loved. You knew what true politeness and style and grace and femininity was — not to mention the glorious tucker you were fed along the way. Most of all, you knew what it is to be truly listened to.

Michael and Suzie said in their email yesterday: "Don't cry because she has gone. Smile because she was here." And her brother Bruce called to "celebrate her life".

That's what Mum would have wanted. She would want us to be happy and smiling. She was disturbed by mass outpourings of grief as well as gloomy chat about the past and always encouraged Dad and I to talk about positive things at the dinner table. "Don't let's talk negative," she'd say.

Well, let's not. Delphine lived and all of us have been touched by her charm. She was a delicate, beautiful lady with a great heart. She would be worried about all of us at the moment — wishing we would get on with our lives and stop moping around. "Come on. Beep beep," she would say. "Get crack'n. That's it. Goody goody gum drops." She'd wish us all the best as we, who love her so dearly, wish the same for her.'

Afterword

We had built our own home in a little Victorian township called Beechworth, (pop.3,000) where I was born. The house stands on a great rocky outcrop and overlooks mountains — snow-covered in winter and purple in summer. I've called the house Delhaven, because for 18 months while Del was still with us, it was.

Beechworth is a tourist mecca, with its heritage-preserved sandstone court-house, telegraph office and prison, which were erected 150 years ago; shop-front roofs extend to the street gutters as they did in the Gold Rush; and its bakery is famous world-wide. A gentleman rides his penny farthing down to the bakery for morning coffee; two Clydesdales pull a stagecoach that Ned Kelly might have held up; for this is where Ned and his gang rode, caroused and robbed.

Having lived in London for 11 years, Cairns for 23, the garish Gold Coast for four and Melbourne for about 10 years, I have come full circle, playing golf on the same course my parents enjoyed, each day passing the hospital where I came into the world.

I write newsletters for the Burke Museum, the golf club, the old peoples' hospital and Neighbourhood Watch; a weekly newspaper column for the local vicar.

I have begun another book — my 18th — on the delicate

subject of Catholic priests and their enforced celibacy. An often tragic story.

Adam, my son, will be married when this book is published and gives me great pride as I read what he writes, see him acting on television and am taken into his plans for a major movie he has written.

And I live by the prayer that I heard for the first time when I was invited to experience an AA meeting:

'God grant me the serenity to accept the things I cannot change; to change the things I can. And the wisdom to know the difference.'

THE END

Books By Desmond Zwar

The Infamous Of Nuremberg, Written For Col.Burton C Andrus, Published In 1969 by Coward-McCann, USA, Leslie Frewin, UK; and in several European countries.

This Wonderful World Of Golf, With Peter Thomson, Published in 1969 by Pelham Books, UK.

The Loneliest Man In The World — the story of Rudolf Hess's Imprisonment, Written For Col. Eugene Bird, Published by Viking USA, Secker & Warburg, UK, and in 10 other countries. 1974.

Vet In The Clouds, with Vet Don Lavers, Published by Granada UK. 1978.

In Search Of Keith Murdoch, Published by Macmillan, Aust And UK. 1980.

The Soul of a School, Published By Macmillan, Aust. 1982.

New Frontiers of Medical Research, Published By Stein & Day, USA, and in Japan.

The Magic Mussel — The Story of a Natural Arthritis Treatment, Published by Ideas Unlimited, Aust., 1983.

The Dame, Published by Macmillan, Aust., 1984.

The Ma Evans Baldness Cure, Woodland Books, USA, 1984.

Golf - The Dictionary, Published by Sun Books, Aust., David & Charles, UK, Tomas Books, Germany, 1984.

Doctor Ahead of His Time — The Life of Dr. Ainslie Meares, Psychiatrist, Published by Greenhouse Publications, 1985.

The Mad, Mad World Of Unisex Golf, Published by Ideas Unlimited, Aust. 1990.

Disgrace! The Saga of The Downfall of Medical Hero, Dr. William McBride.

The Queen, Rupert & Me — A Reporter's Extraordinary Life.

New Releases...Also from Sid Harta Publishers

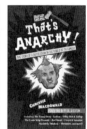

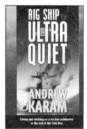

More New Releases

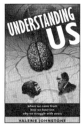
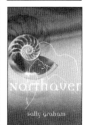
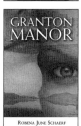

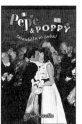

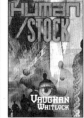
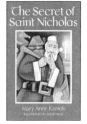

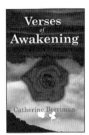   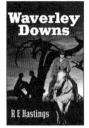

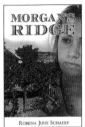  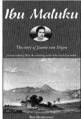 

Best-selling titles by Kerry B. Collison